The Botanic Garden

and

My Old Kentucky Plays

The Botanic Garden and My Old Kentucky Plays

Richard Cavendish

authorHOUSE®

AuthorHouse™
1663 Liberty Drive
Bloomington, IN 47403
www.authorhouse.com
Phone: 833-262-8899

Published by AuthorHouse 12/03/2020

ISBN: 978-1-7283-5891-8 (sc)
ISBN: 978-1-7283-5890-1 (hc)
ISBN: 978-1-7283-5892-5 (e)

Print information available on the last page.

Cover: Constantine Rafinesque, miniature attributed to William Birch (1775-1834)
Back Page: Mrs. Emily H. Tubman

This book is printed on acid-free paper.

Contents

List of Illustrations

Dedication

To Brenda Sims Bartella Peterson, who taught us to demand nothing less than excellence,

To Dr. Charles Haller, who threatened us with Pace, Projection, Pronunciation, but smiled with approval,

and

To Father John, my mentor and great friend, who journeyed backstage with me to the Garden, the Station, the House, the Battlefield, and the Houseboat. For whom I am eternally grateful.

PREFACE

Figure 1

My first exposure to the theatrical stage was probably at The Capitol Theater in my hometown of Frankfort, the capital of Kentucky. The theater was being used to show movies; we called it, "The Picture Show." This is where my family took us to see all the popular movies, and all the old ones that were new to us. It was an ominous auditorium with darkly lit little broken faces on the walls, a massive stained-glass chandelier that hung over our heads, and medieval Spanish castle pillars and doorways that flanked the proscenium. After seeing the movie *Sleeping Beauty*, I was convinced that Walt Disney had designed the interior of our Frankfort Capitol Theater. That stage and auditorium stood as a reminder of a time that had passed. A time of old Kentucky.

It was on this stage that I once tap danced. To have performed live on that old stage, and not as a motion picture from a reel to reel projector, was an amazing experience for me. I was doing what the building had been originally built to do: presenting live entertainment. Looking out over the audience, I could feel the thespian spirits coming alive again. I remember the eerie stone walled dressing rooms in the basement, remnants of the old Major Hall Opera House. That dungeon cellar in my time was filled with young girls changing into new dance recital outfits that all sort of looked alike with feathers and sequins. One little girl, standing completely naked and waiting for her mother to dress her, saw me--a strange boy in silver tap shoes--and quickly made me disappear by pressing her hands over her eyes. At that time, I could not help but relish the attention all the beautiful older girls in fishnet stockings gave me, something enjoyed by other young men over a hundred years before.

The first announced theatre performance west of the Allegheny Mountains was in Kentucky on the campus of Transylvania University in Lexington April 10, 1790, "in the presence of a very respectable audience."[1] Theater was alive in Frankfort taverns as early as December of 1807. The Frankfort Theatre was built in August of 1812, run by Luke Usher of Lexington. [2] Usher invited Samuel Drake to organize a company and blaze the western frontier from New York down the Ohio River by flatboat to Frankfort, Kentucky where they performed in the fall of 1815.
Noah M. Ludlow, one of Drake's players, wrote:

> I have never found a more kind and hospitable people than those in Kentucky, generally, and I have travelled in most all States of the Union. It seemed to me in after years, when I had visited most of the Western, Southern, and Northern States, that Kentucky, as a State, could boast of more high-minded men and beautiful women than any I had ever been in. I have found there more genuine

---

[1] West T. Hill, Jr., *The Theatre in Early Kentucky 1790-1820*, (The University Press of Kentucky, Lexington, Kentucky, 1971), p.9.
[2] West T. Hill, Jr., *The Theatre in Early Kentucky 1790-1820*, (The University Press of Kentucky, Lexington, Kentucky, 1971), pp.22-23.

and unostentatious hospitality than in any other State, and that dispensed by princely men and courtly women, stamped with nobility by the hand of their Creator.[3]

The Metropolitan Hall at 317 St. Clair Street was stage for theatrical performances in Frankfort until it was destroyed by fire in December of 1867, and Major Hall replaced it on Main Street with the Post Office and Barrett's Bookstore on the ground floor. The Major, named after mayor S.I.M. Major, was called The Opera House. For thirteen years, it entertained with such performers as Buffalo Bill and Annie Oakley. But then the hotel next door caught fire and Major Hall burned in November of 1882. The new Opera House that replaced it was located on the same spot but renamed The Capitol Theater and City Hall.[4]

The Capitol Theater was designed by Chicago architect Oscar Cobb, and built by John and Denis Haly in 1883. The scenery was painted by nineteen-year-old artist J. E. Leslie of Cincinnati; the drop curtain he chose was a scene representing the decline of Carthage. It is said that the opening performance was Clara Scott in *Leah the Forsaken.* Touring artists who performed at the old Opera House included Madame Modjeska, Maurice Barrymore, The Four Cohans, E. H. Sothern, Minnie Maddern Fiske, Nazimova, Henry Miller, George Arliss, Marguerite Sylva, De Wolf Hopper, Nat Goodwin, Denman Thompson, Henrietta Crossman, Joseph Jefferson, Madame Schumann-Heink, Rose and Charles Coghlan, Fanny Davenport, Julia Marlowe, and Lily Langtry.[5]

---

[3] Noah Miller Ludlow, *Dramatic Life As I Found It,* (New York: 1966), p.78.
[4] Carl E. Kramer, *Capital on the Kentucky*, (Frankfort, Kentucky: Historic Frankfort, Inc., 1986), pp. 210-11.
[5] *A Century of Progress with Frankfort.* (Frankfort, Kentucky: State Journal, 1950); Kramer, *Capital,* p. 230.

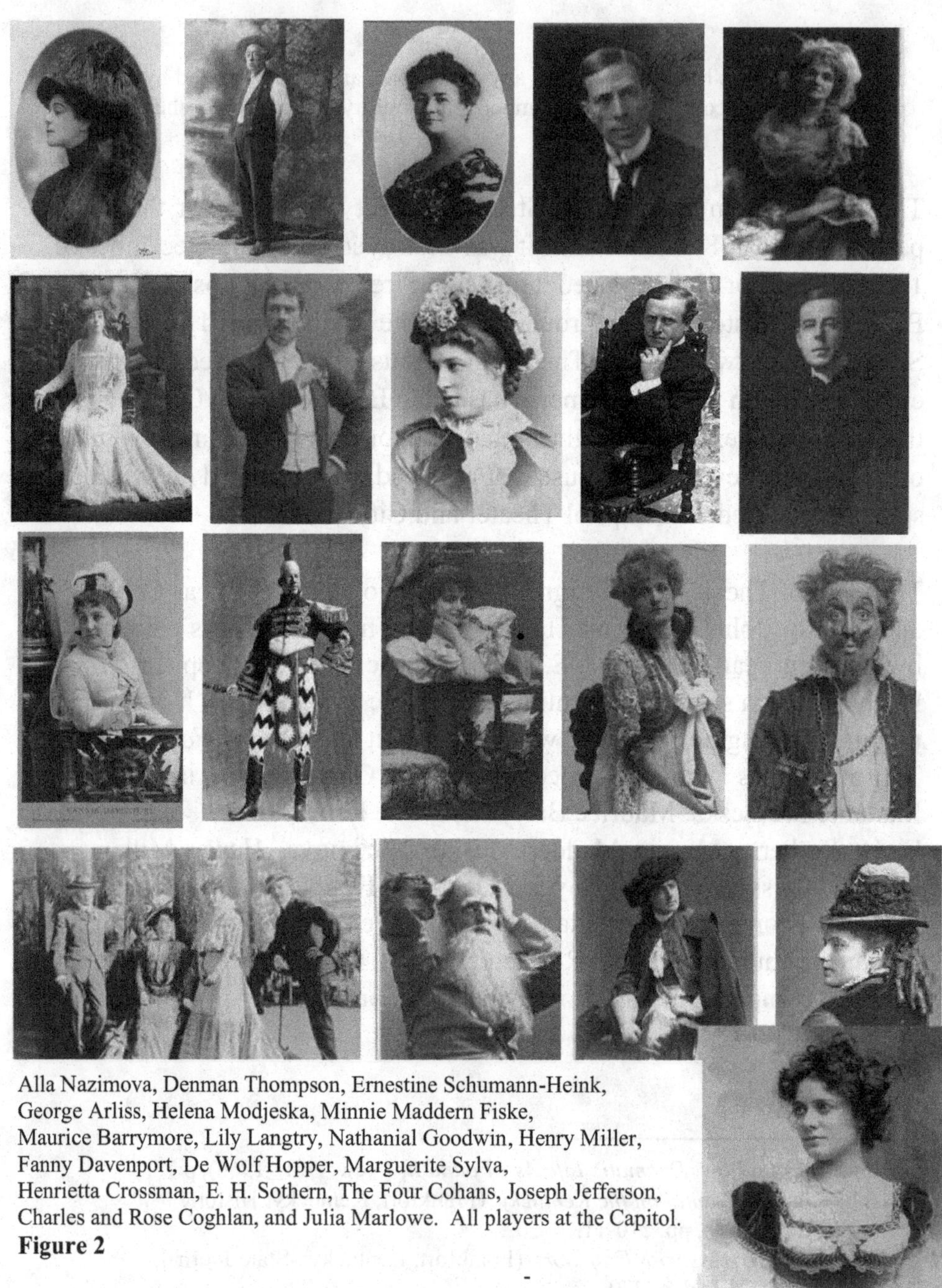

Alla Nazimova, Denman Thompson, Ernestine Schumann-Heink, George Arliss, Helena Modjeska, Minnie Maddern Fiske, Maurice Barrymore, Lily Langtry, Nathanial Goodwin, Henry Miller, Fanny Davenport, De Wolf Hopper, Marguerite Sylva, Henrietta Crossman, E. H. Sothern, The Four Cohans, Joseph Jefferson, Charles and Rose Coghlan, and Julia Marlowe. All players at the Capitol.
Figure 2

Figure 4

Figure 3

Like a lot of our historic buildings in Kentucky, they tore down the Capitol Theater. During the demolition, my Dad, Russell Sr., and I chipped out a tiled crest from what had been the foyer floor. And probably, filled in below the current modern building that stands there now are the stone walls of the old dressing rooms. Some things always remain behind: I know that the cherished memories of that old theatre, remembered by my childhood friends, can never be destroyed. And somewhere, laughter of its long-ago audiences echoes through the night.

Nights of summer theater in Kentucky had a huge influence on me as did the Capitol Theatre. Three of these are among those that have gone upstage to the happy hunting ground in the theatrical sky, due to financial struggle: *Wilderness Road, The Book of Job*, and *The Legend of Daniel Boone.*

The Legend of Daniel Boone, Harrodsburg.

On April 14, 1962, sixty-eight citizens of Mercer County petitioned to Governor Bert Combs for the building of an amphitheater. The amphitheater was dedicated "to tangible progress for the future," said Combs, "at the same time retaining the drama and romance that are so much the history of Kentucky and America."[6]

Harrodsburg Drama Productions, Inc. was formed and *Home is the Hunter* was written by Robert Emmett McDowell. John Cauble was hired as manager, former manager of *The Stephen Foster Story*. Dr. Samuel Selden was chosen as director whose credits in directing included *The Lost Colony* at Manteo, North Carolina, *Wilderness Road,* and *The Stephen Foster Story*. Musical direction was by Ralph Burrier of Princeton, New Jersey and costume design by Lucille Baillie of Kansas City, Missouri. The script portrayed James Harrod, George Rogers Clark, Ben Logan, Hugh McGary, Thomas Slaughter, and John Gabriel Jones as the true heroes of the Kentucky territory. The amphitheater was built in the Pioneer Memorial State Park and *Home is the Hunter* opened June 29, 1963.

Home is the Hunter was replaced by *The Legend of Daniel Boone*, and later attempted to "give a Boone in whom you might recognize yourself. A human, fallible Daniel, the kind that is easier to love and easier to understand. The Boone of our Legend suffers and knows joy. That is enough to make him a hero. For we all suffer and know

---

[6] Dorothy Ann Davis, *Lexington Herald-Leader*, Bluegrass Review Forecast, Section B, Lexington, Kentucky Sunday January 13, 1963.

joy and to the extent that we do it fully, we are all heroes."[7] Rewritten as *Daniel Boone, the Man and the Legend*, it closed at the end of the summer of 2005, to liquidate assets to pay debts. Since then, The Ragged Edge Community Theatre performs in the summer evenings at the amphitheater producing Broadway musicals and the original *James Harrod the Battle for Kentucky*.

The Book of Job, Pineville.

This adaptation of *Job* in biblical verse premiered the summer of 1959, at Pine Mountain State Park. Featured at two World Fairs, Brussels and New York, it toured four continents. *The New York Times* wrote of it, "An awesome and most majestic rendition. The imagination is stirred—the eye magnetized. *The Book of Job* should not be missed."

Figure 5

The makeup and costumes were painted in colorful mosaic, and took hours to apply. It was the gift of Preston and Mildred Slusher, adapted and directed by Georgetown College professor Orlin Corey.[8] Currently, it is being revived, a tribute to one of the oldest dramas in history that must speak to the ages.

---

[7] Jan Hartman, The Power of a Dream, *The Legend of Daniel Boone* program.

[8] "Director of "Book of Job" Sets World Tour for Plays," Lexington Herald Leader, June 21, 1964.

Wilderness Road, A Symphonic Outdoor Drama, Berea.

Commissioned by Berea College for its centennial celebration, *Wilderness Road* was written by Paul Green and coordinated by trustee Dr. Willis D. Weatherford. Under the Presidency of Francis S. Hutchins, Indian Fort Theatre was built in the Berea College Forest and designed by John Lippard to showcase this musical drama. It premiered in the summer of 1955. This was the first outdoor theater in the country sponsored by a college. The play portrayed the early settlers of Daniel Boone's migration through the Cumberland Gap into Kentucky along the buffalo paths and creeks that later became known as the Wilderness Road. It also showed the importance of education in the mountains of Appalachia, the founding of Berea, and the division of family and friends during the

Figure 6

American Civil War. It was the dream of Dr. Weatherford to share the truth about Appalachian culture and the importance of education. *Wilderness Road* paid tribute to Berea's pioneers, who blazed a road through "misunderstandings, passions and persecutions of misguided men, their neighbors even."[9] Due to lack of support and financial difficulties, the drama closed in 1958, and later revived in 1972, during the presidency of Willis D. Weatherford, Jr., before its curtain finally fell.

Thankfully, other outdoor Kentucky dramas survive and continue to inspire, entertain, and educate during the summer months. Some of these are Pioneer Playhouse, *The Stephen Foster Story*, and The Jenny Wiley Theatre

Pioneer Playhouse, Danville.

Pioneer Playhouse, the oldest outdoor theatre in Kentucky, was founded by Col. Eben C. Henson in 1950. Its outdoor stage, dining hall and indoor stage were constructed from salvaged and recycled materials, including the train station set from the MGM movie *Raintree County* that Henson re-purposed into his ticket office. Pioneer Playhouse was the original "state theater" of Kentucky. Henson cast actors from New York City each summer and gave developing playwrights a stage to work out new plays. Past alumni include Jim Varney, Lee Majors, and John Travolta. Henson died in 2004; his daughter Holly carried on the Playhouse legacy until her death from cancer in 2012, and now Robby Henson serves as artistic director working in tandem with his mother Charlotte and sister Heather. Pioneer Playhouse is truly a grass-roots, family-run theater under the stars.

---

[9] Shannon H. Wilson P., *Berea College an Illustrated History*, (Lexington: The University Press, 2006), p. 157.

The Stephen Foster Story, Bardstown.

Figure 7

Under the leadership of Ted Cronk, the first producer, it opened June 26, 1959 in an amphitheater on the grounds of Federal Hill, home of Judge John Rowan, thought to be the inspiration for Stephen Foster's song, "My Old Kentucky Home." The idea to create *The Stephen Foster Story* is credited to Catherine Conner as a Kentucky Tourism project under the administration of Governor Happy Chandler. Foster's song is a terribly sad song about a slave whose only hope is the release of death and the memory of living in Kentucky with a family sold away from him, a song revised into a few verses by the State as its song of home patriotism. Paul Green, Pulitzer Prize winner for his 1927 play, *In Abraham's Bosom*, wrote the play using Foster's famous songs. The 1400 seat amphitheater was erected by the Commonwealth of Kentucky Department of Parks and the people of Bardstown and Nelson County.

My family went to see *The Stephen Foster Story* on a warm summer night. I was completely charmed by its idealistic romance, and Foster's music has never been the same for me. Anne S. Arnold, costume designer, was so kind to loan me several of their costumes for the very first rendition I made of *Sabbath of the Soul,* at First Christian Church, Frankfort in 1973.

The Legend of Jenny Wiley, Prestonsburg.

The Jenny Wiley State Resort Park amphitheater was built for the historical drama *The Legend of Jenny Wiley*, in Prestonsburg, Kentucky. This summer drama told the story of pioneer woman, Virginia Sellards Wiley who was captured by Native Americans in 1789, escaped and returned to her husband. Jenny Wiley State Park opened in 1962.

The Jenny Wiley Theatre was established in 1965, when a group of players from Paintsville, Kentucky presented Rodgers and Hammerstein's *South Pacific.* In 2012, an indoor theatre located in Pikeville was built making it possible to produce musicals, plays, tours, and educational arts programming throughout the year. Michael Cerveris, James Barbour, Sharon Lawrence, and Paige Davis are among its professional alumni actors.

I share with you five of my plays of Kentucky. My old Kentucky plays, because they are historical dramas. I mean nothing but honor to the characters that I have portrayed. Emily Tubman and Emma Watts were both philanthropists that desired no publicity for their kindnesses. Mrs. Tubman would not even allow her name to be mentioned in the interview with the Augusta newspaper just before her death; her name added to the great stained-glass window in the sanctuary of the Frankfort church after her death probably would have displeased her. Mrs. Merritt, Miss Watt's caretaker, first said to me that Miss Emma would not want the attention of a play written about her life; but when I shared my faith with her, she smiled, welcomed me in, and became my comrade. On the other hand, James Neale, Jr. until his death maintained that Emma preferred her privacy. I believe that if one person's life is enriched and helped by the shining examples of these saints, then these great protagonists must be looking down and nodding with approval, not unlike those thespian spirits of the Capitol Theater. "So, let your light so shine before men, that they may see your good works and give glory to God," Matthew 5:16.

Each play must hold a bit of dramatic license. Darsie and Mary Fleming may never have gone to the train depot so late the night before the funeral train arrived; Rafinesque may never have fallen in love with Mary Holley, the wife of the University President; an architect had never been commissioned by the University to build a student center at Elmwood when my play was written and there have never been found letters buried in the garden; Elizabeth may never have had a confrontation with a runaway Union soldier; and Paul Sawyier and Mayme Bull may never have consummated their twenty three year old relationship. And yet, . . . who knows?

Reading a play puts you in the actor's seat. What you do with it, no one will ever do the same with again. It is an amazing unique experience that can never, never be duplicated by even the most sophisticated and multibillion-dollar production staged on Broadway or Hollywood. Just as the simplest production of a play is completely unique to its cast and time and place, so is the reading of a play. And once having read a play, somehow that play becomes a part of the reader, for the reader has become its player. In this same manner, the old Capitol Theater and those magical summer amphitheater nights have colored my writing, friends lost for just a little while.

A play is a living thing once the curtain goes up, who seeks to share its moment in time with you. You be the actor, the director, the costume and set designer, and the entire production staff. This is my play but your performance. Make it your own.

Break a leg.

BIBLIOGRAPHY

"A 'Home Is the Hunter' Scene," *The Harrodsburg Herald,* August 14, 1964.

A Second-Century of Progress with Frankfort. Frankfort, Kentucky: Farmers Bank and Capital Trust Company. First published as *A Century of Progress with Frankfort.* Frankfort, Kentucky: State Journal, 1950.

"Book of Job" To Open At World's Fair, Hart Co. Herald—Horse Cave, May 14, 1964

"Carpenters 'On Stage,'" *The Harrodsburg Herald,* June 28, 1963.

Davis, Dorothy Ann. *Lexington Herald-Leader,* Bluegrass Review Forecast, Section B, Lexington, Kentucky: Sunday January 13, 1963.

"Director of "Book of Job" Sets World Tour For Plays," Lexington Herald Leader, June 21, 1964.

Exploring Kentucky. "Summer Drama Under the Stars!" Summer 1965. Kentucky Historical Society, Theater [Outdoor].

Hartman, Jan. "The Power of a Dream." *The Legend of Daniel Boone* play program.

Hill, Jr., West T. *The Theatre in Early Kentucky 1790-1820.* Lexington, Kentucky: The University Press of Kentucky, 1971.

"'Home is the Hunter' Cast to Begin Rehearsal Sun," *The Harrodsburg Herald,* June 5, 1964.

Kramer, Carl E. *Capital on the Kentucky,* Frankfort, Kentucky: Historic Frankfort, Inc., 1986.

Ludlow, Noah Miller. *Dramatic Life As I Found It.* New York: Benjamin Blom, 1966.

"National Figures To See Debut" *Murray Ledger and Times,* June 5, 1964.

"Opening of Stars Set For Saturday' *Murray Ledger and Times,* June 23, 1964

Patterson, Malcolm. "'Home Is The Hunter' Draws Sell-Out Crowd." *The Harrodsburg Herald*, June 29, 1963.

Shannon H. Wilson P., *Berea College an Illustrated History*, Lexington: The University Press, 2006.

"Stars Shaping Up Well Says Director," *Murray Ledger and Times*, June 6, 1963.

The Botanic Garden

Introduction

Office of the President
Transylvania University
300 North Broadway
Lexington KY 40608
Founded 1780

April 15, 2016

History plays struggle at the edge of fashion. *Hamilton*, the rap musical life of Alexander Hamilton, is today's Broadway rage with tickets costing its cast's weight in rubies. But in spite of their long history in the theater and the incandescence of Shakespeare's kings and princes, history plays only really seem to hold audiences when their stores are full of great arrogance, great dreams and even greater falls.

Lesser histories, those social dramas of ordinary men and women built from smaller battles and inelegant wars, seem more the result of bad luck than bad character or cruel fate. Theirs is so much the stuff of everyday nightmares that we do not easily see why we should want to hear their stories of fortunes reversed, or watch their accidental collisions unfold, or feel their victim's pain. So the arrows miss, so the truth reveals, so the furies arrive, so what.

It is its answer to this last question that makes *The Botanic Garden* so interesting. Cast with unknown or largely forgotten names from American history, set at Transylvania University, the first university west of the Alleghenies and in Lexington Kentucky in the 1820s, and about the struggle to build a liberal, eastern university amidst the full throated Jackson-Clay debates over rights for the common man, the place of the West in American culture, and the role, if any, of any American aristocracy.

Despite the text's potential for vulgar frontiersmen to clash with smug easterners, the playwright gives us so much more to experience as we watch the half-scientist, half-alchemist, half-showman, half-mad Constantine Rafinesque try to explore this western edge of civilization, try to teach his bewildered students the new world's botanic splendor, and try to imagine, with his colleague, President Horace Holley and his wife Mary, what this new civilization might become.

The Botanic Garden offers nothing less than the tragic struggle to bring higher learning to a place and time where it was so needed but seemed so unnecessary. In one sense, Jackson's followers were right. Schooling mattered enormously, but what was needed was practical education. Law, medicine, agriculture, mechanical arts mattered; Greek, Latin, philosophy, humanities were luxuries that threatened potentially the survival of the enterprise.

And yet, Jackson's followers were also wrong. The liberal arts cultivate the mind in ways that the practical arts cannot. The easy contrast would be to say that the practical arts do and the liberal arts dream. But that would be unjust to both. Rather, let it be said that the liberal arts cause us to question the foundations of the problem at hand even as we attempt to solve it while the practical arts focus greater attention on the immediately needed solution. The great tragedy in the 1820s which *The Botanic Garden* so eloquently portrays is that neither side found a way to see or understand or value the others' points of view.

That tragedy also points us to its contemporary power. Our age is not less contentious than the 1820s and our ongoing wars over the nature of and need for higher education echo with terrifying precision those that are enacted in this play. The very headlines splashed across newspapers in Kentucky, on the day that I write this, blare forth once again the struggle over public education's form, and function, and worth.

And while Transylvania University may appear a non-combatant in the struggle, we are not. Our intention to remain committed to liberal learning and to the demand that our students can both reflect and do, that they can both imagine and act, that they can be in and of the world, and not merely its subject or its victim, is daily questioned by those who would substitute workforce development and job creation for our intention to imagine the future and then make it happen.

I will end by saying again: ours is the imagination business, and *The Botanic Garden* is a very contemporary reminder of why we work so hard to keep Transylvania University at the cutting edge of what the world at large is and what it ought to be. I will also end by saying that his alma mater is proud of Russell R. Rechenbach [pen named Richard Cavendish] for bringing this story to life and cultivating in the imagination the garden that sadly could not be cultivated in Lexington all those years ago.

Seamus Carey, President

Dedication

This play is dedicated to Dr. Charles Boewe
Whose brilliance and forbearance
Has rescued the Grecian Bard
From the overgrown pathways of mediocrity
Planted by sometimes but not always good intentioned historians,
To whom without his expertise in discovering the historical Rafinesque
This play could never have been written, and for
whom the playwright is forever indebted.

There is no angry God, the wily foes
Who born of him could fall by envy, pride;
In anger yet retain the stubborn spirit
Of wrath, and wickedness, are never Gods.
The God who made us all, is ever loving,
No one he hates; in pity looks on errors,
On wicked men his equal boons bestows:
If they refuse his loving gifts with scorn,
'This their freewill, the consequence they take;
But if relenting, his holy will they seek
Contrive again to keep, they are restored
By him to fatherly affection, and
His loving care obtain to bless their days.

C. S. Rafinesque *The World: Or, Instability* 2385-97

The Botanic Garden

Characters

Horace HOLLEY
Henry CLAY
MARY Austin Holley
John James AUDUBON, also William BRAND
Constantine Samuel RAFINESQUE, also The MAN
The Revd. James FISHBACK
The Revd. James BLYTHE
The Revd. Robert BISHOP, also GUARD
Dr. Charles CALDWELL
Dr. Benjamin DUDLEY
Dr. William RICHARDSON
HARRIETTE Holley, also EMILIA Rafinesque
John EVERETT, also SOLOMON
Madison JOHNSON, also STUDENT
John TROTTER, also ISAAC Desha
Jefferson DAVIS
Joseph DESHA, also STEWART
MRS. BRADFORD

ACT ONE

Scene One

SUMMER

The sound of approaching horses galloping, birds singing in the trees take us back to an unspoiled time in the wilderness of Kentucky. We see a backdrop of shadowing branches and foliage through whose arches the sun flickers with summer playfulness. It is Nature's own garden outside of Lexington, Kentucky, Summer, 1818. Henry CLAY and Horace HOLLEY dismount their horses and view the terrain.

HOLLEY

"Transylvania."

CLAY

It was the name given to this land. Judge Richard Henderson used the name for his land company.

HOLLEY

"Across the woods." Yes. It's Latin.

CLAY

[Of the vista:]

Our county is named for the great French hero, Lafayette. And our town from the first battle of the Revolution. There's Lexington: the first western town to provide oil lighting in the streets. Hemp is central to our economy. Land prices are similar to Boston.

HOLLEY

Senator Clay, your town has a comfortable and genteel aspect. President Monroe spoke highly of the opportunities here in Kentucky.

CLAY

It's wild and wonderful and waiting to be tamed. *[He takes a deep breath, savoring a fragrance in the air.]* Dr. Holley, do you know what that is?

HOLLEY

[After a ponder]

Ragweed, Senator Clay?

CLAY

There is a spirit here. The Indians call it The Great Spirit. And the land they call The Great Meadow. The land of tomorrow.

HOLLEY

I thought the Indians didn't make their home here.

CLAY

True. They considered the land too sacred. They would hunt game and bury their dead here. You can see the college from here. The cupola of the new Principal Building.

HOLLEY

The architecture of Ancient Greece has survived over thousands of years. It brought us democracy, has dominated the intellectual life of our world. . . There was a garden in Athens—the garden of Epicurus. Men from all over the world came there to sit in the grass and listen and learn his philosophy. A philosophy of pleasure.

CLAY

Kentucky is known for its Bourbon, horse races, and beautiful women. *[Of the buildings in the distance:]* The Virginia Assembly chartered our Seminary in 1780, as a state public school. Undesirable student organizations are forbidden. Dirks, swords, and guns are not allowed on campus. The taverns are off-limits, and students must have permission and be chaperoned to the theatre. *[He considers the view.]* At one time we had over 20,000 acres.

HOLLEY

What happened?

CLAY

The previous President Blythe sold much of it to raise money for the school.

HOLLEY

He resigned?

CLAY

As President, yes. The students hated him. He remains on the faculty.

HOLLEY

The offer I received from your Board of Trustees was withdrawn last year. I thought they viewed my theology "unorthodox."

CLAY

The House has rid itself of them. Our new Trustees are conservatively liberal in religious matters and liberally conservative in political ones.

HOLLEY

But the old ones are still lurking in the woods—this side of it? Like the Indians in the cane break? I cannot be enslaved by religious peculiarities, Senator Clay. I have tried them all and found them nonsense.

CLAY

Then you are a man redeemed from vice and made to practice virtue. Much worthier than all propagations of peculiar doctrines.

HOLLEY

You Kentuckians are very vocal, aren't you?

CLAY

Why do you say that?

HOLLEY

While I was in Washington calling on President Monroe, the Kentucky Representative was introducing a bill before Congress.

CLAY

Small deep sunken eye? That would be Joseph Desha.

HOLLEY

Yes. He was proposing to change the number of stars and stripes on the national flag. It was quite influential.

CLAY

We do not need a reformer, Dr. Holley, but a University President who will captivate the mind for the acquisition of truth of all kinds. If you preach, do it seldom and to exhibit your talents for education. Keep foremost in sight what is the main thing.

HOLLEY

And what is the "main thing," Senator Clay?

CLAY

To make men live better. That's why we're here, Dr. Holley. You have the opportunity to father a university which will endure for ages. The opportunity to prepare the minds of millions of young men–born and unborn–for great principles of science, of morality, and of religion. Take a moment. *[Eager to give him a chance to be entranced by the view]* I'll tend to the horses.

[He is gone]

HOLLEY

Ah, Kentucky . . . land of opportunity. With the power to change the American flag!

[Scrim upstage silhouettes MARY holding an infant in her arms, her daughter of nine years at her side.]

MARY

Come home, Horace. You have missed the birth of your son. Just as you missed the birth of your little daughter when you first went to Boston. They cry for you. I need you.

HOLLEY

Oh, Mary! Our house will be a resort for all who shall have any claims to literature and refinement. The road I am pursuing is the most direct one to useful power, to honorable fame.

MARY

It sounds a bit crowded to me, Horace. Pursue to the road that brings you home.

HOLLEY

But I shall father a university!

MARY

Not in my bed you won't. You shall be father to our children. Come home, Horace.

HOLLEY

Oh, come to Kentucky, sweet Mary . . .

MARY

Come back to our friends here in Boston, Horace. Your position is enviable and secure. You cannot expect to enhance your happiness by taking a less important station in the wilderness of Kentucky.

HOLLEY

The field is wider, the harvest more abundant, and the grain of a most excellent quality! My life has not been half so useful in Boston as it can be here in Kentucky.

MARY

Who would teach at such a school?

HOLLEY

Whoever I chose! I could persuade Benjamin Silliman to join us from Yale. There is a brilliant botanist residing in Philadelphia, Rafinesque, who has lived in Tuscany and France.

MARY

Farmers fear sending their sons to be corrupted by such Europeans. You shall be destroyed by their religious brawl. My children will be scalped by Indians!

HOLLEY

Mary, this is the Nineteenth Century: Indian warfare is a thing of the past. The school was chartered as a public nondenominational institution. We are without rival in the West!

The whole is left for me to arrange. Mary, they guarantee my salary at $3,000!

MARY

Forget your ambitions, Horace. They will serve only to steal your talents and bury them.

HOLLEY

I breathe an atmosphere more agreeable to me in the large view that I take than I have ever breathed before.

MARY

Horace, the air is humid . . . and it smells of ragweed.

HOLLEY

It is a Great Spirit, Mary. There is a spirit that reigns supreme in this place, a spirit of opportunity and I am seduced by it!

MARY

Horace, come home immediately!

HOLLEY

This whole Western country is to feed my seminary, which will in time send out lawyers, physicians, and savants, who will make the nation feel them!

MARY

And our allergies will be grievous. Come home and be a father to your children rather than an allegorical fool who loves a challenge.

HOLLEY

[Using his charm, to its maximum seductiveness:]

Mary . . . *[MARY heaves a heavy sigh]* Mary, my sweet . . .my love . . .

MARY

You promised me that you would delay your decision until you came home and we could talk about it together.

[The scrim fades out]

HOLLEY

Damn it! The Rev. Dr. Horace Holley shall accept the appointment of President to Transylvania University in Lexington, Kentucky, the Athens of the West! *[He huffs a great sigh of frustration]* I must on to the end of it. Ah, dear Senator Henry Clay . . .You may have signed the Treaty of Ghent and been elected speaker of the House of Representatives—you may even succeed as President of our great nation, but you stand corrected! It is not the religious hostility that I will have as challenge to my vision. Oh, no. It is not the urgent expectations of the State. It is not even the savagery of the Iroquois, Shawnee, or Wyandotte. Nor the harsh life of the wilderness on the frontier. No, dear friend. The restraint is but yet greater than all of these. Much greater. It is a man's unnerving persuasion . . . of the woman he loves!

ACT ONE

Scene Two

AUTUMN

The scrim changes to an attic room in silhouette. We see the shadow of a bearded MAN, unclothed, running and screaming, and swinging a broken mallet. AUDUBON appears in nightshirt and cap with a candle, also in silhouette. The MAN is RAFINESQUE.

AUDUBON

Good God in heaven! Be calm, before you bring harm upon yourself! *[He reaches to help the MAN, who collapses into his arms and brings the two of them to the floor.]* There now. Everything is fine. You must have had a bad dream . . . *[The MAN cannot get his breath; he motions frantically about him. AUDUBON holds him down.]* What you need is some soothing music. My Cremona! Yes. I shall play my violin for you. I possess the rarest and most exquisite Cremona you shall every see. And its sound . . . its sound is sheer heaven. It will surely put your mind at peace. *[A bat flies by them, and they duck. The MAN grunts and gestures towards it.]* Shhh. I let no one *touch* my Cremona, but for my wildlife friend, I shall retrieve it–*[The MAN pleads and begs]* Of course you are eager to hear me play—*[The two men duck. The MAN is up and swinging again at the bat.]* What? You want a *bat*? You think it is a rare species? That ordinary *bat*? *[The MAN is on his knees begging again.]* Stop this! It is not decent . . . shivering in the raw like a housed maniac. Robe yourself. *[The MAN covers himself with a blanket.]* I had planned to play my precious Cremona for you. Besides, your running around and around has only frightened it more. You want a specimen that I might prove to you that it is no new or rare species? *[The MAN nods desperately.]* Very well. Calm yourself. Give me the weapon. *[He takes it, waits, watches, swings and the bat falls. The MAN goes for it on the floor. The MAN is up hugging and kissing AUDUBON in gratitude, the blanket falling away exposing his nakedness.]* Now, now! Robe yourself! *[The MAN clutches at the blanket and is once more on the floor examining the bat.]* It was a well-timed tap, if I were to say so myself. Showed skill and precision. 'Played a bit of tennis in my youth—still have the arm for it! Why, I should get me one of these bat swatters. What do you have here, anyway? GOOD GOD! NO! *[He examines it]* MY CREMONA! *[Violently he chases the MAN round the room with his broken violin. As the lights behind the scrim fade out, we hear from the darkness:]*

HOLLEY

That must be Lexington! Where you see the lights!

[Below the scrim, each man carries a candle: FISHBACK, BLYTHE, and BISHOP, dressed in greatcoats and hats, at stage Right. We hear the chattering of a large impatient crowd around them. The night of November 21, 1818.]

FISHBACK

It's colder than a well digger's sack.

BLYTHE

"Constantine Rafinesque" will teach *Botany*. He has been traipsing about the wilderness with James Audubon, the naturalist. Audubon tells some wild stories about him.

FISHBACK

He says to expect an "odd fish." I think Audubon is jealous not to have been recruited to faculty.

BLYTHE

I understand that Daniel Webster has been invited to join us.

FISHBACK

Enrollment has *doubled*. Our students are from all over the country: General James Taylor of Newport has sent his son.

BLYTHE

Rafinesque comes from France and Tuscany. But he was born in Istanbul.

FISHBACK

A Muslim!?

BISHOP

[Who speaks with a thick Scottish accent.]

It will destroy the University. Too many outsiders.

FISHBACK

What they will pay him is criminal. Not even our Governor has such a salary!

BLYTHE

The Legislature expects him to shake hands with the world and bring all their sons to Transylvania.

FISHBACK

[Sarcastically]

Horace Holley is the new Light of the World!

[At Stage Left are assembled CALDWELL, DUDLEY, and RICHARDSON, all in greatcoats and hats, carrying candles.]

CALDWELL

It's colder than a well digger's ass. Did I tell you of the time I met Horace Holley? I was performing a funeral, in Philadelphia. This fellow walked into the room and his mere presence commanded the attention of every man and woman in the place, I expect the corpse as well! After what seemed an eternity, I managed to ask him to be seated. The whole room broke into applause! It was Horace Holley, who is now our new President.

DUDLEY

I wonder if Rafinesque will find the students to fill a class? If we are to expect an "odd fish," perhaps he should teach Agriculture. That way we would know to look for . . . a Croppy.

RICHARDON

No, he should teach European Etiquette. We should expect to look for a . . . "Blue Gill?"

DUDLEY

Maybe he will be asked to direct the school choir?

RICHARDSON

Then we could expect a . . . ?

DUDLEY

A wide mouth "bass"? *[They laugh]*

DUDLEY

It's colder than a witch's tit. You see any sign of them?

BISHOP

It is! The Rev. Holley and his entourage!

[There is a great thunder of applause and cheering as students and faculty recognize the Holley carriage. The front of the scrim bursts into the candle lit windows and roof of the Principal Building of Transylvania. HOLLEY, MARY, HARRIETTE, and EVERETT appear grouped together, having descended from their carriage. EVERETT is a young man and Harriette is girl of ten years holding her infant brother who seems almost as big as she. The men shake hands:]

BLYTHE

Dr. Holley? Mrs. Holley? Welcome to Transylvania.

HOLLEY

Thank you, Rev. Blythe. This is John Everett, one of our young tutors. *[To EVERETT:]* The Rev. James Blythe.

EVERETT

A pleasure to meet you, sir.

DUDLEY

[He tips his hat]

'Evening, and welcome. I'm Benjamin Dudley, Medical School.

HOLLEY

Yes! Good to see you, again, Dr. Dudley. *[To his family:]* Dr. Dudley graduated from this university.

[HARRIETTE, holding her infant brother, drops a blanket. BRAND steps out from the crowd and retrieves it for her. He smiles at her, and she smiles back.]

DUDLEY

Follow me. I'll show you to the Refectory where there is a nice hot meal waiting for you.

HOLLEY

Wallingford, attend to the horses! We're home!

[HOLLEY waves to the crowd and everyone cheers again. He and his party exit on foot. FISHBACK, BLYTHE, and BISHOP remain while RAFINESQUE appears from the shadows. RAFINESQUE is bearded, dirty, and wearing a ragged old hat and coat.]

FISHBACK

[Watching them go, he whispers:]

Holley has made his triumphant entry.

BLYTHE

He was not voted unanimously.

BISHOP

Many opposed him and left the meeting.

FISHBACK

After they left, Mr. Clay took the vote. Is that democracy?

BLYTHE

Horace Holley will unmask himself as he gains ground.

[BLYTHE and BISHOP join the parade. FISHBACK, mistaking the poorly attired RAFINESQUE for a beggar, passes him a quarter and exits with the others. JOHNSON, a young man, appears laughing.]

JOHNSON

They didn't realize that you, too, are a professor?

RAFINESQUE

I'm sure I do not look the part.

JOHNSON

You are an explorer. I can tell. Every good teacher should be an explorer.

RAFINESQUE

And you are quite perceptive. A lad such as you must one day come here to study.

JOHNSON

And a professor such as you must one day come here to teach. What did he give you?

RAFINESQUE

A quarter.

JOHNSON

[Humorously]

Don't spend it all at once!

RAFINESQUE

On the contrary. They paid my very own admission.

JOHNSON

Where can you go for a quarter?

RAFINESQUE

To one of the most amazing and magical places on this earth. A place of beauty like nothing you have ever seen before. The Botanic Garden!

ACT ONE

Scene Three

WINTER

The scrim is lit from behind to show the silhouette of an outdoor duel. We see two men choosing their pistols. We hear the counting of paces. The two men square off and fire. One of them falls. The scrim fades out from behind and is lit from the front to show the Old Seminary, Winter 1820. We hear the sound of chamber music as DUDLEY, RICHARDSON, and CALDWELL enter L in formal evening attire. They toast wine glasses towards BLYTHE, FISHBACK, and BISHOP across the room who toast back their tea cups. It is a party inside the apartment of Horace Holley. EVERETT and MARY stand by the fireplace. There is a small Grecian nude sculpture of a woman set on a pedestal near the mantle.

MARY

Why on earth did they fight a duel?

EVERETT

Something to do with an Irish cadaver in the graveyard. They must have them to dissect. Drake published that Dudley was an ignoramus, so Dudley challenged him to a duel. Drake refused but Richardson fought in his stead.

MARY

[Sarcastically]

What are friends for?

EVERETT

So, they had their duel and Dudley shot Richardson.

MARY

Shot him? Our Dr. Dudley and Dr. Richardson? Of our Medical School? But they seem such good friends.

EVERETT

They are now. Quite the *intimate* of friends. He shot him in the . . . well, in the most intimate of places.

MARY

No . . . ! Such barbarians.

EVERETT

And Dudley, being the constant doctor, applied pressure on the wound to stop the blood. It saved Richardson's life. Of course, he asked permission before he put his hand . . . there. *[EVERETT and MARY have a good laugh.]* But that was before you and Horace Holley came here. With such professors as Rafinesque, your husband will carve out an Ivy League University here in the West.

MARY

Yes. *Poison* Ivy.

EVERETT

Why do you dislike Rafinesque so?

MARY

I find him arrogant and ridiculous. A regular Rip Van Winkle.

EVERETT

When did you see him last?

MARY

Not long ago. And too soon enough.

EVERETT

Then you have not seen him lately. He is quite the Casanova. All the women are smitten with him.

MARY

Oh, please.

EVERETT

And quite a romantic poet. The women here love his deep bows and kissing of hands.

MARY

In Boston we would not dream of being so conspicuous. In Boston every breath I took was a pleasure. The air is different here.

EVERETT

It shows. In your countenance. Your spirits have drawn down and it shows on your face.

MARY

My face–?

EVERETT

Would you deny me honesty? Enjoy this evening. Speak to every woman here—start at one corner of the room and work your way around. The annoyance of such a venture is little compared to the condemnation you will receive if you ignore them. [*He watches RAFINESQUE from a distance]* Strange. Tonight, every girl refuses Professor Rafinesque. *[Suspicious of MARY:]* What have you been up to?

MARY

Nothing. I've just been working my way around the room—as you suggest—warning our ladies that Professor Rafinesque, who has traipsed through all the weeds and woods around, must be infested with the poisonous ivy! I'm sure they would hate to have their lovely gowns spoiled. The same silks and satins that they wear during the day that they wear at night—which all come from Philadelphia ready-made.

EVERETT

There is our Grecian Bard now. *[They look across the room and see RAFINESQUE, handsome and well dressed in evening attire.]*

MARY

It's not the same man.

[RAFINESQUE approaches CALDWELL, DUDLEY, and RICHARDSON and proceeds quickly to kiss them on both cheeks, leaving them stunned beyond movement; when making his way to BLYTHE, BISHOP, and FISHBACK, they flee from him, only to collide before the sculpture of a nude woman.]

BISHOP

Do you not realize that it is a pagan symbol, an idol of the hedonistic fertility rites?

MARY

No, . . . I mean, yes, I knew it was of Greek mythology—

FISHBACK

Does Mr. Holley find it pleasing: such raw display of licentiousness?

MARY

Yes, . . . I mean no,—

BISHOP

He finds her nakedness pleasing!

MARY

It is art. If it offends you, I'll have Jenny cover it.

BLYTHE

You have slaves working for you?

MARY

They have been leased to us temporarily—

BLYTHE

Does Rev. Holley approve of slavery?

MARY

He sanctions humane treatment of them, yes, for work at home and in the fields–until colonization can return them to Africa.

BISHOP

Federalists. Like Henry Clay.

FISHBACK

Mrs. Holley, the Church is being overrun by European thought and wild revivals in the country sides. Separating religion and politics is a product of French atheism. And who do we now have to teach the young impressionable minds of our students, but this Frenchman Rafinesque!

BISHOP

[In his Scottish brogue:]

Just too many foreigners!

BLYTHE

Rafinesque is on a great race to catalogue all plant life on the earth—begun by such as Linnaeus.

EVERETT

[To MARY, explaining:]

Carl von Linne was the Swedish botanist from the University at Upsala. He was of the opinion that all living creatures changed from primitive forms of life.

FISHBACK

An ancient Greek concept that leads to the assumption that we—who have been created in God's image—evolved from animals!

BISHOP

A blasphemy!

EVERETT

Mary, you promised us a song.

BISHOP

Not a tavern song? What is this, a brothel?

MARY

Many of our greatest Church hymns were once tavern songs.

BLYTHE

So . . . you frequent the taverns then?

MARY

No, of course not. But Horace–

EVERETT

[To MARY]

You mustn't keep your guests waiting. Excuse us. *[He leads her away.]*

FISHBACK

Ah! So, our President frequents the taverns!

BISHOP

But not often. Only when he is not at the *race tracks. [The Doctors toast the Reverends with wine glasses; The Revs toast back with tea cups. The Doctors gather to sing with MARY who accompanies them on guitar. Afterwards, there is applause.]*

BLYTHE

Rev. Holley is allowing new and extraordinary ideas to be preached in chapel.

CALDWELL

Equal invitations are given.

BISHOP

You amaze me, Dr. Caldwell.

CALDWELL

[Of his own singing]

Why, thank you. I thought once of singing opera. That reminds me of a story, when I was singing–.

BISHOP

I meant your opinion of equal invitations in chapel. It allows all differing sentiments to blend.

FISHBACK

Such will absolve and hide every religious spot.

BISHOP

And an equal blending of colors produces White. And that is no color at all.

DUDLEY

Ah, but there is none more pure.

RICHARDSON

The famous Mr. Symmes from Cincinnati is engaged to speak in chapel. He proposes the world is hollow, that a steam ship may sail in at one pole and come out at the other. He is certain that he will get an armament from the government to make the discovery.

FISHBACK

My point, precisely. People barely know what party they belong to anymore. *[RAFINESQUE approaches them again; they stand on guard from his affections]* Where do your sympathies lie, Professor Rafinesque? Are you a Republican?

BISHOP

Rev. Holley avoids partisan affiliation.

BLYTHE

[To RAFINESQUE]

What think you of our President Monroe? He is a friend to Holley.

CALDWELL

[To RAFINESQUE]

It is a shame you were not here this past summer when Monroe visited with General Jackson. We had a good time at the Keen's Hotel.

BISHOP

With the protective tariff on the iron manufacturers and coarse woolens, we might as well be under the thumb of King George again!

CALDWELL

Because of the duty on imported cotton, England cannot dominate the sea trade now.

FISHBACK

Yes, but it has caused revenues of foreign sales to increase and our own manufacturing interests to decrease.

BISHOP

Foreign sales have drawn great sums of money out of our country.

DUDLEY

The state banks will not be bothered by it, they will just continue to print more money for themselves.

FISHBACK

And the more they print, the sooner their collapse. It is the Federalists' way of preparing us for another war!

CALDWELL

If you oppose the Federalism of Jefferson, then you support industry and cluttered city life, and the poverty and violence it has caused. The duties add to the expense of slavery–would you prefer it become a necessity? The question now becomes, who is the enemy?

DUDLEY
[With RICHARDSON aside to CALDWELL]

You *support* the duty then?

RICHARDSON
[To CALDWELL]

You are an *abolitionist*?

CALDWELL
No. I just love a good argument and someone has to take the other side. Come, Rafinesque, enlighten us Yanks. What do you think about foreign trade?

RAFINESQUE
[He speaks with a French accent.]

I do not think it wise to lock horns with our proprietors—

CALDWELL
The voice of wisdom!

RAFINESQUE
–in the manner that you did, Dr. Caldwell, with Benjamin Rush, the chief medical figure at the University of Pennsylvania. Such a dispute caused you to flee here for refuge.

BLYTHE
Wisdom, indeed. *[To CALDWELL:]* So, is that why you came to Kentucky?

RAFINESQUE
Nor do I think we should forfeit our most important assets as you did, Rev. Blythe when you sold off the university land and lost the trust of the

student body. Such disbursements caused you to be thrown down from the seat of President and hated. Even if you did dig the pit for the privy.

RICHARDSON

Touché, Professor Rafinesque! Let me pour you a brandy.

RAFINESQUE

Such drink is a precursor of intemperance and death, with misery, diseases, vices, while the wretched life may last in awful curse.

RICHARDSON

Perhaps a cigar—

RAFINESQUE

A latent poison of the mind and soul; leaving upon the body a ruthless curse affixing in trembling nerves, burning blotches, seals of vice, of infamy, and awful fate.

DUDLEY

[Laughing]

Perhaps the Professor prefers a pipe . . .

RAFINESQUE

Nor do I think it wise to choose impulsively our battles as you did, Dr. Dudley in feuding with Dr. Richardson over an Irish corpse. Such a disturbance caused embarrassment to the University and resulted with your hand in his crotch. Everyone seems to be gathering for the next dance, and I am an excellent dancer. [Exits]

FISHBACK

An odd fish, indeed.

BLYTHE

[Attending MARY and EVERETT]

Mrs. Holley. May I have a word? It is about the Frenchman. He is dancing–

EVERETT

Don't tell me. Does religion oppose dancing also?

BLYTHE

He is dancing by himself.

MARY

Rev. Blythe, I have worshiped in the Church of England since I was a child. The God I worship is a God who wants us to live a life in abundant joy! Joy, Rev. Blythe. Maybe that is not something you preach in your pulpit but I was reared on it. Every Sunday. *[She takes a breath. She is proud of her courage. She notices RAFINESQUE.]* Mother of God! He is dancing by himself! *[BLYTHE recoils in horror. MARY rushes to HOLLEY. Whispering loudly:]* Horace! He is dancing. The Frenchman.

HOLLEY

And quite the attraction to all the ladies.

MARY

The ladies are not dancing with him. *[Rapidly]* **He is dancing by himself!**

HOLLEY

So he is! You must not have this, Mary. It reflects badly on you as hostess . . .

MARY

ME?! He is going to send everyone home before we are served supper!

HOLLEY

Surely, he will tire before long . . .

[In great desperation, MARY lunges into the middle of the dance floor, grabs the hand of RAFINESQUE and becomes his dance partner.]

MARY

Good evening, Professor Rafinesque. I am Mrs. Horace Holley, the President's wife. Your hostess.

RAFINESQUE

Is this the American way: the women choose the men?

MARY

No. I just happened to notice that you have no partner.

RAFINESQUE

That is because none can dance as well as I!

MARY

In America the men dance with a partner—a lady partner.

RAFINESQUE

In Greece the men dance with men.

MARY

We are not in Greece. We are in America. So, kindly conform to American customs.

RAFINESQUE

I have asked the ladies, all of them, and strangely they have refused me.

MARY

If you cannot find a partner, perhaps you should sit the dances out.

RAFINESQUE

But I have a partner, and we have only just begun this dance.

MARY

For you and me this dance is over. *[She pulls away and curtsies.]*

RAFINESQUE

Very well. I have some questions to put to the ladies—

MARY

[Pulling him back to her as partner.]

Maybe you had better not. *[They dance.]* I could not help but notice your appearance. You have changed.

RAFINESQUE

You are pleased with my appearance?

MARY

I am . . .glad you decided to freshen up a bit before we eat. Do you not find such dancing tiresome?

RAFINESQUE

Perhaps a dance instructor would be of help to you?

MARY

I am an excellent dancer.

RAFINESQUE

I thought you heavy on the turns.

MARY

It would be less scandalous if you would converse with others concerning their interests and not your own!

RAFINESQUE

Forgive me. Did you erect your O Tannenbaum?

MARY

Yes, no thanks to you. I do not understand why you raised such a protest to our poor fir tree.

RAFINESQUE

It was a cedar tree. And Toxicodendron radicans.

MARY

You and your crazy names.

RAFINESQUE

I warned you but you would not listen.

MARY

The tree is perfect.

RAFINESQUE

I'm sure it is crooked.

MARY

It is not. I had to wrestle with it a bit—

RAFINESQUE

That is something I'd like to have seen. You inside the tree, wrestling with it—

MARY

What? Do you think I am too precious? I'll have you know, I love the woodlands.

RAFINESQUE

Have we something in common?

MARY

Our tree is straight. And when the candles are lit, it will be lovely. I'm sorry that you do not appreciate the German customs.

RAFINESQUE

Martin Luther began the tradition of lighting candles on the Tannenbaum. A symbol, I suppose, that the Christ Child was the light of the world. It is sure to burn down your house. Toxicodendron radicans. If it burns, you must not breath the smoke. Toxicodendron radicans–

MARY

Professor Rafinesque, please speak of something more pleasant. *[They dance.]*

RAFINESQUE

Shall we speak then of sex? I find a comparison of flowers with the gentler sex. Your sex is the flower of mankind.

MARY

Ah! You mean Womanhood.

RAFINESQUE

A woman's hands . . . appear to be made on purpose, as it were, to handle these delicate objects, and to assort blossoms and flowers to adorn and set off their own blossoming charm.

MARY

You have the makings of a gentleman, Professor Rafinesque. There is such romance in nature.

RAFINESQUE

Nature is a beautiful and modest woman. Concealed under many Veils, . . .some of which she throws aside occasionally or allows them to be removed by those who deserve such a high favor. Such is our venture. *[She is not sure of this. They dance]* Forgive me if I have spoken out of turn. I often use the word "venture" when you say "*future*" because I am reminded of the Italian "venturo." The mouth can be a cruel traitor. Plants have no mouths. Nor an internal cavity for the reception of food. Their organs of reproduction perish before the individual plant, while in the animals they last as long. Have you not found this to be true with the reproductive organs? *[MARY is shocked.]* Of course, you have never applied yourself to the study of an individual's mouths and reproductive organs. May I stop dancing now? Your dawdling has succeeded in boring me gravely. *[He attempts to leave her standing in the middle of the room alone, but MARY comes to herself to pull him once more to herself for a dramatic curtsey.]*

MARY

[With her fan]

Professor Rafinesque, if you have no female dance partner, kindly socialize with the other gentlemen and refrain from asking them to dance. I will remind you of who you are: a guest. And I will often need not be reminded of this conversation with you. Bonne nuit! *[In a rage, she exits. HOLLEY arrives.]*

HOLLEY

How did you fare with Mrs. Holley, Professor Rafinesque?

RAFINESQUE

She is quite taken to me. But then, I have a way with women, to my misfortune. Reverend Holley, may I speak with you now concerning the Botanic Garden?

HOLLEY

The Botanic Garden?

RAFINESQUE

It would be my delight! Students need to see and experience the individuals firsthand, watch them grow, examine their survival and procreation. The garden would include a museum, and it would not be terribly expensive. I have traced a plan for it with a retreat among the flowers, a library and greenhouse—*[HOLLEY travels around the room trying to avoid him. RAFINESQUE trails behind him.]* The first botanic gardens of the sixteenth century were appropriated for the cultivation of medicinal plants. Do you know the Botanic Garden in Palermo?

HOLLEY

This is not Palermo—

RAFINESQUE

Every great university has a Botanic Garden.

HOLLEY

I have not forgotten you. *[As he moves to the Dining Room.]* Shall we go through?

RAFINESQUE

I am not hungry, but I shall sit and watch the others. Have you found insects to be a problem with eating this late in the evening? It may be of interest to you to know that the corolla and the bark of the Lombardy poplar drive away the locusts, and bugs are killed by the smoke of the cayenne pepper, the infusion of the acorns or sweet flag, and of the hemp seeds? I could start a fire for you outside the window—

HOLLEY

[Laughing]

Constantine, I'm sure you could have had any fine and distinguished university of your choosing.

RAFINESQUE

I did not wish to teach at a fine and distinguished university. I chose to come here.

MARY

[Having found the solace of EVERETT's company]

I am beside myself with him! "Toxicodendron radicans!"

EVERETT

That's the botanic name for a plant—

MARY

It's a cedar tree. How dare he criticize it.

EVERETT

Toxicod—oh, no. *[He starts to laugh, tries to stifle it, backs away:]* Were there vines growing up in it?

MARY

There was everything growing up in it. But I pulled them all out.

EVERETT

With your bare hands?

MARY

Well, he offered no hand to help! *[She scratches at her gloves.]* What are you laughing at?

EVERETT

I think "Toxicodendron radicans" is the botanic name for *poison ivy.*

HOLLEY

A toast! *[He raises a glass, and everyone follows his lead.]* To Virginia, the provident mother of Kentucky, who early endowed a Seminary of learning in the West for the benefit of her grandchildren. May the daughter, already the head of a numerous and rising family, prove that she inherits the distinguished parent, the Ancient dominion!

ACT ONE

Scene Four

SPRING

A classroom. The Principal Building is projected on the scrim. The young men students set the stage. BRAND and JOHNSON are at the professor's desk.

BRAND

Someone watch the door!

[JOHNSON pulls out a black snake from his pocket, and all the others make a fuss over it. They pass the snake around, each bragging about how best he can handle it.]

TROTTER

I think it's a mean trick to play!

BRAND

Oh, sit down, Trotter! Jefferson Davis is thinking about coming here in the fall. We've got to impress him.

JOHNSON

[To DAVIS, shaking hands.]

Where 'you from, Davis?

DAVIS

I was born here, but we moved away. I came back a few years ago to St. Rose Priory.

TROTTER

[Of the snake.]

What a way to impress a prospective student! *[To DAVIS]* We don't do this kind of thing all the time.

BRAND

Oh, hang it, Trotter, we do, too. It's just for fun. *[Taking the snake, he holds it up to TROTTER's face, who backs away]* Want to hold him?

TROTTER

Get it away!

BRAND

You scared? It can't hurt you.

TROTTER

No, but it can piss all over you. They are heathen, Davis. Like the President of the University. I'm one of the only Christians around.

DAVIS

That's all right. At St. Rose's I was the only Protestant.

[MARY and EVERETT enter to their surprise as the STUDENTS all run and take their seats. JOHNSON crams the snake back into his pocket. MARY has a rash on her face, that she has been doctoring for several weeks.]

STUDENTS

Good morning, Mrs. Holley.

MARY

Good morning, gentlemen. Where is your teacher?

BRAND

Late again, Mrs. Holley.

[The other students chime in agreeing with him.]

MARY

Now, something is going on? What is it? *[They are silent.]* You there.

JOHNSON

[Standing]

Madison Conyers Johnson, Ma'am.

MARY

Mr. Johnson, what are you concealing? Bring it to me.

TROTTER

It's a snake, Ma'am. They were planning to hide it in the teacher's desk!

BRAND

It's just a common black snake.

EVERETT

Can you image how you would react if you were to open a drawer and put your hand on a snake?

MARY

What a cruel thing to do. Our professors have given up great opportunities to come and teach you here in Kentucky. And this . . . this is the day that the Legislature is coming to visit our campus. What if they had entered the room? What if one of them had opened the drawer? *[There is a silence]* Whose class is this?

EVERETT

Professor Rafinesque.

MARY

I'll guard the door! *[EVERETT throws his hands up. MARY guards the door and the STUDENTS with great excitement plant the snake in the top desk drawer.]* Swear on your honor that Professor Everett and I were not involved!

STUDENTS

We swear!

EVERETT

I've got to get to class. *[He shakes his head with a grin and leaves.]*

MARY

I want the members of the Kentucky Legislature to hear him scream from all the way across campus. *[She glances down the hall. With the excitement of a little girl:]* Here he comes! Good luck!

STUDENTS

[Whispering]

Thank you, Mrs. Holley!

MARY

[In return]

Our little secret! Ah, Good morning, Professor Rafinesque! *[RAFINESQUE enters.]*

What a STRIKING appearance you make for your pupils. *[She winks at the students; they try to conceal their laughter.]*

RAFINESQUE

Good morning, Mrs. Holley. Will you stay for the lecture? It will cost you $10.00.

MARY

I must meet with the Legislature and the President shortly.

RAFINESQUE

Shortly? I can understand that he would have no more time than that for you.

MARY

[Ignoring the insult and her rising rage]

Au revoir! I'll just *slither* on out . . . *[She is gone.]*

RAFINESQUE

Good morning, students. Today marks the most important day of your life. The day you become acquainted with Botany! Can someone tell me what the word means: Botany? *[There is no response.]*

BRAND

Perhaps if you wrote it on the board?

JOHNSON

The chalk is kept in the top drawer.

RAFINESQUE

Thank you. *[He opens the drawer, but then closes it]* No one has an idea of what "Botany" means?

JOHNSON

The study of plants?

RAFINESQUE

[Opens the drawer, but then closes it again.]

Ah! And we shall call them "individuals." Consider the very first individuals of this planet, how they developed. Nurtured by sun and rain. Flora and Fauna. These individuals make up the bread you eat, the air you breathe, the clothes you wear, the ground you travel. *[He reaches into the desk and pulls out the snake.]* What's this? Such is the fellow that crawled from the water organisms to join his family on the land. An individual! Who shall we praise for this fine discovery?

JOHNSON

I, sir.

RAFINESQUE

Then you are not afraid to handle him?

JOHNSON

I should say not!

RAFINESQUE

Come! That your classmates might examine him more thoroughly. *[JOHNSON steps forward and holds the snake.]*

TROTTER

[Under his breath]

It's gonna piss all over him.

RAFINESQUE

Do you know the plant which the snakes cannot bear? It is the liguisticum, or lovage; if it is planted in your gardens no snake will come near, and if you rub your hands with this plant you will handle with safety even the most dangerous snakes for it throws them into a lethargy. By this means the psylle, or jugglers of Europe, are enabled to perform many tricks with the vipers. *[Of the reptile]* Does anyone know its name?

BRAND

Why is it important to know its name?

RAFINESQUE

It could save your life by knowing its name! For this is a deadly poisonous viper!

JOHNSON

Poisonous?

RAFINESQUE

One false move could be fatal. I've known brave men struck one moment and dead the next. At least the rattle-snake warns you off. *[RAFINESQUE attempts to write the name on the chalk board.]* The name of this individual is . . . *[Trying to remember it, he writes, erases, and writes again. He pauses. To himself in frustration:]* Oh, what is it? *[The students laugh at his forgetfulness.]* Whatever I forget, I want you to learn! *[It comes to him.]* Ah, yes! *[He writes "Agkistrodon Piscivorus."]* Agkistrodon Piscivorus *[He takes the snake. JOHNSON is relieved.]* Thank you, Johnson. You may return to your seat, you look a little pale. It is always important to eat breakfast. *[To JOHNSON:]* And you may return to your seat, too, Johnson. *[As they realize he was referring to the snake before, the students laugh.]*

JOHNSON

Yes, sir. *[At his seat, he punches BRAND, who punches him back.]* "It can't harm you."

RAFINESQUE

[Kissing the snake]

Yes, back to your seat, Mr. Snake. You will come in handy for dissection later. *[The class laughs and again when he puts the snake back in the drawer. RAFINESQUE jumps on top of the desk. The class finds this odd and stops laughing, they are almost frightened.]* Oh! How can I tell you the life of a traveling Botanist! You meet rough and muddy roads to vex you. And blind paths to perplex you, rocks, mountains, and steep ascents.

[Gradually the lights change, we hear sounds of the wild forests, the stage and scrim are transformed into a wonderland of sylvan mystery as his lecture comes to life!]

You may often lose your way, and must always have a compass with you as I had. You may be lamed in climbing rocks or break your limbs by a fall! You must wade through brooks, rivers, and swamps. In deep fords or swift streams, you may lose your footing and be drowned. You may be overtaken by a storm, the trees fall around you, the thunder roars and strikes before you. The winds may annoy you, the fire of heaven or of men sets fire to the grass of forest, and you may be surrounded by it, unless you flee for your life. In an unhealthy region you may fall sick on the road and become helpless . . .

Many fair days and fair roads are met with a clear sky or a bracing breeze inspires delight and ease, you breathe the pure air of the country, every rill and brook offer a draught of limpid fluid. What a delight to meet with a spring after a thirsty walk, or a bowl of cool milk out of the dairy! What a sound sleep at night after a long day's walk, what soothing naps at noon under a shaded tree near a purling brook!

Every step taken into the fields appears to afford new enjoyments. Landscapes and plants jointly meet in your sight. Here is an old acquaintance seen again; there a novelty, a rare plant, perhaps a new one! You hasten to pluck it, examine it, admire and put it in your book. Then you walk on thinking what it might be, or may be made by you hereafter. You feel exultation, you are a conqueror, you have made a conquest over Nature, you are going to add a new object, or a page into science. This peaceful conquest has cost no tears, but fills your mind with a proud sensation of not being useless on earth, or having detected another link of the creative power of God. For with God, you live in his wide temple not made by hands. Such are the delightful feelings of a real botanist.

[The lights return. The students applaud his performance. It is the classroom once more.]

Forgive me. I get carried away. But if only you could see for yourself: the world of Flora and Fauna. *[He looks out the window, and melancholia fills his soul]* Come! Leave your books.

BRAND

You mean, . . . leave the building?

TROTTER

It is not permitted.

RAFINESQUE

A Botanist sets his own rules. Come. *[He takes his umbrella and is leaving.]* Now, to experience the Garden!

TROTTER

What about the Legislature?

RAFINESQUE

Let them find their own umbrellas! *[There is great delight as all the students follow him out of the classroom.]*

DAVIS

[To JOHNSON:]

We never had anything like this at St. Rose's.

[The stage is bare and the sounds of the students fade out. Silence. Then the voice of HOLLEY nearing the classroom:]

HOLLEY

I do want Members of the Legislature to view Rafinesque's class. Just listen to the reticence of his classroom. You would swear that no one was here at all—*[HOLLEY appears to an empty classroom.]* Jesus, Mary, and Joseph! *[CLAY and MARY appear]*

CLAY

I suppose that makes me Joseph?

MARY

The man's seedlings have sprouted his brain.

HOLLEY

[Examining books on the desk]

This is his class.

MARY

John and I stopped by earlier to say hello, and they were all here then.

HOLLEY

When was that?

MARY

Within the hour.

BLYTHE

[Entering in a dither]

Rev. Holley, Professor Rafinesque has taken a whole army of students off campus!

HOLLEY

Uh, . . . he is a naturalist. I would presume he has taken them to study nature in its original habitat.

BLYTHE

Who gave him permission?

HOLLEY

[After a slight pause]

I did. Senator Clay, ward off the Members of the Legislature. Send them to the Keene Place.

CLAY

We will meet you there.

BLYTHE

[As he exits with CLAY:]

I can assure you that nothing like this ever happened while I was President. *[They are gone.]*

MARY

This is just like when President Monroe and General Jackson visited in July. You let them publish your speech without editing it, and it was a terrible ridicule for the school. They thought you too apologetic.

HOLLEY

General Jackson liked it. He said it made me sound like the common man.

MARY

Yes, it did. Like a Kentucky hillbilly!

HOLLEY

Mary–

MARY

These things represent you to all the people. You need to defend yourself for the good of the university.

HOLLEY

Henry Clay has advised me to keep a dignified silence—

MARY

A dignified silence?

HOLLEY

The high cultivation of genius finds more to enjoy than to suffer.

MARY

The State Legislature has failed to procure the assistance you requested—

HOLLEY

Students from the best of families all over the country are coming to our university in droves. Professor Rafinesque could teach English to the French speaking boys from Louisiana.

MARY

Professor Rafinesque! You haven't found a suitable place for him since he came.

HOLLEY

Mary, you just don't like Rafinesque.

MARY

That is not so. I hate him. There is a difference.

HOLLEY

He is a little rash at times . . .*[Of her face]* It, by the way, has cleared up nicely.

MARY

He's a plague. *[MARY comes and sits on his knee, her arms around his neck.]* Horace, he is an insult and embarrassment to your university. *[HOLLEY starts to respond, she stops him]* Did you give him permission to take his class "across the woods?"*[HOLLEY does not respond]* I thought as much.

HOLLEY

I'll talk to Constantine when he gets back.

MARY

If he gets back. *[She gets up and paces around the desk. HOLLEY stands.]*

HOLLEY

I happen to know that he carries a compass with him at all times. *[MARY holds up a compass from the desk]* Mary, perhaps if you tried a little harder you might actually come to like him. Invite him to dinner: I think the man must live off corn bread and salt pork. Offer to wash his clothes—he would make a much better appearance cleaned up and well fed.

MARY

[MARY looks at HOLLEY several times, tries to speak but cannot, she is so astonished. Then:]

If that is what you think is expected of the President's wife. I shall try to be civil, and to be agreeable, and to look interestingly!

HOLLEY

I could kiss you! *[She looks for the gesture, but it does not come.]* John Everett will be leaving us in a few months.

MARY

What?

HOLLEY

You might as well know now. He is returning to Boston to become secretary to his brother in Europe . . . in the American Legation at the Hague. *[EVERETT appears in the doorway. HOLLEY gives him a look to signal that he has told her.]* I'll meet the two of you at the Keene Place. Leave a message for Constantine on the board, will you, and tell him to go there? So that he will know where we are? *[MARY's stare is one to kill, the absurdity of it all. HOLLEY kisses his finger and plants it on MARY's forehead. As he exits, we see that he is wiping his finger.]*

EVERETT

[When they are alone.]

I should have told you myself. There is nothing for me here, now. The university has trained its own tutors. *[He laughs]* The price for success. I have not the standing to become a professor at such the university as Transylvania has become. *[He pauses, aware of his affections for her.]* I shall write to you from Boston.

MARY

[Holding back her emotion.]

Somehow Boston seems farther away now.

EVERETT

I'll wait for you outside. *[He drops his head and exits.]*

MARY

And I'll be here. *[She looks around]* Yes, here. *[She goes to the window to watch him.]* You go back to Boston with its glittering spires . . .In all the charms of colour, form, and grace . . *[She picks up the chalk and starts to weep, but fights it with a heavy sigh.]* Yes, I'll be here . . . cooking for the lunatic and washing his underwear. *[She writes on the board: "Professor Rafinesque, Go to–" but the chalk breaks. She looks at the words.]* Oh, Professor Rafinesque, the message I'd like to leave you . . . *[She looks for chalk. Opening the desk drawer, she sees the snake, screams, and slams the drawer shut.]*

ACT ONE

Scene Five

SUMMER

We hear urgent rapping on a door. The scrim is lit from the front to reveal the Old Seminary at night. Students arrange furniture for a parlour. The Grecian statue is draped. HARRIETTE, in nightgown, a girl of twelve, appears with a candle. The rapping stops; enter RAFINESQUE.

HARRIETTE

Good evening, Professor Rafinesque. Comment allez-vous?

RAFINESQUE

Tres bien. Merci. Et vous?

HARRIETTE

Tres bien. Merci. Assoies-toi s'il te plait. *[She brings him in and they sit.]*

RAFINESQUE

Vous parlez très bien français. Ce que tu lis?

HARRIETTE

Paul and Virginia.

RAFINESQUE

I love *Paul and Virginia.*

HARRIETTE

It is very sad. Virginia was not very smart.

RAFINESQUE

No?

HARRIETTE

She drowns because she will not take off her dress. I would have taken my dress off! I don't care who was looking. Would you want to drown?

RAFINESQUE

[Laughing]

No, I would not. I was in a shipwreck once and almost did.

HARRIETTE

Oh, tell me about it!

[The clock in the hall chimes.]

RAFINESQUE

I will. But first, is your father home?

HARRIETTE

No, he has gone to the Opera.

RAFINESQUE

Is your mother home?

HARRIETTE

She is running away from him. We must go with her to Boston in the morning. I don't want to go. We shall stay all summer, and leave Father here to speak to the Legislature. He says they are going to give our school a lot of money. *[She whispers]* She has sewn silver dollars in the lining of her dress. Promise not to tell.

RAFINESQUE

No, I won't.

MARY

[Calling from the other room]

Harriette, dear, who was at the door?

HARRIETTE

It is Professor Rafinesque.

MARY

[Whispering loudly]

Tell him we are not home.

RAFINESQUE

I came to speak to Dr. Holley!

MARY

[Entering slowly, reluctantly, wearing robe, nightgown, and cap.]

Good evening, Professor. Harriette, you must get ready for bed.

HARRIETTE

Yes, Mother. *[HARRIETTE leaves]*

MARY

Do you know what time it is?

RAFINESQUE

You have a clock in the hall; I heard it chime. I have come with urgent matters to set before Dr. Holley. It concerns my Garden!

MARY

Rafinesque, we are leaving in the morning.

RAFINESQUE

I shall await his return. *[He sits.]*

MARY

This is not a free house. *[RAFINESQUE stays seated.]*

MARY

Very well. I was just preparing some tea. I'll send Jenny back to bed. Excuse me. *[She exits to do so.]*

RAFINESQUE

[Talking to himself aloud]

President Holley despises the natural sciences and wishes to exclude them. Now, in my Garden we shall grow teas to please King George IV himself.

I shall try and endure yours. To think I first thought you fat and horrid. I was wrong. You are not horrid.

HARRIETTE

[Entering again, quickly and quietly.]

Are you going with us tomorrow?

RAFINESQUE

No. I have much exploring to do this summer.

HARRIETTE

Go with us! The Gratzes are going with us. And Mrs. Wickliffe's nurse. And Mr. Cooper will drive us. I wish you were going with us! *[She sits with him.]* May I come as a guest to your class some day? Do you know Billy Brand? His name is really Gulielmus Moses Brand. He's so terribly smart. Maybe he'll ask me as a guest. He should, don't you think? After all, I'm going to marry him someday.

RAFINESQUE

Does he know this?

HARRIETTE

He's not that smart. And I'm going to have lots of children. And have an orange tree.

RAFINESQUE

Why an orange tree?

HARRIETTE

That way I can just pick an orange and eat it anytime I'd like.

RAFINESQUE

Orange trees don't grow in Kentucky. The winter would kill them.

HARRIETTE

[Disappointed]

Oh. I'd love to have an orange tree. *[She hears her mother and runs off whispering:]*

Bonne nuit!

MARY

[Appearing with a tea tray, disappointed that he has not taken his leave.]

Professor, why do you insist on this garden of yours?

RAFINESQUE

Mr. Clifford's artifacts have been annexed to me. Since I came here, I have endured no salary; I must hunt down audiences and charge them for lectures; I receive only board, firewood, and candles . . .

MARY

[She sets the tea tray, allowing the tea to steep.]

Candles are costly.

RAFINESQUE

I write at night. Mr. Clifford was my only friend and meconate.

MARY

Meconate?

RAFINESQUE

I derived the word myself.

MARY

Are you in the habit of creating your own language?

RAFINESQUE

I derived the word from the name of the patron of Virgil and Horace. Mr. Clifford was a patron to me. If it were not for Mr. Clifford, I would never have come here.

MARY

Remind me to write him a letter of thanks.

RAFINESQUE

He is dead.

MARY

I am sorry.

RAFINESQUE

My fault for having trusted him. I came. Then he died.

MARY

All human beings die, Professor.

RAFINESQUE

To do good to mankind has ever been an ungrateful task. Plants do not betray you.

MARY

Have you been betrayed?

RAFINESQUE

I was shipwrecked off the coast of Cape Montauk. My Josephine, thinking me dead, married another. An actor in the theatre.

MARY

What a tragedy.

RAFINESQUE

No, he plays the comedies.

MARY

[Explaining:]

How tragic your loss.

RAFINESQUE

Yes. I lost all my manuscripts, 200 maps, and drawings, 300 copper plates, and 600,000 specimens of shells, 50 boxes containing my herbal—Why are you laughing?

MARY

I would think that the tragedy was in the loss of a wife, not your botanical effects.

RAFINESQUE

Yes, that was tragic, too.

MARY

I realize that of your past I am much in the dark.

RAFINESQUE

Some things keep best in the dark.

The revolution in France exhausted my paternal relations. Our inheritance fell into the hands of a Mr. Lafleche, who has never settled with neither me nor my brother, but pretended the funds were lost. Oh, but he has realized many. Yes, I have been betrayed.

MARY

[Pouring the tea.]

Light or dark?

RAFINESQUE

Very dark. He was a liar, a traitor, and a thief.

MARY

I meant the tea: do you wish milk or lemon? *[She pours the tea]*

RAFINESQUE

You have lemon?

MARY

We do our best. *[With tongs she places a lemon slice in his cup while asking:]* Lemon, then?

RAFINESQUE

No . . . milk. You have lemons? How extraordinary. *[MARY, realizing her mistake but having lost much care with it all, fishes the lemon slice out of his cup and discards it on a plate. She pours the milk into his cup]* I said, "No milk."

MARY

Oh, . . . *[MARY pours fresh tea into her own cup and gives it to him. She takes the cup with the milk for herself.]*

RAFINESQUE

[Of the lemon:]

Yes, yes. Quite extraordinary. Wherever did you get it?

MARY

[She looks at the jug with puzzlement. Of the milk:]

From the cow. *[She sips her tea. RAFINESQUE waits.]*

RAFINESQUE

I meant the lemon. Yes, I will have it. The lemon. Not the cow. *[MARY dumps the lemon in his cup and continues to sip her tea with frustration; but thankful that the tea ritual is underway–the sooner to end.]* You play the guitar. I read your poems in the *Western Monitor*, the one on the Catskills and Niagara.

MARY

[Referring to her poetry, fishing for a compliment]

And? . . . What do you think of it?

RAFINESQUE

[Referring to the guitar.]

Very fine.

MARY

Thank you.

RAFINESQUE

But I prefer the violin.

MARY

I meant the poems. How did you know they were mine?

RAFINESQUE

Mrs. Mary Holley, did you really think yourself so clever as not to be discovered? They were signed "M," Mrs. Mary Holley. "M." I am no simpleton.

MARY

Who am I to disagree with you, professor? *[After all, her name is Mary with an M.]*

RAFINESQUE

[Proud of his cleverness:]

You first lived in the big house on Mulberry Street. I'm sure that moving into this Old Seminary saves you money.

MARY

It does. And here I am not obliged to give my time to tedious company—*[He now being the exception.]* As a rule. And it gives me a chance to get to know the students. I take care of my children and study. I have discovered that the heart will be quiet in proportion as the mind is active. I noticed that you do not dine with us at High Table.

RAFINESQUE

The food is overpriced.

MARY

Steward Usher is our chef—he serves the same meals in his tavern, "The Sign of the Ship."

RAFINESQUE

More "The Sign of the Wreckage," if you ask me. *[Laughing, she secretly agrees with him.]* Your house is so au . . . *[He struggles to find the appropriate English word]*

MARY

[Attempting to help him.]

Attractive?

RAFINESQUE

What is the word? Au . . .

MARY

Artistic?

RAFINESQUE

Uh . . .

MARY

Unusual?

RAFINESQUE

No. Ugly! Yes, that's the word. Your house is so ugly. *[He sips his tea.]* It needs color. Have you thought of planting roses and jasmine around it?

MARY

I love the smell of jasmine.

RAFINESQUE

You would have to bring the jasmine inside during the winter. I would be glad to plant them for you. And peonies.

MARY

Peonies. *[She is quiet.]* Thank you, Professor. I think peonies are—

RAFINESQUE

–the perfect flower. *[This agreement in thought begins to mellow them both.]* "Paeoniaceae." It is named from Paeon, the student of Asclepius who was the Greek god of healing. But Asclepius was jealous of Paeon and tried to kill him: Zeus protected Paeon by turning him into a flower.

MARY

Have you always been interested in gardens, Professor?

RAFINESQUE

When I was a child, I was sent to live with my grandmother in Marseilles by the sea. I made myself a little garden, in a wild remote place, but my walks there gave me much pleasure. Later, when I was learning Commerce with my stepfather, Mr. Lanthois, we would visit the gardens and museum of an English lady, Mrs. Partridge near Montenero. A single blade of grass will afford us an unremitted enjoyment and might afford us occupation during many years if we were to consider it and study it under all its different points of view.

MARY

We were created to care for the plants and animals.

RAFINESQUE

There are two creation stories in the Bible. One says that plant and animal life were created first and then the human. The Second says that the human was created first and then plants and animals.

MARY

Which is correct?

RAFINESQUE

I do not know, I was not there. I only know that there was a garden. And God planted it in Eden.

MARY

Do you really think that God created everything in six days?

RAFINESQUE

The days of Creation in the Bible are divine "days," meaning long periods of time.

MARY

Precisely!

RAFINESQUE

If you follow the first creation story, we sprang from the water and through time have changed. The world must change by gradual steps. If you follow the second creation story, we were watered and sprang up from the dirt of the Garden.

MARY

So, you believe there is a God?

RAFINESQUE

I believe in a God of love.

MARY

Why would a God of love allow such evil in the world?

RAFINESQUE

Evil is not of God. It springs from deeds of darkness and deceit, by hands that are free to choose. If God acted for each human soul, man could not sin; but God would sin for him! *[MARY finds this idea amusing and smiles.]* From the God of goodness, no evil springs. We are his children–not his slaves–and he has allowed the use of *change*, a will to choose or reject. By holy providence, the fate of men is ruled, not by mere chance, but by happy change.

MARY

"Happy change."

RAFINESQUE

God only desires peaceful creeds; rites of cruelty he hates. Let the Jews and Muslims forbear the use of pork. Let Hindus never eat a holy cow. It is all the same to God. Whether one is sprinkled by water as an infant or immersed as an adult, it is not the sins washed away but the grace that is received. It is but a sad mistake for those who chose to adore only a part of God—a limb—and not the whole of Him who is present at every person's side.

MARY

[The clock chimes. Mary pours more tea.]

Tell me more of this Garden of yours.

RAFINESQUE

In my Garden, people of all walks of life will gather there: health, education, and pleasure will meet at every step. And the only religion there will be the religion of the soul.

MARY

So many evils have been done in the name of religion. I sometimes think God—if there is a God—has set a veil before his face.

RAFINESQUE

Then the world he gave us is but a mirror of himself.

MARY

How is your tea?

RAFINESQUE

It tastes terrible. Like my pulmel.

MARY

Pulmel?

RAFINESQUE

Yes, it is a special tea that I discovered, my own secret recipe. It will prevent consumption. You must try it.

MARY

I don't believe I have consumption.

RAFINESQUE

How unfortunate. How are your children? Miss Harriette's French is very good.

MARY

She is having a difficult time with arithmetic. And little Horace, well, he, like you, prefers the out of doors. If only Horace could find time to take him hunting.

RAFINESQUE

My step-father took me hunting when I was about his age. *[He is suddenly quiet. MARY waits for him to continue. Then:]* The first bird I shot was a Parus. I watched the little thing struggle and die. I will never hunt again.

MARY

You mention a step-father. What of your father?

RAFINESQUE

He was a ship merchant. He died of the yellow fever on a voyage to China. He had wanted to take me with him.

MARY

How unfortunate.

RAFINESQUE

No, had I gone with him, I would have caught the yellow fever and died as well.

MARY

How unfortunate that he died. My father died of the yellow fever from a voyage to West India. Our house and all that we owned went to auction. Then mother married again and my stepfather bought the place back for her. But I grew up with an uncle and his wife. Then I met Horace. Then my stepfather died . . . and mother married again.

RAFINESQUE

I hope for a long life: I wouldn't want to marry your mother. I had a son but he died as an infant.

MARY

Oh, Professor . . . *[She puts her tea cup down.]*

RAFINESQUE

[He is quiet.]

I have a little daughter. Her name is Emilia. She is the age of your little Harriette. I have not seen her for seven years.

MARY

[Her empathy growing:]

Where is she?

RAFINESQUE

With her mother? I do not know. My sister, Georgette, has made inquiries for me through the consuls of Naples and Palermo, but they have proved to be in vain.

MARY

I am so sorry. I did not know. You must not give up hope. Not for your child. Oh, no. Never.

RAFINESQUE

I believe that I have found a friend in you, Mrs. Holley. *[They are silent.]* You leave for Boston in the morning?

MARY

Yes.

RAFINESQUE

You still miss Boston very much.

MARY

Yes.

RAFINESQUE

I miss Philadelphia. And Mr. Clifford.

MARY

I know what you mean.

RAFINESQUE

You are to travel without Dr. Holley?

MARY

The school demands his presence. We will travel with Benjamin and Maria Gratz.

RAFINESQUE

Perhaps you could visit Mr. Everett there? You must miss him very much.

MARY

Yes, I do.

RAFINESQUE

I suspect he was in love with you.

MARY

He was just a friend—a little bit of Boston we brought with us. Unlike you, Professor, I have no great garden of the world to carry me through my days.

RAFINESQUE

Will you come back?

MARY

[She looks down.]

Why do you ask that?

RAFINESQUE

I suspect you will try to find a position for Dr. Holley, there.

MARY

You have a devious mind. *[She grins. He grins.]*

RAFINESQUE

I hope you will come back. You make Kentucky so pleasant for us.

MARY

How kind of you to say that. Thank you.

RAFINESQUE

[Finishing his tea, he sets it aside.]

It is late. I must leave you in peace. It was selfish of me to stay so long. *[He waits for her to rise. She does so and he gets up]*

MARY

I shall tell Dr. Holley that you inquired about the Botanic Garden. *[She walks him to the door.]*

RAFINESQUE

I will check on him for you to be sure he is taking his meals, and getting fresh air. I'm sure he will miss you very much.

MARY

Yes . . . And I him.

RAFINESQUE

Good night, Mrs. Holley. *[He turns.]* I enjoyed your poems on the Catskills and Niagara. I pray you shall have a safe trip with the Gratz family this summer. And that John Everett is in Europe when you arrive, and that no one will offer your husband a position in Boston. And I shall continue to burn my costly candles. . . . They shall be lit in hopes of your return.

ACT TWO

Scene One

AUTUMN

The scrim is lit from behind to reveal the blue silhouette of a graveyard at night. Dark skeleton branches of old trees, tombstones, the figure of SOLOMON digging. We hear the hooting of an owl. The barking of a dog. Sounds of night. October 1822. JOHNSON and DAVIS appear below the scrim, carrying lanterns.

DAVIS

President Holley has a wife?

JOHNSON

Of course he has a wife. She's been in Boston, that's all.

DAVIS

She's been gone a long time.

JOHNSON

Over a year. She heard you were coming so she skipped town. *[BRAND jumps out of the bushes with a wild animal scream. JOHNSON and DAVIS jump.]*

BRAND

I scared the tar out of you both!

JOHNSON

Shhhh! You're going to get us in trouble with President Holley.

BRAND

President Holley has been gone all summer. He went to Boston to bring his wife back.

DAVIS

I bet she doesn't come back at all.

BRAND

We'll see.

DAVIS

[Of the cemetery at night:]

Pretty spooky, isn't it?

BRAND

A few years ago, we came digging for a corpse and got arrested. Even the professors.

JOHNSON

No kidding? What happened?

BRAND

They let us go. They said there was no law that made the corpse private property. No law but the Law from the Scriptures that, "from dust we come and into dust we must return." So, we had to pay *One cent* damages for taking that much *dirt*.

DAVIS

You've actually seen a dead corpse?

BRAND

No, . . . but I've seen a live one! Ooohhhh . . . . *[He moans like a ghost.]* It will be Halloween in another week.

[We hear the scraping of the shovel against the wooden coffin lid]

JOHNSON

Holy ghosts!

[DUDLEY, CALDWELL, RICHARDSON are on the scene behind the scrim in silhouette. BRAND, JOHNSON, and DAVIS exit and make their way in silhouette joining them.]

DUDLEY

That's our treasure, boys! Good show, Solomon—you're a giant of strength. Now then, let's get him out. *[We hear grunting and cursing while DUDLEY, CALDWELL, RICHARDSON, BRAND, JOHNSON and DAVIS assist SOLOMON in pulling the coffin from the ground.]*

RICHARSON

Where's Dr. Rafinesque?

JOHNSON

He's exploring the plants— *[RAFINESQUE appears with a plant in his hand]*

CALDWELL

Shh! Before someone hears us. *[They pull the coffin above ground. With a crowbar they lift the lid.]* Let's wrap him up, boys, and head home.

RAFINESQUE

It doesn't seem decent to rob this man's grave. It's not reverent.

DUDLEY

How else can we train our students to be surgeons unless they have a cadaver to dissect? You know what it's like: you insist on studying live plants.

RAFINESQUE

Yes, but the plants are alive . . .

DUDLEY

Are you suggesting we dissect a living person? Would you like to volunteer?

RAFINESQUE

Ah, . . . no.

DUDLEY

Then shut up and give us a hand. *[As they finish wrapping him, a gunshot is heard. Quickly, the men run and hide, passing the wrapped corpse from one to the other. RAFINESQUE is the last to end up with the corpse; he darts back and forth with it unable to find a hiding spot, resembling a frantic dance with a dummy. He drops it, disappears and all is deadly silent. The GUARD arrives carrying a lantern and rifle.]*

GUARD

Bandits! Show yourselves, you grave robbers! *[There is a knock from inside the coffin. The GUARD, scatters in terror. Silence. Then:]*

RAFINESQUE

[From inside the coffin:]

Would you be so kind as to help me out? The lid is stuck!

CALDWELL

[As they reappear and approach the coffin. Whispering:]

Rafinesque, you are a genius! That fat ass ran with his tail between his legs! *[He picks up the crowbar and tries to pry open the lid.]*

DUDLEY

We haven't got time for that. Let's get out of here before he comes back! *[They pick up the casket and corpse and take them.]*

DAVIS

We never had anything like this at St. Rose's . . .

RAFINESQUE

[As he is carried off in the coffin.]

What's going on? Get me out! What's happening? It's me, Rafinesque!

[The graveyard silhouetted scene dims out as a pool of light downstage reveals HARRIETTE and BRAND as if on their way to class. HARRIETTE is now more mature in appearance, a young woman.]

BRAND

Miss Harriette Holley?

HARRIETTE

Good morning, Mr. William Brand.

BRAND

Did you enjoy Boston?

HARRIETTE

Yes, thank you.

BRAND

You've changed so. *[To his delight, for she is more a woman now.]*

HARRIETTE

It has been a long time.

BRAND

We were wondering if you were ever coming back. I hope that you and Mrs. Holley are here to stay? You are enrolled at the Female Academy?

HARRIETTE

Yes.

BRAND

May I escort you to the Memorial Service of Colonel Morrison? *[BRAND escorts her to a chair that is being brought by Students and Faculty who set up chairs downstage and sit with their backs to the audience facing the scrim where the silhouette of HOLLEY is seen giving his Memorial Address for Col. James Morrison in Chapel, May 1823.]*

HOLLEY

Colonel James Morrison was a Christian in his sentiments and practice, but did not consider the peculiarities of any of the sectarian creeds in religion as necessary to his character. He had large views and philanthropic feelings, and recognized the wisdom, authority, goodness, and impartiality of the Deity in all relations of life. With him a life of virtue was the most suitable homage to the Deity. He knew and felt that the end of all genuine religion is to make men good, useful, and happy. *[As HOLLEY continues, the lights reveal BISHOP seated downstage with the others.]*

BISHOP

[With angry sarcasm]

If one enjoys the education of a University and if one improves it—one is saved and most highly exalted in heaven.

FISHBACK

After all, Morrison has left the school a tremendous amount of money.

BLYTHE

Don't worry, money like that will be tied up in litigation for many years.

[The scrim is lit from the front showing the capital of Washington D.C. The Students and Faculty turn their chairs around to face the downstage, and become members of the crowd with banners displaying: "Republican" and "Whigs." The crowd cheers. February 1824. Henry CLAY speaks downstage.]

CLAY

Thank you, dear friends of President Adams. As his Secretary of State, I will endeavor to do my duty in this office, and if God grant me life and health, I will disappoint and triumph over my enemies. We shall prevent Mexico and Columbia from seizing Cuba or Puerto Rico. We shall suggest a canal across Mexico and Central America that will open its doors to all the ships of the world at equal tolls. I shall personally be your representative of our Republican type of government that has brought blessings to our United States. *[The crowd cheers.]* And if any man should falsely make a certificate of public stock of the United States, every such person shall be deemed guilty of felony punished not exceeding five hundred dollars, imprisoned and confined to hard labor.

DESHA

[Appearing from the crowd, he is angry.]

Henry Clay! The Kentucky delegation had directed you to cast vote for Andrew Jackson! Instead, you voted for John Adams so that he would name you his Secretary of State. I accuse you of corrupt bargaining! *[A banner reading, "Jackson Democracy" appears. The crowd chants: "Traitor to the West!" "Unholy Corruption!" "Judas!"]* One of Mr. Clay's emissaries made the same offer to General Jackson but he refused! *[The crowd is loud. A stuffed dummy is carried out, a sign around its neck reading "Henry Clay." The scrim is lit from the front in torches and flames as we hear the shouts of the crowd: "Bargain and Corruption!" and "Willful Turncoat!"]*

CLAY

No! Listen to me! If you had wanted Jackson as your President, you would have elected him and not put the responsibility on the House—*[The crowd rushes off with CLAY pleading after them. From the dark we hear the voice of President HOLLEY:]*

HOLLEY

What are the first operations of the mind of a child in the dark? A sense of weakness–dependence—invisible agency—something above them. These are the rudiments of religion.

[The scrim is lit from the front to show the Principal Building. Winter 1824. HOLLEY appears in academic gown before the scrim. The students have brought in desks for a classroom and are seated.]

HOLLEY

Since the Dark Ages, men have set curses. It was their only means of retaliation from unfair and often cruel treatment. Take for example, the monastic estates confiscated by King Henry III. They are haunted, or some believe. *[There is a playful ghostly moaning among the students. HOLLEY laughs.]* We all like a good ghost story, don't we? But many of the new owners of those estates met ghastly ends. Why? Was it because of the curses left on them? All superstitions and personifications of mythology point to religion and immortality as their foundation. *[TROTTER raises his hand to speak. HOLLEY acknowledges him and he stands.]*

TROTTER

Divine justice is not superstition. The curses of a righteous man who has been treated unfairly is honored by God. If indeed God is a just god.

HOLLEY

Trotter poses a wise question. "Is God just?"

JOHNSON

[Raises his hand and stands.]

What of the earthquake in Lisbon? Thousands were killed and many praying inside the Church. Was God showing them justice in the collapse of the ceiling?

TROTTER

For their sins, yes. *[The students argue.]*

HOLLEY

Good. Good. Open discussion is the manner of the Greek fathers. What we have addressed now is the theory of "Original Sin," "Predestination," and even "Gnosticism." Concepts from the Judeo-Christian tradition.

JOHNSON

[Raising his hand and standing.]

But we are all sinners, are we not?

TROTTER

For the righteous it was not the hand of God.

DAVIS

What was it, then?

TROTTER

The devil, of course.

JOHNSON

That sounds as incredible as the medieval curses. A man with horns and a tail who is the scapegoat for the mistakes of humanity. How convenient for the irresponsible man. And a pitchfork! The symbol of the farmer—all an attempt by the upper classes to berate the lower. That's what the word "pagan," really means, is "farmer."

TROTTER

You deny the existence of Satan?

JOHNSON

Are we not made almost equal to the angels—isn't that what the Scripture says?

HOLLEY

I think what Johnson is saying is that he denies easy explanations for complex questions; that modern man must accept responsibility for his own actions. *[He laughs.]* A religious man who believed in the depravity of humanity put up at the same public house with a Quaker for the purpose of lodging all night. After supper, they were shown into the same room where upon the first man knelt beside the one bed and prayed, confessing himself a sinner and deserving God's greatest punishments! The Quaker took his hat to retire. "Are you not to rest with me tonight?" asked the pious man. "No, sire," answered the Quaker. "I cannot sleep with such a scoundrel as thou confessest thyself to be!" *[The students all but TROTTER laugh and exit. FISHBACK appears.]*

TROTTER

[To HOLLEY:]

You advocate free conscience in your classroom yet you ridicule my opinions! *[To FISHBACK]* Mr. Holley ridicules religion! He puts our Savior on the level of Socrates!

FISHBACK

Is this the truth?

HOLLEY

The truth is that Mr. Trotter has not turned in his essay, and has been fined twice already.

TROTTER

I did not have time to finish it Saturday.

HOLLEY

Then why didn't you finish it on Sunday?

TROTTER

It was the Sabbath. I will not break the commandments—

HOLLEY

[To TROTTER]

I order you to finish that theme and turn it in or you will not be eligible for graduation. *[TROTTER leaves, FISHBACK follows him. BRAND approaches HOLLEY.]*

BRAND

President Holley, I will graduate at the end of the term, sir.

HOLLEY

I would say you will, William. Congratulations.

BRAND

And I am old enough now to join my father's business . . .

HOLLEY

I would say you are, William.

BRAND

And, sir, . . . I have come to ask your permission, sir. I love your daughter, Harriette . . .

HOLLEY

I would say you do, William.

[The scrim upstage is lit with the Principal Building. MARY walks with JOHNSON downstage.]

MARY

I was sorry to hear that Jeff Davis is leaving us.

JOHNSON

[With disgust]

I'm not. Maybe he'll like West Point better.

MARY

What's this? You and Jeff have been great friends. *[JOHNSON says nothing.]* His father has died, and his fate is in his brother's hands. That's not his fault. He has no say in the matter. Don't you think he would rather stay here? *[JOHNSON starts to tear up. DAVIS crosses carrying his suitcase.]* Go to him.

JOHNSON

I can't.

MARY

Weigh it out. Which is heavier, your pain at losing a friend, or his at losing a father? *[JOHNSON goes to DAVIS]*

DAVIS

I'm going back to the farm.

JOHNSON

I'm sorry to hear about your father's death.

DAVIS

My brother doesn't share my father's feeling about our school. *[He puts his hand out to shake]* I guess this is goodbye? *[JOHNSON grasps his hand to shake, but the two fall into an embrace. They weep together, as brotherly love is severed.]* I shall miss you, Jeff. It won't be the same here without you. God go with you. *[JOHNSON takes a suitcase in one hand, his arm around DAVIS, and they cross the stage together and exit. The scrim slowly goes to black as we hear HOLLEY's voice in the classroom, trailing into the dark:]*

HOLLEY

Religion is founded deep in our nature. Why else would there be so many quarrels, imposition practiced and submitted to, but that it proves its importance. If our immortality is not true, we can make nothing of the great scheme of things. If there is no immortal mind, then there is no God.

ACT TWO

Scene Two

WINTER

We hear the wail of HARRIETTE. The scrim is lit from the front showing once again the Old Seminary with candles at night. Students change the scenery. HARRIETTE lies in her dressing gown upon a sofa, covered with quilts, and is attended by MARY and MRS. BRADFORD. Dr. DUDLEY, CALDWELL, and HOLLEY stand on the other side of the room L, talking among themselves. It is New Year's Eve, 1824.

MARY

Maybe it is a good thing the wedding is postponed: the guests could never have made it through this blizzard.

MRS. BRADFORD

Try and eat something. Maybe some cake? *[HARRIETTE wails again.]* I didn't mean *that* cake.

CALDWELL

[To HOLLEY]

How did you find things at Monticello?

HOLLEY

Thomas Jefferson's head is full of his own university. But he told me to beware our new governor.

CALDWELL

Joseph Desha. He ran on the Relief ticket; the aristocracy will not accept him.

HOLLEY

I sat at table with Mrs. Taylor in Newport and she and her guests were all for Andrew Jackson.

MARY

If Jackson takes office, we will all be wearing strictly homespun.

HOLLEY

John Quincy Adams and John C. Calhoun and Henry Clay—three of my best friends, and all running for the Presidency against Old Hickory.

MARY

What a year this will be. General Lafayette has accepted our invitation.

HOLLEY

The General plans to shake hands with the nation. Harriette's fiancé, William Brand, is on the committee for the Ball. We shall all pray for a speedy recovery.

MRS. BRADFORD

I didn't think you believed in prayer?

HOLLEY

I don't believe in using it, as the pious do, as an excuse not to work.

CALDWELL

[In an attempt to comfort HARRIETTE]

This storm reminds me of the one we met on the ship Electra–when we sailed for France to bring back our library. *[He sits by HARRIETTE]* Ladies and gentlemen dropped to their knees and betook themselves to prayer. I rushed up the gangway, against the current of water that was still pouring in on us, and the first object that arrested my eye was a fine sailor washed overboard, still clinging to the end of a piece of timber. "Hold on but a single minute, my good fellow," I called, "and you shall stand where I am standing!" Lucky for that sailor that I had not been off in prayer with the others!

MRS. BRADFORD

Maybe you were the answer to their prayer.

MARY

[Whispering to DUDLEY as HOLLEY joins them in ear range.]

Professor Rafinesque has a secret recipe that he calls "Pulmel." He claims it has miraculous powers of healing. Perhaps we should try it?

HOLLEY

What? Some witch doctor's potion?

DUDLEY

If the fever breaks, there is nothing to worry about: she'll be up in a week.

MARY

And if not? *[DUDLEY is silent.]* What harm could it do to try?

DUDLEY

Perhaps you should speak to Rafinesque.

HOLLEY

Don't worry. She'll be fine.

MARY

[Secretly to HOLLEY]

I can always tell when you are lying. Thank you for it.

CALDWELL

[Peering out the window]

Hark! The Bridegroom cometh!

MRS. BRADFORD

William Brand? He mustn't see the bride the night before the wedding!

HOLLEY

William is much smarter than that; besides, the drifts are six feet in places.

CALDWELL

Someone is coming up the walk. Or some *thing*—

HOLLEY

What idiot would be out on a night like this?

RAFINESQUE

Good evening, everyone! *[He appears half frozen, for his greatcoat has covered a large potted plant. He is exuberant.]* A perfect night for a wedding:

the world covered in white! *[To HARRIETTE:]* And the bride! 'Never so lovely as on her wedding day. *[Only MARY is amused. HARRIETTE gestures for RAFINESQUE to come closer. He goes to her. She tries to speak, but her throat is sore. RAFINESQUE cannot understand what she is saying:]* Je ne comprends pas. *[She gestures for him to come closer. Closer. She speaks. But he cannot hear and understand her. He kneels and moves closer. She is right in his face when she says hoarsely and slowly:]*

HARRIETTE

I am very *contagious. [RAFINESQUE, quickly but politely, backs away. He covers his face with a handkerchief.]*

MARY

Harriette has been ill. The wedding has been postponed for another week.

RAFINESQUE

I am sorry. You must try my Pulmel!

MARY

Could she? We were just discussing it. *[RAFINESQUE pulls out a small bag. To MRS. BRADFORD]* Would you be so kind as to brew this for Miss Harriette?

DUDLEY

It's quite all right, Mrs. Bradford. *[MRS. BRADFORD exits with the tea to the kitchen.]*

MARY

Thank you, Dr. Rafinesque. *[To the others]* Our good Professor has received his doctorate from the University at Bonn. And he has been hired as Librarian and Secretary.

MRS. BRADFORD

The Legislature insisted on reducing tuition by cutting the professors' salaries. So, Dr. Holley advised the trustees that a professor of Natural History and Botany was not needed. It was the very thing that rallied support to keep Professor Rafinesque, and with a yearly salary!

MARY

He is also keeper of our Museum, soon to be included in his Botanic Garden. He has received permission to purchase the land for it.

RAFINESQUE

Every major university in Europe has a Botanical Garden annexed to it. We render ours both Medical and Agricultural, securing lasting benefits to the country. There shall be two great sales, spring and fall, from the trees, plants, seeds, wines, drugs, cattle and animals raised–

HOLLEY

Constantine, may I see you in the other room? *[As they move off to the side.]* The seller has demanded payment in gold. Not the Commonwealth notes—the money that was over-printed.

RAFINESQUE

But I only have Commonwealth notes.

HOLLEY

He will take gold or no sell of the land.

RAFINESQUE

Why didn't you tell me?

HOLLEY

I thought he could be persuaded. I thought I could persuade him. I was wrong. *[RAFINESQUE is quiet.]* The Commonwealth notes are worth only half their specie. Many people have lost their life savings. But you've got time on your side. People will buy shares . . . if this garden is as good as you say it is. We started the Law School with the selling of subscriptions: you can do the same with your Garden. *[With encouragement to a disheartened RAFINESQUE:]* It is the first of its kind this side of the mountains . . .

MARY

[Having found them.]

Harriette was asking about the poem.

HOLLEY

Come. *[HOLLEY puts his arm around RAFINESQUE. They return to the other room. MRS. BRADFORD has returned with a pot of tea. She pours a cup for HARRIETTE and holds the cup for the girl to drink. HARRIETTE grimaces at the taste.]*

RAFINESQUE

[All assemble round him to hear the reading]

My Epithalamium . . . *[He has fallen into great despair over his Garden]* . . . it is just a foolish poem.

HARRIETTE

[Holding the cup herself.]

Please, I want to hear it.

MARY

Listen everyone, Dr. Rafinesque is going to read the poem that he wrote for William and Harriette.

RAFINESQUE

[He takes a paper from his coat. It is his poem. He unfolds it, unfolds it again, etc. the work getting bigger and bigger and bigger as those in the room groan:]

I shall read just a few lines.

HOLLEY

[Whispering to CALDWELL]

There is a God.

RAFINESQUE

[Reading his poem]

"Jovial friends and festive crowd . . .

[He sighs heavily thinking of the Garden.]

Now assembled in the hall, Join the minstrel, at his call a nuptial chorus sing aloud.

HARRIETTE

Why are you sad?

RAFINESQUE

Because . . . because a little girl I once knew has grown into a lovely young woman.

HARRIETTE

[Blushing. She puts her fingers to her lips and blows him a safe kiss. It is the thing that gives him courage.]

Please, I want to sit up and hear his poem. *[MRS. BRADFORD attends to her with a quilt. HARRIETTE sits by the covered plant.*

RAFINESQUE

[Now he reads, vigor and dramatic flair growing with every word.]

The green holly and thistle in garlands are blended;
The fond joys are beginning, the sorrows are ended;
Since the thistle and holly have lost all their thorns
And the crown that they weave, the fair bride now adorns.

[He bows and they applaud, but his strength is gone.]

HARRIETTE

[Having uncovered the gift]

Oh, Mother, look. He brought me an . . . *an orange tree*!

RAFINESQUE

It needs another week to bloom–

HARRIETTE

And I shall be married in a week. Oh, thank you, thank you!

HOLLEY

An orange tree? In Kentucky? But orange trees cannot live in this climate.

HARRIETTE

Oh, Papa, this one will!

MARY

Now, that's the first time I've seen a smile on your face since—*[She feels her daughter's forehead]* The fever . . . Horace, the fever is gone. Her fever has broken! Charles! *[CALDWELL examines her, MRS. BRADFORD and HOLLEY cluster at her.]*

MRS. BRADFORD

It is a miracle.

CALDWELL

Constantine, it is confirmed: we must have you in the medical college.

MRS. BRADFORD

You see. Our prayers were answered.

RAFINESQUE

I'm afraid I belong to my Garden, doctor. But it will produce medicines that you need.

HOLLEY

You have been the best medicine for our Harriette. How can we ever thank you?

RAFINESQUE

You can all buy shares in the Botanic Garden? *[They laugh.]* Ten-dollar installments? Five years to pay. Shareholders have first preference at the Fall and Spring harvest sales.

HOLLEY

Put me down for one share.

CALDWELL

Dr. Dudley and I will buy five.

MRS. BRADFORD

And John and I will pledge as well.

RAFINESQUE

John?

MRS. BRADFORD

As in Bradford. John Bradford? As in Chairman of the Board of Trustees? The Trustees who granted your yearly salary? I am Mrs. Bradford.

RAFINESQUE

What a pleasure to meet his mother!

MRS. BRADFORD

He is my husband.

MARY

[Bringing a wrapped gift, she presents it to RAFINESQUE.]

It is from Horace and me. Open it.

RAFINESQUE

[Opening the box, he brings out a coat of tails.]

It is beautiful.

HOLLEY

Merry Christmas, Constantine.

MARY

Try it on. *[He quickly tries it on. MARY fusses with it on him to make sure the shoulders and sleeves fit.]*

HOLLEY

Your students measured you while you were lecturing. *[Everyone laughs in good humor.]*

RAFINESQUE

Thank you.

HOLLEY

No, Constantine, it is you we thank tonight.

MARY

It fits perfectly. *[She twirls him around to face her.]* But I warn you: no grass stains. Not one!

HOLLEY

Dr. Rafinesque must look his best when he tours our State Representatives through his Garden.

MARY

[With pride]

The Botanic Garden.

HOLLEY

A toast! *[They all raise glasses.]* To my wife Mary with whom tonight marks our anniversary of twenty years! To my daughter Harriette's good health and her wedding to William Brand: To Scotland, England, and Kentucky. A union of the security of the thistle with the evergreen of the holly and the abundance . . .of cornfields of the West! And to the Transylvania Botanic Garden Company! Happy New Year!

ACT TWO

Scene Three

SPRING

The scrim is lit from the front revealing the trees of a great garden. RAFINESQUE is surrounded by his students DL, with CLAY and BRAND, all having fun examining an ant farm. It is Spring, 1825, the Garden.

RAFINESQUE

It is an "ant farm," because they are farmers. *[The students laugh.]* Just look how they work the soil and gather their harvest. Farmers. They also have lawyers, and doctors, generals, and privates . . . Look over here, we have a great battle going on. Oh, no! Look out! *[The students laugh.]* There goes a physician to care for the wounded soldier. *[The students laugh again. But the lecture hour is over.]* You should be heading back now. *[The students groan.]* You mustn't be late for your next class. *[The students exit; CLAY and BRAND remain.]*

CLAY

Even the ants are farmers in your garden?

RAFINESQUE

Here we will find all productions of earth that until now have been scattered throughout the country.

CLAY

How is that possible?

RAFINESQUE

With our greenhouses. Experiments can be made to ascertain the best mode of cultivation. Instruction will be given to farmers calculated to improve agriculture in Kentucky and the Western States.

BRAND

The public will pay twenty-five cents admission.

RAFINESQUE

In this Garden a single item can be grown to cover all of the Garden's annual expenses! Poppies.

CLAY

Poppies?

BRAND

For Opium.

CLAY

Rafinesque, you are a genius.

[The scrim is lit from behind showing the silhouette of SOLOMON digging.]

RAFINESQUE

There: the serpentine walk.

CLAY

But summers can be hot in Kentucky and dry . . .

RAFINESQUE

Irrigation. We have discovered two springs. *[Pointing, envisioning his dream]* And there: a fountain. And there: another! There: cherry trees, raspberries, weeping willows, cotton trees . . . Locusts in the front and in the main alley. There: a small but elegant building erected with portico. There: aviaries that will cage the most exotic of birds. There: bowers. There: a museum and library. Our garden will unite utility with pleasure. Affording a pleasant resort and delightful walk to the Citizens and Ladies . . . Solomon! Would you be a good chap and see if the Shakers have arrived with the seeds, roots, and silkworm eggs? *[SOLOMON exits. The scrim is lit from the front again showing the trees of the Garden.]* Thank you, Solomon. Solomon has been digging the central circle of our Garden.

CLAY

Do you not use the African slaves?

RAFINESQUE

In Europe the Negro gentry are placed in seats of honor.

CLAY

But Colonel Meade was to send you one of his slaves—

RAFINESQUE

Billy! I sent him on an errand days ago and he has yet to return. *[He bends down and examines string.]* Stewart has laid the meridian line all wrong! Too short, now the string is wasted! He does mischief in the garden. I suspect he is stealing shrubs and selling them. And seed is missing.

CLAY

Let me help you. *[He joins him on the ground and with a pocket knife works the string.]* I had a garden when I was a child. My best friend lived in it. He showed me this trick.

RAFINESQUE

Who was that?

CLAY

An old Negro who used to show us rascals where to find the best fish, the best berries, and fox-grapes . . .

RAFINESQUE

He was a slave?

CLAY

A runaway. We used to take him food. He would tell us stories. There you are! Your string is good as new. *[He has rescued the string.]*

RAFINESQUE

That is amazing. Thank you. *[He marvels at the trick that lengthened the string.]* What became of the old man?

CLAY

One day the constable hunted him down like a wild animal through all of our secret ponds and meadows. They killed him. *[After a silence.]* Dr. Holley agrees with me that colonization could restore them to what is rightly theirs.

BRAND

Father says that President Adams is a fortunate man to have you as Secretary of State, Senator Clay.

CLAY

John Adams is up at sunrise reading five chapters of the Bible while I am up until sunrise gambling, drinking wine, and smoking cigars.

BRAND

Without Senator Clay's vote as Speaker of the House, John Adams would not have been elected. And the President knows that.

CLAY

Governor Desha would have had the Kentucky Delegation cast vote for Andrew Jackson. I'm afraid I have made quite an enemy of Desha in going against his direction. And Jackson's nephew, Andy, and my son are both students here.

RAFINESQUE

And Governor Desha's son . . . what became of him?

BRAND

He killed a man. They filed for a second trial.

RAFINESQUE

Our new Governor will be glad to know that my Garden will offer sources of agricultural wealth to our State.

CLAY

The New Court would have the debtors pay with worthless bank notes; we, the landowners, must eat the cost in the end. They need a better idea.

RAFINESQUE

If the money a person saved would be used by the bank to loan to others, but paid through certificates that would grow in value—what would you think of that? Whole companies could be designed for the sole purpose of management and distribution.

CLAY

Go on.

RAFINESQUE

I call it "The Divitial Invention." It consists chiefly in rendering bank stock and deposits and savings circulative by divisible certificates. If a new Divitial Bank can be established in every State, the amount of stocks for them might be 50 million, which at one percent only for patent right would be half a million!

CLAY

You must patent this invention of yours. Come to Washington with me, and we shall see it patented. And put me down for two shares in your Garden. I love a gamble. *[CLAY and BRAND exit. STEWART is suddenly behind him with a knife to his throat.]*

STEWART

I'm leaving this bloody job, so cough up my money now or I'll plant you alongside the rest of your seedlings!

RAFINESQUE

Stewart? You are drunk again!

STEWART

My money or your throat?

RAFINESQUE

How many times have I told you that you must not drink while on this job?

STEWART

What? I'm about to cut your ugly throat and you preachin' to me about the evils of drink?

RAFINESQUE

I shall gladly provide you with your two weeks pay—

STEWART

We agreed on a month's pay!

RAFINESQUE

You worked two weeks, and you deserve two weeks, not a penny more—

STEWART

I say I'm going to cut your bloody throat—

RAFINESQUE

You put one drop of blood on this coat and you will have to answer to Mrs. Holley! You shall not have more than you have earned—*[SOLOMON appears and hits STEWART over the head with his shovel. JOHNSON grabs the knife, as RAFINESQUE jams STEWART in the ribs, hits him across the face, and STEWART falls over. Taking the knife, he then throws some paper money to STEWART.]* There, you thief. And be gone with you! *[STEWART grabs the money and runs.]* Thank you, Solomon. *[SOLOMON, whose back has been to the audience, nods and with his shovel exits.]*

JOHNSON

'You all right, sir?

RAFINESQUE

I have not shown you a good example.

JOHNSON

I thought he deserved the beating, sir.

RAFINESQUE

No, I mean the money. I gave him the worthless Commonwealth notes.

[JOHNSON laughs. RAFINESQUE joins him in the laugh.] Thank you, Johnson, for coming when you did.

JOHNSON

Stewart was drunk again, wasn't he?

RAFINESQUE

He gets mean when he drinks. Yet Solomon drinks all the time and is good through and through. How much longer have you at University, Johnson?

JOHNSON

I graduate next month.

RAFINESQUE

And you will be a lawyer?

JOHNSON

I guess so, sir.

RAFINESQUE

My son would have been about your age . . . had he lived. *[JOHNSON knows not how to respond to this.]* You know that your examinations will be tight and rigid, and you will not pass if you miss one question?

JOHNSON

Yes, sir. *[RAFINESQUE affectionately slaps him on the back. JOHNSON exits to join the others. MARY appears in a large straw hat, carrying a basket with one hand, a bouquet of flowers in the other.]*

MARY

I've come for my tour of the Botanic Garden. *[She puts the basket and bouquet down and weaves her arm through his.]*

RAFINESQUE

Yes. And there will be two floors of fine fossils and plants. Here we have the dry specimens of all productions cultivated in the Garden. Medical roots and drugs . . . fruits and seeds . . . soils and minerals. Plants and insects from the museum in Vienna. Agricultural and horticultural implements and products.

MARY

And Mr. Clifford's collection!

RAFINESQUE

[He stops and remembers his friends and is saddened.]

Yes.

MARY

[Pretending and pointing]

And the library . . .

RAFINESQUE

Yes. Our Library with books of agriculture, gardening, domestic economy, Veterinary, Botany, Mineralogy . . . *[Playfully, he reaches for an imaginary book from an imaginary shelf, and hands it to her. MARY pretends to open it.]*

MARY

How I love the smell of leather!

RAFINESQUE

A lecture hall for practical demonstrations.

MARY

Quiet! Dr. Rafinesque is about to speak!

RAFINESQUE

And a Central Circle bordered with marsh mallow.

MARY

[She stops him.]

Careful. You'll step on the peonies.

RAFINESQUE

An alabaster white fence—*[He attempts a running jump]*

MARY

–Six feet high! *[He stops short!]* And a gate. *[She opens it for him.]* This Garden is a gateway to the world! *[They laugh. MARY spreads a blanket and opens the basket.]* I thought today we would dine in Marseille. And tomorrow Sicily. Then Pisa and her tower, and taste all her wines! *[She produces a bottle of wine from the basket and cork screw. She hands it to him.]* But none can compare to the wines of the Botanic Garden! A finer export than hemp, and a competitor to the French. Mixed with water, of course. *[He takes the bottle and cork screw. She sits on the blanket and brings forth her bouquet.]* Let us not forget the *flowers* . . . Such flowers.

RAFINESQUE

Sincere emblems of sweetness and beauty, they serve to say the simple truth.

MARY

There is a Botanic Garden in everyone's life. And if not, there should be. *[She tosses him a quarter. He laughs.]*

RAFINESQUE

My first customer! *[MARY takes off her hat and raises her parasol. He joins her on the blanket, and they laugh together. The foliage on the scrim fades away to the Old Seminary, May 16, 1825. People have gathered to honor Lafayette in the Holleys' apartment. HOLLEY leads them in a toast.]*

HOLLEY

A toast! To Marquis de Lafayette: the son of the father of our beloved country. The beloved brother to our sons of liberty. *[There is much cheering]* And to our fair maidens: the roses of peace entwined with the Laurels of victory. *[Cheers again.]*

CALDWELL

[Entertaining RICHARDSON and DUDLEY with a tall tale:]

The wife and young daughter were seated in the carriage, and the horses being frightened, dashed off down the street with the carriage pitching the coachman and jerking the reins from his hands! I seized the reins, which were now rather sailing in the air and instead of attempting to stop the horses, which I perceived to be impossible, I determined to run alongside of them and restrain their speed. Being sufficiently swift to foot, I found no difficulty in doing this. Fortunately, at the distance of perhaps two hundred paces I observed that a wagon filled with hay was so arranged slantingly across the street and that barrier presented our only discovered place of safety. When I had brought our race to termination, and handed down the woman and child to safety, she asked if I were hurt. I had no time to think of myself—instead, I inquired as to the safety of the horses!

HOLLEY

[Addressing the audience.]

We shall continue in procession to where accommodations have been made for your dinner, followed by a stop at the Female Academy to be named in your honor. This evening we shall enjoy a grand ball at the newly built Grand Masonic Hall.

MARY

[Playing her guitar, the STUDENTS accompany her to the tune of "Strike the Cymbal:"]

Welcome Lafayette
Let sounds of myriads sound!
With us uniting
For Freedom fighting,
Our arms with victory were crowned.

[Amidst much applause, the crowd exits leaving MARY and RAFINESQUE left behind.]

MARY

You will leave for Washington with Senator Clay?

RAFINESQUE

Yes, to patent The Divitial Invention.

MARY

Take this with you. *[She hands him a letter]* May it keep you safe and bring you luck.

RAFINESQUE

From the Italian Peninsula.

MARY

It is addressed to you, "Constantine Rafinesque," . . . from Emilia Rafinesque, your daughter.

ACT THREE

Scene One

SUMMER

The scrim is lit from behind showing us the silhouette of EMILIA Rafinesque. She speaks with a thick Italian accent.

EMILIA

My dear and loved Father, I cannot possibly describe to you the inexpressible pleasure which I have experienced in seeing for the first time your handwriting, how many tears I have shed reading and rereading the tender lines dictated by your paternal solicitude. My dearest prayers have therefore been heard. A father, whom they had always taught me to love, whom an absence of so many years has not been able to remove from my heart, calls me into his arms. *[She is brought an infant, whom she takes and holds in her arms.]* I had become second actress in Teatro Fenix; and then in Rome first actress where I yielded to the importunity of a young English nobleman, Sir Henry Winston. I was not far from loving him when he deserted me. You have a granddaughter, Enrichetta. I have paid with many tears for my error. My mother, whom I love, tells me that it is my duty to visit my father in the woodlands of America. But how can I do so when that mother has a boy of six years old and my stepfather is too old to support the family? Goodbye, my dear Father; your Emilia repeats every day your name. She will try with her conduct, with her tenderness, to cancel the past, to beautify the ending of her career. I beg you to send your paternal benediction and with tears I kiss humbly your hands and call myself your tender daughter Emilia Rafinesque.

[Lights go out on the scrim. The scrim is lit with the Old Seminary. HOLLEY enters, tired and irritable.]

HOLLEY

What is the news from Rafinesque in Washington?

MARY

Senator Clay has been unable to meet with him and give him the signature he needs for his patent.

HOLLEY

Henry plays life like he plays the card table. His son has gambled away his money with that hare-brained scheme to cure hemp.

MARY

The Secretary of Treasury gave Professor Rafinesque a very satisfactory interview. And the Superintendent of Patents found his Divitial Invention novel and important. He stopped to see President Adams and he–

HOLLEY

John Quincy Adams has been the reason for Henry's downfall. Henry Clay is now the enemy of our Governor, and that makes our school his enemy as well. *[Of the flowers in the room]* Look at all these flowers he brings you. It looks like a jungle in here!

MARY

He brings them to us both.

HOLLEY

He brings them to you! His Botanical Garden does not look as well. Have you been out to see it lately? It's going to ruin.

MARY

He left others in charge—

HOLLEY

Rafinesque had best get back here soon, or there won't be any more flowers!

MARY

Rosa canina. It has a name.

HOLLEY

It has hurtful thorns.

MARY

Professor Rafinesque says they are there to protect itself.

HOLLEY

[Laughing]

You're serious.

MARY

It would be foolish to have such beauty and not protect it.

HOLLEY

You think the thorns are there for a purpose?

MARY

It knows that something might want to hurt it. Such individuals survive.

HOLLEY

And what of the ones that have no thorns?

MARY

They will not. *[With a letter opener she begins to open the next letter.]*

MARY

Please, Horace. Address these slanders of the Governor. Let the public know the truth—

HOLLEY

We have been over and over this—

MARY

But sometimes silence is not dignified. Remember how they twisted your remarks at Colonel Morrison's Memorial? It was harmful to the school–

HOLLEY

I will not live subservient to Joseph Desha. These people don't know art and culture. They've been so isolated from the rest of the world for so long. Andrew Jackson is their hero, why? For killing 2,500 Englishmen at New Orleans! The Constitution is a law for the peoples as well as for their representatives!

MARY

General Jackson is your friend.

HOLLEY

The Old Court of Jefferson and Clay was regarded as Master to the people. Andrew Jackson would have the New Court be regarded as Servant. A slave if you ask me! *[As MARY reads her letter:]* Another letter from John Everett? *[He ponders]* I'm coming to believe he was much smarter than the rest of us, to get out of here when he did. So, what does your boyfriend say of the latest books and theatre in Boston?

MARY

John is dead.

HOLLEY

No . . . *[He grabs the letter from her. MARY sits.]* Poor John. Is that the only escape?

MARY

At twenty-five years old . . .

HOLLEY

[He sighs heavily. He goes to the statue and pulls off the veil]

I'm tired of being ashamed. I'm tired of everything being of the devil. I used to think like that. I used to be one of them: those who go about the country braying as asses and telling God what poor Hell deserving scoundrels they are, burning brimstone under the noses of people. Well, I'm not going back there . . . no matter what the cost. Shame is the devil. And to the devil with shame. And to the devil with them all! *[He pours a drink and holds it to toast.]* A toast! To the sleeping partners who dreamed of wealth and honors, but woke to a house of fire, and escaped in nakedness and shame!

[The lights go out downstage, as the silhouette of EMILIA is once again revealed behind the scrim.]

EMILIA

. . . Oh, Father, if Heaven will grant me the favor of living near you, all my efforts will be to give thanks to a tender father for the love he has shown to me; and in what way can I show thanks if not to love him, serve him and to soften the last moments of his life? Tears obscure my sight. Oh, Father, love always your daughter and do not forget her ever. I kiss humbly your hands and call myself your tender daughter, Emilia Rafinesque. Postscript: My mother has two children whom their aged father cannot maintain. Please have the kindness amidst your financial prosperity to send some allowance year by year for my mother who has given me an education worthy of you.

[The scrim light goes out.]

ACT THREE

Scene Two

AUTUMN

The scrim is lit from behind showing the silhouette of a student at a lectern. Below, on stage, chairs are set as an auditorium with members of the cast seated. The STUDENT who speaks is JOHNSON.

STUDENT

Our President gives instruction to two classes daily, superintends the government of the institution in all its departments and ramifications, and receives his pay as usual in commonwealth wages. Notwithstanding all the efforts of political and religious fanatics to pull him down, to keep away students, and to injure the institution, his university flourishes, and the number of students continues to increase. *[There is a slight stir in the crowd.]* Our president stands as yet erect amid the storm, enjoying as heretofore the confidence, esteem, and love of his pupils and fellow citizens. And we can avouch, that we have seen Mr. Holley at the Theatre and Ball Room, and that his conduct at those places, has uniformly been that of dignity and decorum.

As to his politics, we believe there is more genuine republicanism in his little finger than in the whole bench of New Court Judges. At least his religion picks no man's pockets.

MARY

[To HOLLEY in a whisper]

Horace, do something.

HOLLEY

We advocate freedom of ideas—

STUDENT

Jacobin conspirators have commenced war upon this man with charges of Dandyism, Deism, and Federalism. *[The crowd stirs. STUDENT speaks faster.]* Our students have been brutally criticized by our Governor: yet, look at his own son. An innocent man is en route to marry his fiancée and is brutally murdered! And to this day his son has not been brought to justice. Is to slander and to vilify all who will not bow to the New Court, the Governor, and the Governor's son excellent proof of democracy and high-toned republican zeal?

[DESHA gets up from the crowd. Enraged, he faces HOLLEY who stands. DESHA turns to exit and is in the path of CLAY who stands. DESHA rushes away in fury. HOLLEY steps C; he turns to the audience:]

HOLLEY

A toast! To Transylvania University. That education which makes statesmen and patriots. And those statesmen and patriots who support education. *[On the scrim we see the Capitol Building of Kentucky. It is the meeting of the Kentucky Legislature in Frankfort weeks later, Fall 1825. HOLLEY speaks to them.]* I appeal to you, members of the Kentucky Legislature. There are too many misconceptions formed in relation, not only to religious sects, but to people and nations, differing from ourselves; such as Jews, Mohammedans, and Pagans. There exists extravagance that marks feelings of nationality and sentiments of republicanism. It must be properly tempered and moderated by a practical acquaintance with other nations and forms of government. *[The scrim is lit from behind revealing a silhouette of the Kentucky Legislature sitting in tribunal. HOLLEY wipes his face with a handkerchief.]* Our personal and local jealousies, our political contentions and religious divisions have impaired these results in our University. This is a State institution, declared so repeatedly and solemnly by the State itself, assembled in its representatives; you must doubtless refuse to let it pass out of your hands. What then is the result? Plainly this: you must endow it amply, and endow it speedily or bear the disgrace of its decline, and perhaps its fall. Individual efforts have heretofore chiefly maintained it, and large subscriptions have been collected from among friends and neighbors. This resource is exhausted, or nearly so; and especially the motives are wanting, which are to rekindle private exertions. The number of friends of learning in Kentucky must be multiplied before Transylvania can be placed upon an eminence suited to the liberal course of studies and policies which has been pursued in it for the last eight years. *[There is silence. DESHA appears.]*

DESHA

If it pleases our members, allow me, your Governor, to speak. *[The scrim fades out as the audience becomes the Legislature.]* This institution has been a favorite of the State, and has drawn with a liberal hand upon the funds of the people. Yet in its benefits it has not equaled the reasonable expectations of the public and for several years its expenditures have been extravagant in amount. A compensation has been allowed to the President twofold higher than is paid the highest officers of our State government, and wholly disproportional to the services rendered. To make up these extravagant allowances, the prices of tuition are raised to a very high rate, which effectually shut the door of the University to a large majority of the young men of Kentucky. The only motive a republican government can have to foster such an institution is to bestow on all men the blessings of a liberal education. But as this University is now managed, it seems that the State has lavished her money for the benefit of the rich, to the exclusion of the poor, and that the only result is to add to the aristocracy of wealth, the advantage of superior knowledge.

HOLLEY

With due respect, raising tuition was an immediate consequence of the Bank relief policies. When the charters of the independent banks were repealed, we lost all interest on the shares bestowed to us. Tuition increase was our last resort.

DESHA

Women are admitted to the lectures!

HOLLEY

Because the gentlemen students listen better when ladies are present—

DESHA

This liberality ceases to unite the confidence and affections of the people!

HOLLEY

Our graduates have multiplied—

DESHA

So they have. The current enrollment is 666. The mark of the Devil himself! *[We hear much commotion.] Foreigners* flock to your school, as their dollar will double itself in this country and they can live on half the sum. The religious sectarians want their land back and you have not produced so much as a theological department for them. *[To the Legislature:]* I say let the fines of the county court that are presently being appropriated to this university be given instead to build highways and bridges. Dividends for roads may be used to further the public schools—the schools of the people and not of the elite rich! *[The lights reveal only DESHA and HOLLEY]* I would have thought you at the race track this morning? Your wife home alone again. The foreign botanist running at free range? They say he's a Mohammedan and lived with a woman in France, who bore him children out of wedlock. Bastard children. And you leave your wife alone at home with that infidel. Your life is cuckolded, Horace Holley, and you offer this as an example to our youth!

[There is much laughter. HOLLEY attempts to lunge at DESHA but is held back by the crowd, and as he struggles to free himself, all the lights go to black. EMILIA appears in silhouette on the scrim.]

EMILIA

My dear Father, if you desire my happiness, if you desire that I leave this profession which I scarcely exercise, first because I hate it, and second because not even my physique can stand it, it depends on you alone. If you wish my daughter I will send her to you; if you want me with her I will come; if you want me to come with my mother I am sure that you will find her very different from what you imagine her. Since writing this letter to you our manager has abandoned our company, and the war has broken out. Now my mother has been left a widow with three children. I am their support now. The voyage to Italy will cost—I would seek position there and take contract as soon as I arrive. My fate is in your hands; and I pray your benediction be upon your obedient daughter, Emilia.

ACT THREE

Scene Three

WINTER

The scrim is lit front to show the Old Seminary. The parlor is filled with blooming potted plants. 1825. MARY sits playing her guitar. RAFINESQUE enters hurriedly, tattered and dirty. MARY is immediately glad to see him.

MARY

Constantine, it is so good to see you! Harriette and William just shared with me their joyful news–

RAFINESQUE

Mary, I must speak to you!

MARY

She is in the family way. They are so happy–

RAFINESQUE

There are students living in my rooms!

MARY

Rev. Holley has had to accommodate twelve Preparatory students. We had not heard from you in weeks, and the term has started.

RAFINESQUE

All of my effects have been thrown into one room!

MARY

You had three rooms–

RAFINESQUE

Don't you understand? Someone has broken into my rooms! There is a thief among us!

MARY

We expected your specimens to be in the Botanic Garden by now. Wasn't that what you planned? In the museum?

RAFINESQUE

[Quieting down.]

Yes . . . but . . . I was detained. I needed Senator Clay's signature.

MARY

But you got it?

RAFINESQUE

Yes . . .

MARY

Splendid! Then you got the patent?

RAFINESQUE

Yes.

MARY

[Taking his hands.]

I am so happy for you. You must build that dream of yours!

RAFINESQUE

My dream . . .

MARY

It is so neglected. You must build your museum—

RAFINESQUE

In time it will be put into operations in all countries of the world, and we shall reap its profits!

MARY

The Botanic Garden!

RAFINESQUE

No, no, no. *[He laughs.]* "The Divitial Invention!"

MARY

But Constantine, your Garden . . .

RAFINESQUE

But when my Divitial art is well understood, money will be as plentiful as labor and property is now. I shall market my Pulmel around the world! I must. You see, Emilia thinks me renowned.

MARY

So, with money you shall woo her? *[She releases his hands]*

RAFINESQUE

Money is everything in this selfish world, and money must be made somehow.

MARY

How much money have you sent her?

RAFINESQUE

I have requested that she travel to my sister, Georgette.

MARY

Has Georgette heard from her?

RAFINESQUE

Georgette insists that Emilia will deceive me and teach me that she is something unfavorable. As for my Garden, perhaps the managers can attend to it during my absence by walking there occasionally in the cool of the mornings and evenings! Even it has betrayed me. *[He takes her hands.]* Oh, but what a great Bank my Invention will establish in Mexico. It shall form a company to unite the Pacific and Atlantic Oceans by canal.

MARY

Is this the coat we gave you? So tattered and stained?

RAFINESQUE

[He burns with madness:]

Mary, I have an invention that can destroy a thousand men in arms, a mile off . . . secretly available to any government that grants my privileges.

MARY

[Backing away]

It could have been a wonderful Garden.

HOLLEY

[Entering]

So, Professor Rafinesque . . . you have decided to come back to us.

RAFINESQUE

[Running to HOLLEY.]

Dr. Holley, I must report a theft! My rooms . . . all of my books—

HOLLEY

Students needed your rooms. They were not being used—

RAFINESQUE

They were given to me to store my artifacts, my plants—

HOLLEY

And you abandoned them.

RAFINESQUE

I was delayed in Washington. I came as quickly as I could—

HOLLEY

Did you? How?

RAFINESQUE

Through the Alleghenies—

HOLLEY

How through the Alleghenies?

RAFINESQUE

[With excitement]

I was able to inspect the prehistoric monuments in Circleville–

HOLLEY

You *walked* the Allegheny Mountains.

RAFINESQUE

The trip to Washington was more costly than I had anticipated–I had to borrow money to get back. How dare you invade my rooms without seeking my permission!

HOLLEY

Were you anywhere to be found, that permission might have been sought?

RAFINESQUE

But my plants!

HOLLEY

I thought that's why we gave you the Garden. The Garden you have deserted like everything else. Like everyone else. We have waited for you for months.

RAFINESQUE

Urgent business detained me–

HOLLEY

This University is your only urgent business.

RAFINESQUE

You went through my things . . .

HOLLEY

They are the University's things–

RAFINESQUE

Yes! You went through my things to steal my plans!

HOLLEY

Don't be ridiculous.

RAFINESQUE

You did! Thief! Villain! *[RAFINESQUE throws himself at HOLLEY. They wrestle. MARY screams for them to stop. CALDWELL comes in and pulls RAFINESQUE off of HOLLEY.]*

HOLLEY

If you don't calm down, I will have you removed from your position and removed from these premises!

MARY

Horace, please–

RAFINESQUE

[To MARY, out of breath.]

I have a carriage waiting, Mary. We will go to Philadelphia. I've devised a plan for Emilia to take a position in the theatre in New York City!

HOLLEY

Emilia . . .?

RAFINESQUE

She has promised me.

MARY

Constantine—

RAFINESQUE

Come with me. Come with me now. You know I love you. *[There is a silence. MARY does not move.]*

HOLLEY

Mary, you must attend to our guests. *[MARY drops her head and obliges her husband.]*

RAFINESQUE

[Going after her]

No! The carriage is waiting. Come with me, Josephine!

HOLLEY

Josephine? *[RAFINESQUE realizes the mistake he has made, and stops. It is as if the universe and all its planets have tilted, swirled, and come to a halt.]* I'm sorry, Constantine . . .

RAFINESQUE

No . . . don't be. For you see, *[Rising from the ashes.]* I have someone . . . someone who will keep her promise. Someone who will not divide her affections. Tell me, which is the greater betrayal, do you think? The one of the body, or the one of the heart? *[Lights fade away on HOLLEY and the Old Seminary. RAFINESQUE stands alone. He raises a glass, his suppressed anger and hurt surfacing, as the light grows slowly red:]* A toast! To your University. And your State. And your Church. And you! That the walls of each built in ambition, jealousy, betrayal—in human pride–shall collapse upon themselves. I leave this curse behind. For I dare not take it with me.

ACT THREE

Scene Four

SPRING

Immediately the scrim shows a prison cell lit in red light silhouette, with ISSAC Desha. He stands with a knife held high, brings down the knife across his throat and falls. GUARD enters and goes to ISSAC. DESHA enters and stands R.

GUARD

The Governor's son! He's killed himself! Get the doctor!

DESHA

No, guard. . . leave him alone. I said, leave him. In this prison cell amidst humiliation. Isaac is in God's hands now. *[The GUARD stands; hesitantly he retreats from ISSAC. DUDLEY enters with his medical bag and goes to ISSAC to treat him.]*

DUDLEY

He is still breathing—

DESHA

Let him die in peace. *[DUDLEY takes a knife and tube and begins to cut into ISSAC's neck]* What are you doing!

DUDLEY

He cut into his windpipe. I'll just insert a tube so he can breathe—

DESHA

Leave him in peace! He is my son.

DUDLEY

Good God, do you want him to die? *[DESHA gives no answer. He inserts the tube.]* Now then, he can breathe. Your son will live.

DESHA

He could not face the gallows. You should have let him die.

DUDLEY

But sir—

DESHA

Governor! I am your Governor. And this is my son. And you. . . Who are you that you condemn my son now to gruesome humiliation and execution?

DUDLEY

I am Dr. Benjamin Dudley. Of the Medical College of Transylvania University.

[The red lights fades to white as the silhouetted figure of EMILIA takes its place Center one last time. The other actors are gone.]

EMILIA

I am now notified that you have established a contract with the Impresario of the Italian Opera in New York and that I am engaged in the quality of supplement to sing, gesticulate and recite in all kinds of opera in all the cities of the United States north of Virginia. The pay is double that in Italy. I shall voyage from Livorno to New York with my little daughter of about six years, beautiful as the angels. At last, we are coming to you. I kiss humbly your hands, and sign myself until our reunion, your affectionate daughter, Emilia Rafinesque

[The lights behind the scrim fade out; the front of the scrim shows the trees and foliage, weeds of the Garden left unattended.]

EPILOGUE

SUMMER

The Garden, years later. The lights return to the back of the scrim and we see through it to JOHNSON, an adult in business attire, with a walking stick, hiking through the weeds. Downstage stands the silhouetted figure of a man. This phantom-like creature wears a black cape with a large straw hat that hides his face. It is a cool early morning, mist in the air.

JOHNSON

Hello! I seldom find anyone here. Most people think this place is haunted. *[Lights reveal the Phantom who turns towards the audience and we recognize him as RAFINESQUE. But intentionally he keeps his presence from being recognized by JOHNSON.]* A spirit once lived here; man scared it away. It was once The Botanic Garden. Of the University.

RAFINESQUE

The University. I read that it burned.

JOHNSON

Yes. From the roof down, so everyone got out. Cash was a student then. Cassius Clay. A slave boy who shined his boots fell asleep with a candle. *[With a gleam of suspicion.]* Or so he told it. You have to know Cash. *[Remembering]* Classes kept right on going after the fire and they started to rebuild . . .until the cholera came and so many of the people of the town had to leave. It was a dark time.

RAFINESQUE

Were you living there at the time?

JOHNSON

I was married then. To Cash's sister. We were expecting our first child. I lost her in childbirth.

RAFINESQUE

[To himself]

I never wanted that. *[To JOHNSON:]* And the child? *[JOHNSON can only shake his head.]* I am sorry.

JOHNSON

I named him Constantine. After a professor I had once. *[He is silent for a moment.]* This was his garden. It was a magical place, full of dreams.

RAFINESQUE

'Sounds like a fool.

JOHNSON

Not Professor Rafinesque. He brought the world to us here: France and Tuscany. And Greece. *[Sadly]* It was never the same after Professor Rafinesque left. Every time I tread a single blade of grass, I think of him.

RAFINESQUE

You must marry again. And you will have more children.

JOHNSON

No, not I. What about you? Have you a family? *[There is a pause.]* Do you have children? *[RAFINESQUE can only shake his head. They wait in silence.]*

JOHNSON

I guess we are destined to be two old bachelors. *[They laugh.]*

RAFINESQUE

I understand that President Holley died of the Yellow Fever.

JOHNSON

Yes, just after he resigned. He went to Louisiana to start a college there and he and Mrs. Holley both caught the fever. It left her very weak. She says it does her good to walk this Garden. She comes back to visit Harriette and the grandchildren. They rebuilt the College–from the money that Colonel Morrison had left, and they named it after him. But Shryock, the architect, claims he has yet to be paid. They keep fighting over it. It has quite destroyed him.

RAFINESQUE

And Governor Desha? His son had killed a man.

JOHNSON

The Governor pardoned his son, and it ruined his career. Then his son went to Texas. He killed another man there. Some people say this place was *cursed. [He stops.]*

RAFINESQUE

What ends a curse, do you think? Forgiveness? "The rarer action being in virtue than in vengeance?"

JOHNSON

A place of learning is always a place of questions. Without the right questions, there are no answers.

RAFINESQUE

Nothing good comes from a garden of weeds.

JOHNSON

But I did, sir. And greater minds than mine. Cassius now serves on the Kentucky House of Representatives. And of course, his uncle, Henry Clay, had been a student here. And Stephen Austin. And Jefferson Davis will go to Congress. I'm going to teach here–I've been accepted to the faculty of the Law Department. Who knows, we may just change this weedy old world! It opened our eyes to a new light. And in that light, we pass on the light.

RAFINESQUE

In Lumine Illo Tradimus Lumen.

JOHNSON

[In agreement:]

In Lumine Illo Tradimus Lumen.

RAFINESQUE

So, . . . you and Mrs. Holley come here to walk and remember the Garden. *[This pleases him.]*

JOHNSON

And sometimes King Solomon.

RAFINESQUE

"King Solomon"?

JOHNSON

The grave digger. The drunk.

RAFINESQUE

He dug the Garden.

JOHNSON

That's right.

RAFINESQUE

Why do you call him "King?"

JOHNSON

When the cholera came, he buried all the dead: it saved the town. They said it was in the water. But Solomon . . . well, water never touched his lips. *[They laugh.]*

RAFINESQUE

Time brings justice to us all.

JOHNSON

[Seeing the Garden as it might have been.]

People from all over the world were to come to this garden. And there would be plants from all over the world. Everyone would have loved it. And everyone would have come. I think it was a time too big for us. A time that outgrew itself. From the heavens it must have come. And it can never be again. *[With renewed vigor.]* But we were lucky just to have experienced it for whatever brief moment.

RAFINESQUE

[Checking his watch]

I must meet the stage within the hour.

JOHNSON

I've enjoyed talking with you. *[He laughs]* Don't forget to pay your twenty-five cents before you leave! *[He stops for a moment, thinking there is something familiar in this stranger. This pilgrim, a ranger from far countries. Then:]* Adieu! *[He exits.]*

RAFINESQUE

Adieu! *[The scrim is lit from the front to project the Garden with trees, foliage, weeds. RAFINESQUE takes off his hat and cape and we see that he is older, heavier, and balding. RAFINESQUE, alone, walks the garden. He takes a deep breath, and in it he once again recognizes the spirit of the Garden. It leads him to lower his eyes in reverence, and there he notices a tiny flower at his feet. He stoops down to cradle the flower.]* Paeoniaceae. Were you hiding from the jealous gods of healing? You possess no desire to harm. You have no wings to fly from me. No legs to run from me.

Cursed be the bards who sing the deeds of war. But not you. You are the peaceful heroes, . . . to lessen wars or drive them from the earth, To lessen toil, or pleasure new procure: These will deserve our praise, their names endure.

CURTAIN

POSTSCRIPT

Transylvania University blossomed in the nine years of the Horace Holley administration, from 1818-1827. It offered a law school and its medical school was ranked second in the nation. A library was developed from books bought in Europe after the French Revolution. The University's enrollment quadrupled and its faculty included European masters such as Constantine Rafinesque, whose dream was to provide a Botanic Garden, as Palermo's Orto Botancio was just walking distance from where he had lived.[1] When Holley took the Presidency, only 22 students had graduated in 15 years. By the time he resigned, over 600 students had graduated. The College of Law graduated 44 students in 1823. The Medical school went from graduating 1 student to 281 students in 1826.[2] Transylvania was heralded as the Harvard of the West.

Horace Holley was born February 13, 1781, in Salisbury, Connecticut, to the merchant and founder of the Holley Iron dynasty. He attended Yale University and was influenced by the charismatic President of the University, Dr. Timothy Dwight. Dwight, a Calvinist, stated his beliefs in his first baccalaureate address: *"You will find all men substantially alike, and all naturally ignorant and wicked. You will find every man pleased . . . to indulge, without restraint, and without degree, both appetite and passion."*[3] Holley

Figure 8

[1] Charles Boewe, private notes to author, March 28, 2013.

[2] Walter Wilson Jennings, *Transylvania, Pioneer University of the West* (New York: Pageant Press, 1955), pp.112-114; Robert Peter, *A Brief Sketch of the History of Lexington, Kentucky, and of Transylvania University*, (Lexington, Kentucky: 1854), p. 16; Charles Boewe, *The Life of C.S. Rafinesque, A Man of Uncommon Zeal* (Philadelphia: American Philosophical Society, 2011), p. 161.

[3] Kenneth Silverman, *Timothy Dwight* (New York: Twayne Publishers, Inc., 1969), p. 97.

left Yale to go to New York to study and practice law, but after one year returned to Yale to study theology under Dwight in preparation for the ministry.

While singing with the Yale College Corps, he serenaded and fell in love with Mary Austin of New Haven, Connecticut.[4] After he graduated and was licensed to preach, Horace and Mary were married at the Phelps' home on New Year's Day, 1805. The following September, he was ordained by the Western Consociation of Fairfield County, Connecticut.[5] From 1805-08, Horace served the Congregational Church in Greenfield Hill, Connecticut. But his new wife challenged his literal interpretations of the Scripture and predestination beliefs. Gradually, Horace's theology evolved into a more liberal approach to Christianity, an approach embraced by the Unitarians. In 1808, he became pastor of the Hollis Street Congregational Church in Boston as Unitarian, where he became a popular orator. He served as military Chaplain for Colonel Messenger's Regiment during the War of 1812.[6]

On December 13, 1808, while Horace was away in Boston being considered for call to the South End Church, Mary gave birth to their daughter, Harriette Williman, in the New Haven home where she had been born. On July 19, 1818, while accepting his call to the presidency of Transylvania University in Lexington, Kentucky, Mary gave birth to their son, Horace Austin, in Boston.[7]

---

[4] Charles Caldwell, *A Discourse on the Genius and Character of the Rev. Horace Holley, LL.D.* (Boston: Hilliard, Gray, Little and Wilkins, 1828), pp.121-133.

[5] Milo Milton Quaife, *Proceedings of the Mississippi Valley Historical Association*, ed. (1914–1915), p. 124.

[6] Horace Holley to Mary Holley, October 3, 1814 (Lexington, Kentucky: Horace Holley Collection, Transylvania).

[7] Oliver Seymour Phelps, and Andrew T. Servin, *The Phelps Family of America and their English Ancestors,* No. 5228, 5229 (Pittsfield, Massachusetts: Eagle Publishing Company, 1899); Rebecca Smith Lee, *Mary Austin Holley a Biography*, pp. 66, 112.

Horace Holley accepted the position of president at Transylvania University and arrived with his family in Lexington, Kentucky on November 24, 1818. President Monroe, General Jackson, General Lafayette, and the Earl of Derby were among notables entertained by the Holleys at Transylvania. Horace's frequent attendance in Lexington society at horse races, opera, and gambling games, especially with politician Henry Clay, made him unpopular with puritanical factions, many of whom financially supported the University. Also, many of the Presbyterian clergy were displeased with Holley's theology and his inability to provide a theological college for the University. Rural families feared sending their sons into the larger towns to be educated. After Joseph Desha became governor of Kentucky, he accused Transylvania of having become a hotbed for aristocracy, and favored state highways with dividends from turnpike investments devoted to a public education system. [8] The withdrawal of state funding necessitated lowering Holley's salary, and he resigned. The Holleys then moved to New Orleans, Louisiana, where Horace began an academy for elite sons of Louisiana farmers; however, these families disapproved of Holley's proposal to take their sons out of the country to see the world on a "grand tour," and the academy failed. He then attempted to start a local college, but yellow fever took his life July 31, 1827, during a vacation trip to New York aboard the steamboat Louisiana. Holley was buried at sea while his wife struggled to survive the illness herself.

Figure 9

[8] Thomas D. Clark, *A History of Kentucky* (Lexington, Kentucky: John Bradford Press, 1960), pp. 217-221.

Figure 10

Mary Phelps Austin Holley was born October 30, 1784, in New Haven, Connecticut. She was the daughter to Elijah Austin, a physician and shipping merchant, one of the first Americans to open trade with China in the port of Canton. After her father died of yellow fever in 1794, her family home was sold at auction and Mary went to live with her uncle, Timothy Phelps. There she studied music and art.[9]

Mary, with the help of Dr. Charles Caldwell, published a biography of her husband's life, honoring his memory, that helped to dispel the negative reputation that some had bestowed upon him during his lifetime. As a widow, Mary worked as governess for the Hermogene Labranche family in New Orleans. Her daughter Harriette and son-in-law William Brand had ten children; therefore, much of Mary's life included visiting her grandchildren in Kentucky, and visiting her brother, Henry Austin, and their cousin, Stephen F. Austin in Texas. A musician on piano and guitar, Mary wrote and published her music and songs. The first book on Texas written in English was Mary's *Letters from Texas* published 1831; it was the first book to call the world's attention to the Texas Colony. She published poems and songs, and wrote *Texas: Observations, Historical, Geographical, and Descriptive* in 1833, and *Texas* in 1836. Throughout the years she would be reunited with successful and professional men who had once been spellbound lads of her husband's romantic theories of education at Transylvania.[10]

---

[9] Rebecca Smith Lee, *Mary Austin Holley a Biography* (Austin, Texas: University of Texas Press, 1962), pp. 4-5, 10-20; K.S. Latourette, *The History of Early Relationships between the United States and China,1784-1844* (New Haven, Connecticut: Yale University Press), 1917, p.39.

[10] Rebecca Smith Lee, *Mary Austin Holley a Biography,* pp. 359-360.

After a dispute with William Brand in which he protested that her difficult son was not welcomed in their Elmwood home, Mary left Lexington with her son to resume her duties as governess of the Labranche family at their Good Hope Plantation and there she contracted the yellow fever again. Before her death, she was reported to have said, "I see worlds upon worlds rolling into space. Oh, it is wonderful!'[11]

Figure 11

Constantine Samuel Rafinesque

was one of the most colorful professors during the Holley administration and left the university shortly before Holley resigned. Constantine acquired his name from his birth place: Constantinople on October 22, 1783. His father, Francois George Anne Rafinesque, was a French merchant of Marseilles, and his mother, Magdeleine Schmaltz was "Grecian born, but of a German family from Saxony."[12] His earliest memory was among flowers and fruits, and voyages with his parents destined him to be a traveler.

---

[11] Mattie Austin Hatcher, *Letters of an Early American Traveler: Mary Austin Holley, Her Life and Her Works, 1784-1846 (*Dallas, Texas: Southwest Press, 1933), p. 92; Rebecca Smith Lee, *Mary Austin Holley a Biography,* p.361.

[12] Constantine Samuel Rafinesque, *A Life of Travels and Researches in North America and South Europe* or *The Life, Travels and Researches of C.S. Rafinesque, A.M. PhD.*, (Philadelphia, PA: 1836), p.1; *Précis ou Abrege des Voyages, Travaux, et Recherches de C. S. Rafinesque*, original French version with introduction by C. Boewe (Amsterdam: Georges Reynaud, and Beverly Seaton, North-Holland Publishing Company, 1987).

In 1791, his father of the mercantile firm Lafleche and Rafinesque, set sail for Mauritius and China and upon his return two years later contracted yellow fever and died in Philadelphia. After a mob burned the house of Lafleche, his mother fled the French Revolution to Livorno, Tuscany where Constantine was privately tutored and showed an early interest in botany. [13]

In 1802, he arrived in Philadelphia where he worked in the counting house of Quaker John D. Clifford who became his closest friend. Here he began his wilderness expeditions on foot. Three years later he sailed for Sicily where he traded, worked as secretary to the American Consul, and published classifications of plants and animals; he believed he might have been permitted by Thomas Jefferson to accompany Lewis and Clark in their great expedition had he not returned to Europe.[14] Working for himself exporting plants for medicinal purposes, he became financially independent, later turning the business over to his brother.

He considered himself lawfully married to Josephine Vaccaro who bore him a daughter, Emilia, in 1811, and a son who died in 1814. Their marriage would not have been recognized by the Catholic Church, if Constantine had been a Protestant and Josephine a Roman Catholic.

In 1815, he set sail for America, but was shipwrecked off Long Island, the coast of Connecticut, where he lost most of his prized possessions and writings, a severe detriment to his finances; during this time Josephine Vaccaro married an actor in the theatre. In New York City, he helped establish the Lyceum of Natural History. While seeking a professorship at the University of Pennsylvania, he was met by his friend John D. Clifford who had moved to Lexington, Kentucky; Clifford invited Rafinesque to join the faculty of a newly designed Transylvania University. In 1818, he set on a western tour of 2,000 miles that brought him down the Ohio River collecting specimens. In Henderson, Kentucky he met the wildlife painter John James Audubon on the Green River.

---

[13] Constantine Samuel Rafinesque, *A Life of Travels* (Philadelphia, PA: 1836), pp.5-8.
[14] Constantine Samuel Rafinesque, *A Life of Travels* (Philadelphia, PA: 1836), p. 24.

Audubon wrote the tale of killing a bat for an unnamed Rafinesque, who had been swinging his host's favorite violin in its pursuit thinking the bat had belonged to a new species.[15] In Lexington, Rafinesque studied fossils and antiquities, and stayed with Clifford who promised him a Professorship at the Transylvania University. Clifford also promised to travel every year on vacation with Rafinesque to increase Clifford's museum and collections.

On the 25th of April, 1819, Rafinesque accepted the appointment to "the Professorship of Botany and Natural History in the Transylvania University," becoming the first teacher of Natural Science in the American West.[16] But when Clifford died the following year, it left Rafinesque without protection from the University President Horace Holley and suspicious Presbyterian factions at the time, and he pursued Thomas Jefferson for professorship of Natural History in the newly formed University of Virginia but was denied. In 1822, Transylvania University awarded him an honorary M.A. degree, and probably also an honorary doctorate. He also received an equivalent to a doctorate from the Kaiserliche Leopoldina-Carolinische Deutsche Akademie der Naturforscher then in Bonn. He became Librarian to the University, curator of the University Museum which housed the collections of Clifford, and Secretary to the Faculty. He taught the Lexington townspeople French, Italian, and Spanish. A pioneer in the education of women, he encouraged them to attend his lectures. Of the campus life, he wrote: "The intrigues of the University will be an episode of my memoirs; there was little subordination among the Students, and the Professors were far from being friendly to each other."[17] He attempted to publish *The Western Minerva*, a quarterly journal offering essays on Science, the Arts, and Literature.

---

[15] John James Audubon, *The Eccentric Naturalist* in *Ornithological Biography,* Edinburgh, 1831; Richard E. Call, *The Life and Writings of Rafinesque* Publication No. 10 (Louisville, Kentucky: Filson Club, 1895), pp. 26-27.

[16] Constantine Samuel Rafinesque, Letter to Robert Wickliffe Esquire, Chairman of the Board of Trustees of the Transylvania University, Lexington, Kentucky, from Philadelphia, PA, April 25, 1819.

[17] Constantine Samuel Rafinesque, *A Life of Travels* (Philadelphia, PA: 1836), p.67.

In 1824, Rafinesque began the construction of The Botanic Garden, forming the Transylvania Botanic-Garden Company of which he placed himself as superintendent. Located east of the town of Lexington and near the estate of Henry Clay, it was his plan to cultivate and sell opium from it to pay for the annual expenses of the Garden.[18] He pursued the history, language, and archaeological studies of Native Americans, and was familiar with ancient monuments near the Elkhorn River and the Shaker village of Pleasant Hill. He left the University in 1826, to return to Philadelphia, where he taught at the Franklin Institute.[19]

He advertised, as a cure for tuberculosis, a medicine he manufactured and named, "Pulmel"; and beginning in 1827, for three years wrote of it in *The Saturday Evening Post*. Although never releasing its complete recipe, he simply stated that it was "a chemical compound of several vegetable, saline, and alkaline principles"; for years its marketing became for him a financial success.[20]

James Haines McCulloh, Jr. and Rafinesque were the leading American experts on Mayan hieroglyphics for the early nineteenth century.[21] He believed that ancient monuments had been buried by "atmospheric dust" that fell constantly on the earth, that would generations later be

---

[18] Dr. Robert Peter, *The History of The Medical Department of Transylvania University,* No. 20, Prepared for Publication by his Daughter, Miss Johanna Peter, John P. Morton and Company-- Printers to the Filson Club (Louisville, Kentucky: Filson Club Publications, 1905), p. 17.

[19] Constantine Samuel Rafinesque, *A Life of Travels* (Philadelphia, PA, 1836), p.67; Constantine Rafinesque, letter to his sister Georgette Rafinesque, November 20, 1826, (Philadelphia: Rafinesque Family Archives, Letter 295).

[20] *The Saturday Evening Post*, December 29, 1827; Constantine Rafinesque, *The Pulmist, or the Art to Cure and to Prevent the Consumption* (Philadelphia: 1829); Charles Boewe, The *Life of C.S. Rafinesque, A Man of Uncommon Zeal* (Philadelphia: American Philosophical Society, 2011), p. 271-273.

[21] Charles Boewe, The *Life of C.S. Rafinesque, A Man of Uncommon Zeal* (Philadelphia: American Philosophical Society, 2011), p. 335.

understood as aerosols.[22] He published overseas, in such journals as the *Annales Generales des Sciences Physiques* in Brussels.[23]

At a time when there was no common currency and banks were collapsing, Rafinesque's remedy was his "The Divitial Invention": "divitial" meaning "leading to wealth." Using divisible paper tokens as freely exchangeable units that earned interest, his plan was a method of honest banking that would put an end to conspicuous practices and even eliminate poverty. Communistic communities like New Harmony, Indiana would thrive by it, using profits to build libraries and schools.[24] A Divitial Bank in Philadelphia opened in June 1835, and for two years earned 17% for its clients.[25]

Having discovered a new kind of artillery that would destroy "one thousand men and arms one mile off, or sink a large Ship of War," he offered it to any foreign government in exchange for granting patent or privilege for his Divitial Invention.[26] Rafinesque offered the Invention to the minister to Mexico, Joel Poinsett, and the King of England, George IV, although Rafinesque considered himself "a friend of peace" and detested the militia and those who made it their profession to kill.[27]

The search for his daughter, Emilia Rafinesque Winston and

---

[22] Rafinesque, "Thoughts on Atmospheric Dust," *Silliman's Journal*, vol. 1, 1819, pp. 397-400; Charles Boewe, A.C.S. *Rafinesque Anthology* (Jefferson, N.C: McFarland, 2005).

[23]Leonard Warren, *Constantine Samuel Rafinesque, A Voice in the American Wilderness* (Lexington, Kentucky: The University Press of Kentucky, 2004), p.87; Charles Boewe, private notes to author (May 25, 2013).

[24] *The New Harmony Gazette* (Indiana, New Harmony: May 17, 1826).

[25] Constantine Samuel Rafinesque, *Safe Banking including the Principles of Wealth* (Philadelphia, Pa., 1837), p.58.

[26] Constantine Rafinesque to Joel R. Poinsett, Lexington, Kentucky, May 5, 1825, Letter 246 (Pennsylvania: Historical Society of Pennsylvania).

[27] Constantine Rafinesque to George IV of England, Lexington, Kentucky, May 5, 1825, Letter 245 (Kansas: University of Kansas Library); Constantine Rafinesque to Antoine Simon Auguste Rafinesque [his brother], Philadelphia, July 15, 1832, Letter 357 (Paris, France: Rafinesque Family Archives).

granddaughter Enrichetta, resulted in correspondence with Emilia in Italy from 1830 to 1834.[28] To bring her to the United States, he drew up a contract in April 1834, with the Impresario of the Italian Opera in New York, for his daughter to be engaged to sing and act in all the cities north of Virginia with payment of at most $150 every month for ten months, September 1834--June 1835. Absorbed by the responsibilities left her at the death of her stepfather, Emilia seems to have remained in Italy; in the codicil of his will dated June 15, 1835, he alluded to her as bereft of him and "in the power of rapacious relatives."[29]

Rafinesque's last fourteen years were spent in Philadelphia writing and publishing. In his lifetime, he named 6,700 plants and wrote numerous papers and books. In 1833, he published *Walam Olum*, an epic poem translation of the Lenni Lenape, which told of their migration from Asia over the Bering Strait to the banks of the Delaware River, leaving them with the name "Delaware Indians"; although the genuineness of *Walam Olum* is debated by such scholars as David M. Oestreicher."[30] In 1836, he published *A Life of Travels in North America and South Europe.* His 6,000-line poem *The World, or Instability* written in 1836, set forth his cosmic views of religion, science, and the arts.

Rafinesque admired Carl von Linnaeus (1707-1778), who made revolutionary advances in the classification of plants, animals, and minerals. Linnaeus proposed a "sexual" or "artificial" system of

---

[28] Letters of Emilia Rafinesque to C. S. Rafinesque; Tunis, December 11, 1831—January 28, 1834 (American Philosophical Society).

[29]Francis W Pennell, *"The Life and Work of Rafinesque," Transylvania College Bulletin, Rafinesque Memorial Papers, October 31,1940*, Vol. XV September, No.7 (Lexington, Kentucky: Transylvania College, 1942), L. A. Brown, Editor, pp. 45-53, Rivafinoli contract dated April 1834, Rafinesque Papers, The American Philosophical Society.

[30] *Walam Olum or Red Score, The Migration Legend of the Lenni Lenape or Delaware Indians*, (Indianapolis, Indiana: Indiana Historical Society, 1954);
Charles Boewe, *The Life of C.S. Rafinesque, A Man of Uncommon Zeal*, (American Philosophical Society, Philadelphia, 2011), pp. 362-364; David M. Oestreicher, "Unmasking the *Walam Olum*: a 19th Century Hoax," *Bulletin of the Archaeological Society of New Jersey*, no. 49 (1994), pp. 1-44.

classification which Rafinesque sought to improve upon with a more "natural" system that addressed specific varieties. J. B. de Lamarck (1744-1829), first formulated in detail the modern hypothesis of Evolution. Rafinesque had outlined a hypothesis of Evolution but offered no hypothetical mechanisms to explain the constant changes in organisms.[31] He was never able to explain the origin of new species, and his conception of geological time was unfortunately based on the Bible. His concept of "instability" was for him a law of nature, that everything is gradually changing. These early biological theories, based upon years of costly expeditions, discovery, and study of prehistoric fossils predated Darwinism but went without development, based on the evidence of his writings that survive.

Samuel Hood wrote Rafinesque's last will on September 18, 1840, while Rafinesque lay dying; Hood swore that Rafinesque dictated it, but signed it himself as Rafinesque was too weak and died the next morning.
Peter Brulte, the fruit seller whom Rafinesque had accused of persecuting him in life, confiscated the belongings of Rafinesque after his death.
The housekeeper Lucy Lyon testified that there had been gold in the room at the time of Rafinesque's death.[32]

Rafinesque died on September 19, 1840, of gastric carcinoma at the age of fifty-seven. For years, sad and desolate tales circulated about the details of his death and burial: dying alone, his belongings sold to pay for the expenses of a meager funeral and burial, most of his manuscripts destroyed, Dr. James Mease rescuing his body from being sold for possible dissection and lowering it out of a window for burial in a pauper's grave. Asa Gray wrote the obituary of Rafinesque in an attempt

---

[31] Ash Gobar and J. Hill Hamon, *A Lamp in the Forest: Natural Philosophy in Transylvania University 1799-1859*, (Lexington, Kentucky: Transylvania University Press, 1982), pp.96-97, 108-117.

[32] Dictated Will of Constantine S. Rafinesque to and written by Sam Hood, September 18, 1840; Notes taken possibly by the probate clerk concerning sworn testimonies of Mr. Hood, Lucy Lyon, objected by Mr. Hirsh (September 23, 1840); Charles Boewe, *The Life of C.S. Rafinesque, A Man of Uncommon Zeal* (Philadelphia American Philosophical Society, 2011), pp. 407-410.

to destroy his reputation, and to become America's premier botanist himself.[33] It was not until Dr. Charles Boewe challenged these tales that a more realistic end to this great man has been uncovered. Rafinesque lived and died in a rented house at 172 Vine Street and was attended daily by the Philadelphia physician Dr. William Ashmead; he died in the presence of Dr. Mease and Lucy Lyon. An autopsy was performed by Dr. Edward Hallowell.[34] Constantine S. Rafinesque was interred in Ronaldson's Cemetery, a quaint little garden cemetery for visitors to the city. But as years passed, the garden fell into neglect and lack of space required corpses buried on top of one another. In 1914, Henry C. Mercer, of Moravian Pottery and Tile Works of Doylestown, Pennsylvania created a concrete memorial with inscription to commemorate and preserve the site. But in 1923, for fear of this cemetery becoming altogether lost, Transylvania librarian Mrs. Charles F. Norton started a movement to bring his remains back to Lexington. Two other corpses had been buried above his corpse, and the second was taken.[35] What was thought to have been his remains at the time were brought to Transylvania University and buried in a special crypt in Old Morrison on Derby Day 1939.

Many theories have been made about the knowledge of Rafinesque built upon his works that survived. If indeed numerous writings and theories were destroyed after his death, we are helpless to speculate on the full genius of this colorful character. He promised to share the "intrigues of the University" of Transylvania as an episode in his memoirs which have never been found.

For many years students at Transylvania University remembered the life of Rafinesque with Halloween celebrations of bonfires, parties, and

---

[33] Charles Boewe, *The Life of C.S. Rafinesque, A Man of Uncommon Zeal*, (American Philosophical Society, Philadelphia, 2011), pp. 416-417.

[34] Charles Boewe, *The Life of C.S. Rafinesque, A Man of Uncommon Zeal*, (American Philosophical Society, Philadelphia, 2011), pp. 399-400, 408.

[35] Ronaldson Cemetery Interments: Lots," II, 249; Charles Boewe, The *Life of C.S. Rafinesque, A Man of Uncommon Zeal*, (Philadelphia: American Philosophical Society, 2011), pp. 434-435.

humorous "Rafinesque Awards" from a hooded Rafinesque Society, in attempts to ward off the curse he had placed on the university. In his *A Life of Travels* Rafinesque wrote of his demise at the university:

> I took lodgings in town and carried there all my effects; thus leaving the College with curses on it and Holley; who were both reached by them soon after, since he died next year at sea of the Yellow fever, caught at New Orleans, having been driven from Lexington by public opinion; and the College has been burnt in 1828 with all its contents."[36]

In the will dictated to Sam Hood, the day before his death, Rafinesque did "hereby express my forgiveness of all my enemies as in duty bound to do . . ." It is enough to say that the true curse of Rafinesque has survived him to this day: one that denounces ignorance and the lack of respect for all living things.

---

[36] Constantine Samuel Rafinesque, *A Life of Travels,* (Philadelphia, PA, 1836), p. 78.

BIBLIOGRAPHY

Allen, James Lane. *Flute and Violin and Other Kentucky Takes and Romances.* New York: MacMillan Company, 1919.

Audubon, John James. *The Eccentric Naturalist* in *Ornithological Biography.* Edinburgh: 1831.

Boewe, Charles. *The Life of C.S. Rafinesque, A Man of Uncommon Zeal.* Philadelphia: American Philosophical Society, 2011.

Boewe, Charles. Private notes to author. March 28, 2013.

Caldwell, Charles. *A Discourse on the Genius and Character of the Rev. Horace Holley, LL.D.* Boston: Hilliard, Gray, Little and Wilkins, 1828.

Call, Richard E. *The Life and Writings of Rafinesque.* Louisville, Kentucky: Filson Club Publication No. 10, 1895.

Clark, Thomas D. *A History of Kentucky.* Lexington, Kentucky: John Bradford Press, 1960.

Clay, Cassius. *The Life of Cassius Marcellus Clay. Memoirs, Writings, and Speeches, Vol. I.* Cincinnati, Ohio: J. Fletcher Brennan & Co., 1886.

Gobar, Ash and Hamon, J. Hill. *A Lamp in the Forest: Natural Philosophy in Transylvania University 1799-1859.* Lexington, Kentucky: Transylvania University Press, 1982.

Hatcher, Mattie Austin. *Letters of an Early American Traveler: Mary Austin Holley, Her Life and Her Works, 1784-1846.* Dallas, Texas: Southwest Press, 1933.

Holley, Horace. Letters to Mary Holley. Lexington, Kentucky: Horace Holley Collection, Transylvania University, Jefferson, Thomas. Letter to Rafinesque. Dec.15, 1804.

Holley, Mary. "On Leaving Kentucky." Lexington, Kentucky: *Kentucky Reporter,* March 10, 1827;

Mrs. Holley's scrapbook. Lexington, Kentucky: Transylvania University.

"Index to Transylvania University Students from early 1800s – 1970s." Lexington, Kentucky: Transylvania University.

Jennings, Walter Wilson. *Transylvania, Pioneer University of the West.* New York: Pageant Press, 1955.

Johnson, Rossiter. *Twentieth Century Biographical Dictionary of Notable Americans.* Vol. I-X. Boston, MA: The Biographical Society, 1904.

Latourette, K.S. *The History of Early Relationships between the United States and China, 1784-1844.* New Haven, Connecticut: Yale University Press, 1917.

Lee, Rebecca Smith. *Mary Austin Holley a Biography.* Austin, Texas: University of Texas Press, 1962.

The New Harmony Gazette. New Harmony, Indiana: May 17, 1826.

Oestreicher, David M. "Unmasking the *Walam Olum*: a 19th Century Hoax." *Bulletin of the Archaeological Society of New Jersey*, 1994.

Peattie, Donald Culross. *Green Laurels, The Lives and Achievements of the Great Naturalists.* New York: The Literary Guild, 1936.

Pennell, Francis W. *"The Life and Work of Rafinesque." Transylvania College Bulletin, Rafinesque Memorial Papers, October 31,1940*, Vol. XV, No.7, Lexington, Kentucky: Transylvania College, 1942.

Peter, Robert. *A Brief Sketch of the History of Lexington, Kentucky, and of Transylvania University.* Lexington, Kentucky, 1854.

Peter, Dr. Robert. *The History of The Medical Department Of Transylvania University.* Filson Club Publications No. 20, Prepared by Miss Johanna Peter. Louisville: John P. Morton and Company, 1905.

Phelps, Oliver Seymour Phelps and Servin, Andrew T. *The Phelps Family of America and their English Ancestors.* No. 5228, 5229. Pittsfield, Massachusetts: Eagle Publishing Company, 1899.

Quaife, Milo Milton. *Proceedings of the Mississippi Valley Historical Association*, ed. 1914–1915.

Rafinesque, Constantine Samuel. *A Life of Travels and Researches in North America and South Europe*, or *The Life, Travels and Researches of C. S. Rafinesque, A. M. PhD.* France, 1833.

Rafinesque, Constantine Samuel. Dictated Will of Constantine S. Rafinesque to and written by Sam Hood, September 18, 1840; Notes taken possibly by the probate clerk concerning sworn testimonies of Mr. Hood, Lucy Lyon, objected by Mr. Hirsh, September 23, 1840; *Profiles of Rafinesque*, 2003.

Rafinesque, Constantine Samuel. Letter to George IV of England. Lexington, Kentucky: May 5, 1825, University of Kansas Library, Letter 245.

Rafinesque, Constantine Samuel. Letter to Antoine Simon Auguste Rafinesque [his brother]. Philadelphia, Pennsylvania: July 15, 1832. Rafinesque Family Archives. Paris, France: Letter 357.

Rafinesque, Constantine Samuel. Letter to Joel Roberts Poinsett, May 5, 1825.

Rafinesque, Constantine Samuel. Letter to Robert Wickliffe Esquire, Chairman of the Board of Trustees of the Transylvania University, Lexington, Kentucky. Philadelphia, PA, April 25, 1819.

Rafinesque, Constantine Samuel. *On Botany (1820)*. Edited with an Introduction and Notes by Charles Boewe. Frankfort, Kentucky: The Whippoorwill Press, 1983.

Rafinesque, Constantine Samuel. *Safe Banking including the Principles of Wealth.* Philadelphia, 1837.

Rafinesque, Constantine Samuel. *The Pulmist, or the Art to Cure and to Prevent the Consumption*. Philadelphia, Pennsylvania, 1829

Rafinesque, Constantine Samuel. *The Saturday Evening Post*, December 29, 1827;

Rafinesque, Constantine S. *"Thoughts on Atmospheric Dust," The American Journal of Science and Arts/Silliman's Journal*, vol. 1. New York: J. Eastburn and Co. / New Haven: S. Converse, 1819.

Rafinesque, Emilia. Letters of Emilia Rafinesque to C. S. Rafinesque, Tunis: December 11, 1831—January 28, 1834, American Philosophical Society.

Rivafinoli contract dated April 1834, Rafinesque Papers, The American Philosophical Society.

Ronaldson Cemetery Interments. Ronaldson Cemetery, Ninth and Bainbridge Streets, Philadelphia, Pennsylvania: Lots, II, 249.

Silverman, Kenneth. *Timothy Dwight.* New York: Twayne Publishers. Inc., 1969

"Walam Olum or Red Score" The Migration Legend of the Lenni Lenape or Delaware Indians. Indianapolis:

Indiana Historical Society, 1954.

Warren, Leonard. *Constantine Samuel Rafinesque; A Voice in the American Wilderness.* Lexington, Kentucky: The University Press of Kentucky, 2004.

Wright, John D. Jr. *Transylvania: Tutor to the West.* Lexington, Kentucky: The University Press of Kentucky, 1975.

[illegible] Jan 1 April 1826. Rafinesque Papers. The American Philosophical Society.

Ronaldson Cemetery Internments. Ronaldson Cemetery, Ninth and Catharine Streets, Philadelphia, Pennsylvania. Lot [illegible]

Silverman, Kenneth. *Memory Quest.* New York: [illegible] Publishers, Inc., [illegible]

Weslager, [illegible] "The Migration Legend of the Lenni Lenape." *Delaware Indians.* Indianapolis: Indiana Historical Society, 195[illegible]

Warren, Leonard. *Constantine Samuel Rafinesque: A Voice in the American Wilderness.* Lexington, Kentucky: The University Press of Kentucky, 2004.

Wright, John D. Jr. *Transylvania: Tutor to the West.* Lexington, Kentucky: The University Press of Kentucky, 1975.

Sabbath of the Soul

Introduction

The central character in *Sabbath of the Soul* is Emily H. Tubman. A young widow in pre-Civil War America, she found herself in the midst of a blood-stained culture struggling to recognize people held in bondage as fellow human beings. She witnessed this struggle with her eyes, her intellect, her spirit, and her conscience.

It was across this landscape of despair that winds of change began to blow. "The Dark and Bloody Ground" is the title of the first chapter of church historian Richard M. Pope's book, *Lexington Theological Seminary: A Brief History*. The title, while perhaps not an exclusive reference to the bloodshed of the Civil War, is a reminder that the College of the Bible came into existence at the end of this bloody, divisive conflict about the future economy of the South and the engine that fueled that economy – slave labor.

The College of the Bible eventually became Lexington Theological Seminary, established in 1865, nearly 20 years after Tubman began working for the freedom of others. Since its inception, the seminary has been dedicated to the idea of an educated clergy and laity to lead and guide God's church and communities. The seminary's mission is to prepare faithful leaders for service in God's church and mission in the world. It is a covenant graduate theological seminary of the Christian Church (Disciples of Christ).

A student of the Disciples' Stone-Campbell heritage and a charter member of First Christian Church of Augusta, Georgia, Tubman's life and legacy bears witness that she not only understood the work of God, but engaged the work of God to liberate those held captive and provide for the motherless and the poor. Her soul bears witness that the work of freedom in Christ is the work of liberation for all.

The final chapter of Pope's book about Lexington Theological Seminary is "A Light on a Hill." It speaks to the hope and promise of those who dared to believe in 1865 that an institution to educate God's people could prevail. I imagine Emily H. Tubman all those many years ago, somewhere in Frankfort, Kentucky, embodying a light on a hill to her family, friends, church, slaves, wounded soldiers, and community.

I invite you to join me as the extraordinary life of Emily H. Tubman is revealed in Richard Cavendish's play, *Sabbath of the Soul.*

Charisse L. Gillett
Lexington Theological Seminary
9/15/17

Sabbath of the Soul

Characters

SOJOURNER of the night
MARY Fleming
George DARSIE
EMILY Thomas Tubman
RICHARD Tubman
LOUISA Thomas, also MINNIE Fleming
Caroline AMERICA Thomas, also KATE Fleming
ANN Thomas, also ELLEN Thomas
Alexander CAMPBELL, also Phillip FALL, also SUITOR
GUS Dawsy, also PORTER
YOUNG LANDON Thomas Jr., also Paper BOY
LANDON Thomas Jr., also SUITOR

ACT ONE

It is late. The old train station appears lonely; the gas lamps have gone out and the streets are dark and empty. Frankfort, Kentucky, June 1885. It is a station weary and worn, whispering a time that has outgrown itself. We hear the sounds of the summer night: locusts in the trees, pigeons roosting, crickets, but there are no sounds of human life. Until a solitary figure approaches, all alone, dressed in black, carrying a single bag of luggage. This is MARY Fleming, a woman in her mid-twenties. She is apprehensive; there is a sad childlike innocence about her. Tired of carrying the bag, it has been heavy, she sets it down upon the platform, looks out into the night, and looks up into the heavens.

MARY

I know you, Sagittarius. And if I draw a line from you, I find Capricorn. It looks like a smile. But the rest of you, I do not know your names.

[A sad tune is heard sung nearby. Startled, MARY looks around and we see for the first time in the Depot shadows a figure sitting there on a bench, as if it has been there all along, but we, like MARY, have not noticed it. This person is whom we shall call the SOJOURNER of the night. The SOJOURNER finishes singing.]

SOJOURNER

Only when it's dark do the stars appear. *[We cannot see the face as it is heavily veiled in black lace; the voice sounds sometimes African and at others only Southern. But for the black dress and gloves, we might have presumed it to have been a man. This SOJOURNER is content being alone, unlike MARY, but like MARY is in possession of a single piece of luggage as well.]* You forgot the three sisters. Just there in a line.

MARY

[Startled that she has been addressed from the shadows in the night]

What?

SOJOURNER

In the sky there . . .

MARY

Oh. *[She looks up and sees them.]* Yes. Yes . . . .

SOJOURNER

You look as though you have lost something. *[MARY turns and stares, as though this is very familiar.]* It must be something precious . . . *[This brings back a memory—from long ago; but MARY's troubled mind cannot retrieve it.]* Would you like to sit? It's a long time before that train arrives.

MARY

No. But thank you. *[And then]* You scared me. I thought I was alone.

SOJOURNER

[Simply and without apology]

You are not.

[MARY paces to L. unable to make sense of the remark. George DARSIE enters from R. A man in his thirties also dressed in black, carrying a luggage bag. He is a nice-looking man, but there is something very hostile about him. A haunting anger, which is fed by the presence of others at the depot as he has expected to find himself alone. With an effort, upon noticing the two women, he tips his hat. MARY smiles. SOJOURNER nods.]

DARSIE

The next train . . . It is not to arrive until sunrise?

MARY

Yes, that is correct. *[There is a long pause as each wonders why the others are there]*

DARSIE

We have a long wait.

MARY

Yes, I expect so.

DARSIE

[He marvels at the irony of it and feels compelled to explain.]

I thought I would wait here. I know I'm early . . . But I thought I would wait here . . . for the train.

MARY

I thought I would do the same. *[DARSIE and MARY look to SOJOURNER, who only smiles back at them.]*

DARSIE

[How very strange.]

I expected the train station to be abandoned at this time of night.

MARY

The hour is past midnight. A strange time of night . . .

SOJOURNER

The morning and night sleep at this hour. This strange, empty, nothing time. . . .

[DARSIE would like to sit, but there is but one bench half occupied by the SOJOURNER. Half empty. As if having read DARSIE's mind and he knows it, she gestures for him to share the bench. He smiles in short polite decline and looks away; her response shows no surprise. He wishes there were newspapers, and light, so that he might read.]

SOJOURNER

If there was a newspaper, and more light, you could read. *[DARISE stares at her.]*

MARY

I never read the paper. The news is always too depressing.

SOJOURNER

[She sings]

Same train carry my mother
Same train carry my sister
Same train be back tomorrow
Same train . . .

[There is a silence. As though the song is another weary traveler who has suddenly joined them. Another soul shrouded in black with its own luggaged agenda. She sings:]

Same train–

Sing it with me? *[DARSIE turns away from her]*

MARY

It is such a sad song. Please sing another. *[To herself]* I can take no more sadness. *[Much brighter]* She is on the train. Bringing Spring back with her. Lilacs and wisteria. It is always sunshine and laughter when she comes. That's why I'm here. I've come to welcome it. I couldn't sleep. I couldn't wait any longer for it.

DARSIE

The lilacs were beautiful this past spring. *[He knows that autumn will soon be approaching]*

MARY

Before the train came through town, she would come by carriage. How many days that must have taken! Always she would sit up properly and never let her back rest against the seat. "Sit up straight, Mary," she would say to me, "Always be proud of who you are." *[We hear the town clock strike the hour of One in the distance.]* They brought a grandfather's clock with them from Virginia, strapped to a horse. Back when her father was the first land registrar of this new state–when George Washington was President. *[She thinks of how long ago that was, and how it must have been.]* George Washington . . . can you imagine? And that old clock still keeps time. *[Reminding us that every second that passes never comes back.]* In their house, there. *[She gestures]* There on "Washington Street." *[She looks out into the dark town, so asleep.]* Every street has a *name*, doesn't it? *[To DARSIE]* Are you from here?

DARSIE

I've been here a few years. *[And then:]* Long enough.

MARY

That street there is Holmes Street.

SOJOURNER

This world is not our home.

MARY

[Correcting her:]

"*Holmes* Street." I don't remember exactly why, but somehow Mr. Holmes was the reason that Frankfort became the capital of the State.

DARSIE

He bribed them with land and building materials. Kentucky needed the money.

SOJOURNER

[She laughs]

"Holmes" is its name. Your point is well taken.

DARSIE

He had bought the land from Wilkinson for 300,000 pounds of tobacco.

MARY

General James Wilkinson.

DARSIE

That's right. Wilkinson named the streets.

MARY

Did he?

DARSIE

Many of them after his military friends. Montgomery Street after the brigadier general in the Continental Army. Clinton Street after General George Clinton, vice president under Thomas Jefferson. Madison Street after Governor George Madison who died in office after only a few months. Lewis Street—

MARY

–After General Andrew Lewis.

DARSIE

That's right. St. Clair Street is named after General Arthur St. Clair from Scotland, who served under Washington and became a hero in the battle of Quebec. *[He laughs]* And Miro Street–he hoped to flatter the Spanish General Don Esteban Miro. Wilkinson wanted Kentucky to separate from the Union and become part of Spain. The lower end of the Mississippi River belonged to the Spanish and it was important to the Kentucky settlers.

MARY

Wasn't he the one that tried to get George Washington removed from his post?

DARSIE

Yes. Had he succeeded, we might be saying "Buenas noches" instead of "Good Night."

MARY

She always spoke of this town. Its streets. Everyone all the way down to the river. Down where they call it the "Craw." *[The thought brings back a memory that frightens her.]*

SOJOURNER

"Craw?" That's a funny name.

DARSIE

Crawfish Bottom. It's where the freed slaves settled—the only land they could afford, land that floods when the river rises.

MARY

General Wilkinson never really lived here, did he? He built a large log house for his wife, Ann, but she was afraid of the Indians. He sold the log house to Colonel Love and to this day they call it "The Love House." *[She laughs, for she enjoys remembering these things, it is sheer delight to tell them. "The Love House" is the perfect name.]* Ann Street there he named after his wife.

DARSIE

Yes. Where the church is. Where it once burned. *[He remembers it. She remembers the telling of it, and together they look into the dark streets to see the church steeple. The thought of it silences them.*]

MARY

This street is Broadway . . . but before propriety it was Market Street. There was a large farmers' market down there in the middle of the road—before the train came through: that was the street that she knew when she was a little girl.

DARSIE

It went all the way down to Wilkinson's most principal street. Its name being the most prestigious of them all! *[DARSIE and MARY must share a secret, because SOJOURNER's look betrays her ignorance. They laugh and tell her the name together:]* "Wilkinson Street!"

SOJOURNER

Named after himself!

DARSIE

Wilkinson Street led to Leestown.

MARY

The first settlement on the river!

DARSIE

Yes, named after Captain Hancock Lee. The ford there was the main crossing from Louisville to Lexington; that's where Stephen Frank was killed. That's how Frank's Ford became the name of the town.

SOJOURNER

Not the *first* settlement.

MARY

No, but it was–

DARSIE

The Woodlanders and Mississippians lived here first. Their descendants were the Iroquois, Shawnee, and Cherokee.

MARY

Well, yes, . . . everyone knows that. *[But those native inhabitants do not seem real to her.]* But they never settled here. They found the land too sacred. They believed no one could own it, only the Great Spirit. That was their name for God. The Great Spirit.

SOJOURNER

Your point is well taken. They used this land as their hunting ground . . . and to bury their dead. Only God owns the place of eternal rest.

[There is a silence.]

MARY

[Continuing in her attempts for cheerfulness]

The Weisiger House used to be where the Capitol Hotel is now. *[She looks upstage]* She went to all the balls there. She was so beautiful. The painter Matthew Jouett begged her to sit for him there when she was just sixteen. *[With great fondness]* He painted LaFayette and all the Kentucky dignitaries, and so, he painted *her*. *[With surprising disgust:]* She *hated* it. 'Stored it in the attic. I've begged her to hang it but she won't. *[Yes, she has recaptured the radiance of lilac and wisteria.]* I want to remember it. All of it. All of the names of all of its streets. Every one. I want to hear it all, tell it all. Smell the honeysuckle in bloom again. When she left this town for the first time. *[We hear a stringed orchestra from another room, another time. MARY laughs, beckoning it to come.]* She was my age. She was my age when she and her brother Western accepted the invitation of Colonel Nicholas Ware to spend the winter in Augusta, Georgia. Western had just made application for license to practice law. The Wares were Georgia society, people of wealth. They left this town on horseback, her winter wardrobe in saddlebags. I want to go there, to all the streets she traveled, and remember their names.

[We hear the stringed instruments of a ball. The lights change, and RICHARD Tubman appears. He is a handsome man, in his fifties, dressed in evening attire of 1818. It is the back veranda of Colonel Nicholas Ware's mansion in Augusta, Georgia. RICHARD leans against the balusters, looking up at the stars, troubled. EMILY Thomas, a woman in her twenties, dressed in a ball gown enters from inside the house upstage and notices him. She stops. She closes the door and the music behind her.]

EMILY

You look as though you have lost something.

RICHARD

Ah . . . Good evening. *[He smiles at her, then turns back to the stars.]*

EMILY

It must be something precious . . . It has kept you from joining us inside all evening.

RICHARD

Precious. Yes, that it is.

EMILY

[She looks out over the balcony and is suddenly on guard.]

Oh, no! You haven't seen me. Please—*[She turns to rush back into the house but sees someone who makes her quickly hide UL. A SUITOR enters in a hurry from DL as another SUITOR enters from the house, causing them both to collide. RICHARD is quick to point to the Right. Grateful, the SUITORS dash in that direction, one trying to out-race the other.]*

RICHARD

You can come out from behind that wisteria. They are gone.

EMILY

I am grateful to you. And quite embarrassed.

RICHARD

You are not pleased with the Season here in Augusta?

EMILY

I was at first. But it has quickly become tiresome.

RICHARD

You are not from Georgia, are you?

EMILY

How can you tell?

RICHARD

Your accent. You are from the North.

EMILY

I came with my brother as guests of Colonel Ware. To spend the winter. His niece and I are close in age. *[She frowns in displeasure]* She has lost something most precious–her heart to one of the local Augusta gents, and received a proposal for *marriage* in return.

RICHARD

And you have not?

EMILY

Not a one. *[But she is not disappointed] Several* . . . unfortunately. One young man has offered me half of his estate in exchange for my hand.

RICHARD

And you are displeased?

EMILY

Most assuredly displeased! Why not the whole estate for both hands? *[They laugh together.]* You are not a native of Georgia–I can tell by *your* accent. It is farther North than mine.

RICHARD

Colonel Ware has invited a young attorney from Kentucky to manage my estate. Thomas, I believe the name is. And he insists that I make the acquaintance of the young man's sister.

EMILY

Miss Emily Thomas?

RICHARD

The very same. Are you acquainted?

EMILY

With Miss Thomas? *[She considers this opportunity. Thinking before she speaks. Sauntering about in hopes of finding her voice and scheme.]* I should hope that *I am*. You say that he spoke of her to you?

RICHARD

Yes.

EMILY

Did the good Colonel speak of her . . . beauty?

RICHARD

No. No doubt she is a young girl looking for a rich husband with the face of a mule and the figure of a wagon to match.

EMILY

[Suddenly quite offended, she recovers to protect herself]

Are you so certain!

RICHARD

Has Nicholas Ware not suggested one of the Georgia gents for you?

EMILY

A man from Maryland.

RICHARD

Richard Tubman?

EMILY

The very same. Are you acquainted?

RICHARD

With Mr. Tubman? *[He considers this opportunity. Thinking before he speaks. Sauntering about in hopes of finding his voice and scheme.]* I should hope that *I am*. You say that he spoke of him to you?

EMILY

Yes.

RICHARD

And did the good Colonel speak of Mr. Tubman's . . . accomplishments?

EMILY

No. No doubt he has an accomplished bald head, rotund belly, and broken teeth—all both of them–is as old as Methuselah, and looking for a young bride.

RICHARD

[Suddenly quite offended, he recovers to protect himself]

Are you so certain?

EMILY

I've avoided meeting him all night, which has been quite easy, as he has yet to be introduced. He's probably out there somewhere still trying to get down from his horse.

RICHARD

Well, then, . . . fortunately for the two of us we are free from such obligations. But I hear that Mr. Tubman is not so old, and quite a gentleman.

EMILY

I hear that Miss Thomas is not so poor, and quite a lady. *[They both look at the other in agreement, but as they turn their faces away to the stars, we see each roll his/her eyes in doubt and disgust.]* The night is warm here. At home it must be cold and snowing.

RICHARD

Bonfires by the frozen ponds. Ice skating . . . *[The thought tantalizes, conjuring a tinge of nostalgia and homesickness for them both.]*

RICHARD and EMILY

Snow makes the world so clean . . . *[They laugh at their shared thoughts.]*

RICHARD

I do not miss the winters in Maryland.

EMILY

[Calculating]

And does your wife miss the winters in Maryland?

RICHARD

Not a one. Winter or summer. *[Explaining:]* Her bones rest in the ground there.

EMILY

I am so sorry.

RICHARD

Thank you. But winters melt into springs. Over and over. And then another summer. .

EMILY

I know that when my father died, part of my world died with him. Were you married long?

RICHARD

Long enough for my world to die with her.

EMILY

Did you have children?

RICHARD

Just one. With her also beneath the snow.

EMILY

[After a silence, not knowing what to say.]

You were fortunate to marry for love. When I marry—*if* I marry—it will only be for love.

RICHARD

You would marry a poor man for love?

EMILY

Were I to marry a poor man, he would no longer be poor.

RICHARD

[Her charm makes him laugh.]

What makes you think I married for love?

EMILY

Didn't you?

RICHARD

We were young and it was expected of us.

EMILY

My mother married for love and it broke her heart. I may not marry at all. It seems so difficult to live with one's self much less another human being. I could be a successful woman and remain unmarried like Mother. And she has been alone in the world for many years. Perhaps you will marry again?

RICHARD

The first time just about killed me.

EMILY

You sound like Mother. I want to believe that love is not something to be measured out. Limited and prudently dispersed. It must be more expandable. With plenty to go around. So that the more you give of your heart, the more you have.

RICHARD

There is an old story of a clown searching for something beneath a streetlamp. They ask him where he dropped it. He points to the darkness far off.

EMILY

[Trying to understand the fable.]

Why? 'Would he look for it nearby under the streetlamp when he dropped it far off?

RICHARD

[Exactly. Nodding and continuing the story:]

"Then why look for it here?" they ask him. "Because here is where the light is," he answers. It may be that the older we get, the less we care to venture out in the darkness to find our heart.

EMILY

Maybe it is best not to look for it at all. Maybe it is best just to wait for it. For if we are looking, we might miss it when it passes us. And love is always passing by. I hope you will again wait for it.

RICHARD

For it to come back?

EMILY

Surely it has never left.

RICHARD

How did you come to be so wise at your age? You were educated in Kentucky?

EMILY

By Mrs. Margaretta Brown. Our Senator's wife. They live in a most beautiful house named "Liberty Hall." Every house should have such a name. And every street, and every person! My middle name is "Harvie." It means "worthy." And with my first name they spell "worthy laborer." Sometimes, . . . when life is lonely, and the world has turned a most . . . *[She laughs] beautiful* shade of lavender, I think of the name I was given, who gave it to me, and who wore it before me, or I write it down and look at it and say to myself, "Worthy laborer, old girl, earn your name this day! Claim your inheritance!"

RICHARD

My name means "Ruler."

EMILY

You must be a man of great strength to fit into such a name.

RICHARD

It's just a name . . .

EMILY

Oh! But a name is a scepter passed down through the generations. Then it becomes our turn. And we must hold it up in its splendor, or let it fall and tarnish . . . as they all watch down upon us.

RICHARD

"They?"

EMILY

The great cloud of witnesses that wore it before us.

RICHARD

I suppose you are right.

EMILY

Margaretta had a little daughter, Euphemia. I loved her dearly. Euphemia means "All-praised." She was named after the Saint–

RICHARD

Saint Euphemia. 'Martyred for her faith. They put her in the arena with wild lions but they only licked her wounds. The bears were not so kind.

EMILY

My little Euphemia died last year. Margaretta has grieved so. Margaretta's aunt came to comfort her. Mrs. Varick. Mrs. Margaret Varick. Margaretta was named after her: Margaretta means "Little Margaret." The journey from New York was too much for Mrs. Varick and she fell ill and died.

RICHARD

How sad. To lose a child and a dear aunt.

EMILY

I saw her. Just weeks after her death. Mrs. Varick. In the garden. It was as if she had come back to help Margaretta and fulfill her intentions. Do you believe in such things?

RICHARD

Did the aunt love her?

EMILY

Very much so. The aunt was the only mother that Margaretta had ever known.

RICHARD

I believe that love never ends.

EMILY

I believe in God. And God is love. We had no church in our town. Margaretta and Mrs. Love started a church for the children in the garden of Liberty Hall. Then the town built a church for the different denominations to use. The Baptists and Presbyterians took turns using it. They got along fine, until the Methodists asked to use it. You're not Methodist, are you?

RICHARD

No. Episcopalian.

EMILY

Oh, that's even worse. *[RICHARD laughs.]* No—I mean, the different groups had a hard time accepting the Methodists much less the Episcopal Church: that's the Church of England.

RICHARD

So, they couldn't get along? What happened?

EMILY

It burned down. I don't think that God burned it down. But . . . *[She is silent.]*

Sometimes it takes a fire to cleanse us.

RICHARD

God is silent at times. Like those stars.

EMILY

My brother, Western, has lost his heart to one of your Augusta ladies.

RICHARD

I hope for him a long and plentiful life with her.

EMILY

Plentiful? I wonder. Her family name is "Few." I must make investigations of Miss Emiline Few.

RICHARD

I can save you the effort.

EMILY

You know them?

RICHARD

They were loyalists, like I, until we became disenchanted with the King. We are all strong patriots. No, I would think your brother's blessings are many if he has indeed stolen the heart of Miss Few.

EMILY

You will like my brother Western; he is a hard worker. Do you have a farm in Maryland?

RICHARD

I did. But I have moved my interests here and plan to make the South my home.

EMILY

Will you grow wheat?

RICHARD

The finest.

EMILY

Not cotton?

RICHARD

Some cotton, yes.

EMILY

I've seen the slaves working the cotton fields. It is as barbaric as the slaves back home in the hemp fields.

RICHARD

I suspect you are a libertine.

EMILY

Does that offend you?

RICHARD

No. It delights me. *[They stare at one another for a moment.]* Tell me about your Kentucky home.

EMILY

I come from a little river town. It connects us with the rest of the world. Although the river can be so shallow you ford across it. That's how our town got its name. There is a little island in the middle: my brothers and I love to fish from it. It is called Fishtrap Island. You see, long ago the Indians would pull a net across to the island, a V-shaped trap that would gather up the fish as they swam. That's how our island got its name. A certain Mr. Hawkins developed a plot to navigate it. He created the most impressive wax replica of the river. My brother Landon and Margaretta's son made quite a name for themselves with that model.

RICHARD

Did they help build it?

EMILY

No. They helped eat it. They snuck in one night and chewed it to bits. They knew that Hawkins' plan was to pad his own pockets, and they both had a sweet tooth for beeswax. But no one listened to my brother and the dam was built and Mr. Hawkins got his money and gristmill—until the whole thing fell apart much like the model and he was run out of town. And our Fishtrap Island was safe. My brother Landon is studying to be a lawyer. He and Mason Brown rode off to Yale and we haven't seen them since.

RICHARD

Mason Brown?

EMILY

Margaretta and John Brown's firstborn.

RICHARD

Ah. The brother of the young girl that died. Euphemia

EMILY

Yes.

RICHARD

I can tell that you miss your family and friends up in Kentucky.

EMILY

Yes. But I find comfort in thinking that these same stars that shine down on us are shining down on them tonight as well. *[They look away at the stars.]* I like to think of my father being one of those stars. And little Euphemia. And your wife and child . . . they are surely the brightest of the stars in heaven! *[She observes the depth of his melancholy.]* Only when it's dark do the stars appear.

.

RICHARD

Yes.

EMILY

Shame on you! I haven't seen you dance this evening. There are many young ladies without a partner.

RICHARD

And how would you know?

EMILY

I was watching you from inside. You have not joined the party all evening. I kept watching for you to come join us. Forgive me. I speak my mind too candidly.

RICHARD

But you dance the minuet beautifully.

EMILY

And how would you know?

RICHARD

I was watching you from out here.

EMILY

How silly of you. *[Their eyes are fast upon one another.]* Funny . . . It seems as though I've known you before. But that's not possible, is it?

RICHARD

No. Have you ever been to Maryland?

EMILY

No. Have you ever been to Kentucky?

RICHARD

No.

EMILY

You must come. Come see Kentucky.

RICHARD

Your little river town and Fishtrap island. And your Liberty Hall.

EMILY

In the spring, of course. When the dogwoods are in bloom. *[She pulls her eyes away from him.]* Supper will be served. Perhaps we should go inside?

RICHARD

Why should I? When here is where the light is. *[They laugh. And stop. They look deeply at each other. They laugh again. EMILY opens her fan and moving away fans herself.]*

EMILY

You take my breath away, sir.

RICHARD

I have yet to make my salutations to Colonel Ware. Will you introduce me?

EMILY

'My pleasure. I would be most honored to introduce you. *[They start inside. She stops and turns.]*–Ah—but who may I say I am introducing?

RICHARD

Richard Tubman of Maryland.

EMILY

[Curtsying]

How do you do? I am Emily Thomas of Kentucky. It is a pleasure–*[At the same time they discover they have been conversing all along with the very ones they have criticized. It makes them laugh. Then so very quickly they pull away in horror and embarrassment]* I am so sorry—

RICHARD

Forgive me—

EMILY

Mr. Tubman?–

RICHARD

Miss Thomas?–*[They laugh again. And again. And that laughter chases away the horror and embarrassments.]* I am old enough to be your father.

EMILY

And how would you know my age? A lady's age, Mr. Tubman, must always remain one of her best secrets.

[They laugh again. But the attraction between them is too great, and EMILY fans herself and moves away while RICHARD moves away as well. Each rolls eyes away from the other at the strong feelings that bewilder them.]

RICHARD

This has been a night of losing one's heart. For Colonel Ware's niece, and for your brother and Miss Few. And for me. You asked me if I had lost something. Something most precious. I thought I had, until tonight. I thought God had been silent, but I was wrong. I've had it all along. And now . . . *[He laughs at the absurdity of it.]* Now I want only to give it away. Maybe a heart is not meant to be kept. Am I speaking nonsense?

EMILY

[She pauses. Then courageously but carefully advances:]

Having found it, you seek to give it.

RICHARD

Yes.

EMILY

And having given it, you are once more without it.

RICHARD

[Sadly]

Yes.

EMILY

Perhaps, if I were to give you mine, there would be no loss.

[They gaze at one another with pleasure. She offers her hand, and he takes it and kisses it. DARSIE and MARY replace them, simultaneously taking in a deep sigh over the romance they have remembered. Once again, their thoughts are back with them at the train station.]

DARSIE

So, you await the train of Mrs. Tubman?

MARY

Yes.

DARSIE

She has always been a widow since I've known her. Traveling with her sister Louisa. I never knew her husband.

MARY

She and Richard Tubman married that same winter in Augusta, and rode with his caravan of slaves here to tell Emily's mother. Her brother Western, stayed in Augusta and married, leaving their mother with just the two girls at home: Louisa Ann and Caroline America.

SOJOURNER

The three sisters.

[The time and place change to a bedroom at the Thomas House in Frankfort. AMERICA is a young preadolescent, LOUISA an adolescent, both dressed in petticoats. LOUISA is on the floor, her ear pressed to the boards. EMILY enters dressed in traveling clothes.]

EMILY

Louisa Ann! Shame on you.

LOUISA

Shh! *[She turns and sees EMILY]* God's britches, Harvie! Do you realize what this means for us? Now that you are married . . . *[To her sister, Caroline America.]* It is our turn, America! *[With another thought:]* What a scorching day, to welcome you home—but cast it aside! Harvie is our Deliverer!

AMERICA

I don't ever want to get married!

LOUISA

Just wait, America, you will change your mind. Oh, Harvie, what did Mama say when you told her you were married? Was she boiling mad?

AMERICA

Louisa said she called you every name in the book!

LOUISA

America!

EMILY

You heard Mama cursing?

LOUISA

No . . . but I knew what she was thinking just the same. *[She brings out a white wedding dress and prances around with it, modeling it in front of her]* Look, Harvie.

AMERICA

Is that Mama's wedding dress! Louisa Ann, Mama's going to tan your hide!

LOUISA

Not if she doesn't find out. That is if no one tells her. Look, Harvie, she must have been about my size. It will fit perfect—can you even believe that Mama was ever married?

EMILY

"Perfect*ly*" . . . "It will fit perfect*ly*."

LOUISA

That's what I said. It will be perfect*ly*. Oh, but what a betrayal: you should have worn it first. But Louisa shall wear it for you! And then you, America!

AMERICA

I hate wearing dresses.

LOUISA

You will wear this dress when you marry. And you will marry, America! *[To EMILY]*

Oh, the service you have rendered your shackled little sister. Poor little America, the poor dear had surrendered all hope. Not to mention the service you have rendered to the despaired men of our region!

AMERICA

I shall wear trousers and boots to my knees.

EMILY

Dear little Cat, promise me you will never change.

LOUISA

Oh, she'll change all right. Look at you, Harvie. You've changed. You have a glow. A glow of a married woman. I almost didn't recognize you.

EMILY

If only mother would change. Richard is talking to her now.

[We see RICHARD and ANN Thomas at R, as though they were downstairs.]

ANN

You marry my daughter without my permission.

RICHARD

We seek your blessing now.

ANN

My husband is gone, Landon is away at college, and Western married and living in Georgia. And now Emily.

RICHARD

I will make her happy.

ANN

You will break her heart. Like mine has been broken. You will never understand until it happens to you. I pray that it never happens to her.

RICHARD

What are you saying–that it is better never to have loved at all?

ANN

It is precisely because I love my daughter, I will not have her heart broken.

RICHARD

She will be here every spring and summer. I promise.

[We see EMILY, LOUISA, and AMERICA at the bedroom, L]

EMILY

Now that I am a married woman, Louisa, you must call me "Emily."

LOUISA

Mrs. Emily Tubman. Yes. Oh, Harvie, tell me how it was. You know . . .

EMILY

Louisa Ann!

LOUISA

Between us girls. Oh, Harvie, it is your responsibility as the eldest. You can't send poor America out in the Lion's Den unarmed.

AMERICA

I'm not afraid of lions!

LOUISA

Oh, Harvie, was there a . . .struggle?

EMILY

"Emily" . . .

LOUISA

"Emily," yes, yes! But, Harvie, was there a struggle? I wouldn't struggle.

EMILY

No, you're right: but *he* would.

LOUISA

You are a brutal older sister. Tell us! Oh! Show us your ring! Yes . . . *[EMILY shows them her hand]* I thought the man was rich. You got gypped!

EMILY

The wedding was sudden. Richard has three large uncut diamonds he wants to make into a ring for me. But I told him, I'd just as soon have this one.

LOUISA

I'd have taken the rocks! Now, you promised to tell. America is dying to know. *[She pulls AMERICA down to sit and listen with her]*

AMERICA

What? I know all about it.

LOUISA

No, you don't. Emily, you promised!

EMILY

When did I promise?

LOUISA

What! Promise breaker!

EMILY

Louisa Ann . . .

LOUISA

[Pleading]

Please . . .

AMERICA

Please . . .

EMILY

Caroline America! Oh, all right. We met at a ball there is Augusta. Richard had been invited—

LOUISA

Not when you met. You know . . . *[whispering]* . . . the wedding night.

EMILY

[Taking a deep breath, continues]

Promise not to tell.

LOUISA and AMERICA

[Rapidly]

Cross my heart, hope to die, stick a needle in my eye.

EMILY

All right. The lights are out. You are already beneath the covers. Is this what you want to hear?

LOUISA and AMERICA

YES!

EMILY

[She exaggerates the tale]

You suddenly feel a presence with you in the room: you are not alone. The door closes. It locks. You hear footsteps . . . coming towards you. Closer and closer. You hear . . . breathing. His breathing. You can smell him approaching. It is too late, his shadow leans over your tiny bed and you hear his voice . . . the hot whisper in your ear: *[She imitates the childlike voice:]* "Someone's been sleeping in my bed, and there she is right now!" *[EMILY and AMERICA laugh. LOUISA is not amused]*

AMERICA

I know this story, Louisa. "The Three Bears!" *[LOUISA listens at the floor again]*

EMILY

Louisa Ann Thomas, I absolutely forbid you to listen in on their conversation. That is spying! It is indecent, unladylike, uncharitable–

LOUISA

[Raising her head]

He just invited Mama to live with you in Georgia. *[EMILY is down with her ear to the floor, LOUISA and AMERICA join her.*

[We see RICHARD and ANN again at R, as though downstairs.]

ANN

You promise to bring her back home each summer?

RICHARD

And we will take you with us for the winter!

ANN

Just be there for her. Promise me that.

RICHARD

I promise.

ANN

[Taking his hands, she looks deeply into his eyes]

I mean: always.

LOUISA

[At L, up dancing, ecstatic]

Sweet day in heaven! Mama adores him! We are free and shall all be wed . . . just like regular folk. We shall live gloriously . . .and trade privileges for favors! We shall all live happily ever after with diamonds and babies a plenty. And Mama will come live with us all! *[There is a pause. They produce fans, opening them simultaneously. We see that they all have a sudden change of heart. They fan themselves. With great disappointment:]* Hot as Hades today!

[It is the train station again. Once again, the years have passed away in the night mist.]

DARSIE

So, the promise began. Winters in Georgia and summers in Kentucky. Mother and daughter were baptized together in the Kentucky River by Brother Silas Noel. But she refused to tell of a conversion experience which was the custom at the time.

MARY

[Gayly]

She danced the minuet with General Lafayette when he made his tour of the United States. She planned the banquet at the Planters Hotel and placed a special coverlet of hers on his bed. They led the minuet together, and he refused to dance with anyone else. *[Sadly]* Why don't they dance the minuet anymore?

DARSIE

Its old fashioned. Besides, no one remembers it.

MARY

I remember it. I was taught it by my teacher when I was a child.

DARSIE

[He laughs]

So was I.

MARY

But do you remember it?

DARSIE

Surely, it is true. *[He does the steps]*

MARY

Yes! The minuet. You know it.

[SOJOURNER hums "Slumber My Darling" as DARSIE and MARY dance the minuet together. Distanced from one another and reluctantly at first, but slowly they join together and take hands. For a moment they enjoy themselves and dance. They laugh and turn and bow and courtesy.]

DARSIE

[While doing the steps]

It was the fashion for the men to show off their calves.

MARY

And the women their ankles! *[They laugh and dance and bow and courtesy. The dance comes to its end, as does their memory of it. They are suddenly embarrassed by the brass familiarity]* Forgive me. But it was good to laugh again!

SOJOURNER

[Her music changes to:]

Same train carry my mother
Same train carry my sister
Same train . . .

Is it not a funeral train that we await?

[Silence]

DARSIE

This will be her final trip.

MARY

[Remembering]

We attempted the trip several times. But she grew ill . . .

DARSIE

When her casket is carried from the train, the church bell will ring. The procession will go straight to the cemetery. Brother Philip Fall is to give a prayer and . . . I . . .

MARY

Please let us remember the minuet again. Let us laugh. I know that if I were to cry one more tear, the levee of my heart will break and I will drown in my sorrow.

DARSIE

I understand.

MARY

[Bitterly]

No . . . You cannot begin to understand. You . . . are to give a prayer . . . at the grave?

DARSIE

Yes.

MARY

You are . . . *[DARSIE does not respond. He turns away. Suddenly aware]* You are the minister here. Here at her church. I thought you were familiar. Brother Phillip Fall.

DARSIE

[Annoyed]

No. . .

MARY

I mean, Brother Tyler.

DARSIE

[With great annoyance]

No . . .

MARY

My apologies—*[For she does not remember]*

DARSIE

[With greatest annoyance]

Darsie.

MARY

[She ponders this name]

No . . . that's not it.

DARSIE

No, I am. George Darsie.

MARY

Are you sure?

DARSIE

I should think I should know who I am!

MARY

But it doesn't sound right. Like Jane Austen's Mr. Darsie? *[She is confused by this]* I did not recognize you.

DARSIE

It is dark. And late. . . .

MARY

No, I didn't connect you with that name. Mr. Darsie is supposed to be handsome. You know what I mean. He was young . . .ger. You look so much older than I remembered you.

DARSIE

[Inescapably flippant]

I have aged considerably since meeting you.

SOJOURNER

From the moment we are born we start this journey, don't we? We make our reservation, and we wait for it to arrive?

MARY

[To DARSIE]

Why have you come at this hour?

DARSIE

I . . . could ask you the same question.

MARY

And I might answer it, were I to know you better.

DARSIE

I was thinking perhaps that you are a relative?

MARY

Yes. Her nephew's fiancée.

DARSIE

The nephew Landon. From Georgia. The elder Landon's son. I didn't recognize you . . . *[He is puzzled by her face, and tosses his chuckle aside, and with it his forgetfulness. Then in an attempt to laugh at himself and all of this with good nature:]* Me being so old and all.

MARY

[Tired]

I didn't mean it like that.

DARSIE

I came to this town at the wish of Mrs. Tubman: that's why I took the church here. She heard my appeal for world missions. She gave a handsome gift to help the poor and sick in other countries, and . . . to spread the gospel.

MARY

[Pondering his choice of words.]

The gospel.

DARSIE

The good news.

MARY

[Bitterly, for she knows what the word means]

Where is the "good news?" There is no news that is good anymore.

DARSIE

"Come to me, ye who are weary and heavy laden. And I will give you rest for your soul."

SOJOURNER

Even the soul must find rest.

MARY

My soul is weary beyond reproach. It will never rest again.

DARSIE

Perhaps Mrs. Tubman's soul is at rest this Sabbath night.

MARY

[Correcting him]

Friday.

DARSIE

It is after midnight; it is Saturday now.

MARY

Yes. It is Saturday. But not Sunday.

DARSIE

No, not Sunday. As I said.

MARY

You said Sunday.

DARSIE

With all due respect, I believe that you are mistaken. I said "Sabbath."

MARY

Yes, you did.

DARSIE

[Confused]

That's what I thought.

MARY

You meant Saturday. You said tonight was Sunday.

DARSIE

No. I said "Sabbath."

MARY

Yes, you did. But it is *not* Sunday.

DARSIE

No, you are correct: the Sabbath is not Sunday.

MARY

But it is!

DARSIE

The Sabbath begins at sundown, on Friday night. In the Bible, Sabbath refers to Saturday.

MARY

No, it doesn't. The Sabbath is Sunday.

DARSIE

It is a common mistake—

MARY

I believe I know when the Sabbath Day is!

DARSIE

Pope Sylvester declared Sunday "The Lord's Day," never the Sabbath. Saturday has always been the Jewish Sabbath, the day of rest.

MARY

I've never heard this before.

DARSIE

[Sarcastically, and a little cruel, but only to the grievous event:]

Well, after all, you don't read the papers.

MARY

When did this happen?

DARSIE

In the Fourth Century. Sunday celebrates Resurrection. Saturday commemorates rest from Creation.

MARY

I don't believe that is correct.

DARSIE

Then don't believe me.

SOJOURNER

If you can't trust the preacher, who can you trust?

MARY

Well, preachers don't know everything.

DARSIE

What a relief!

MARY

I shall . . . look it up. Later. Good Lord, the world is coming apart at the seams. Mrs. Tubman is dead and they've changed the Sabbath and no one told anyone!

DARSIE

What difference does it make?

MARY

What difference does it make? It makes a lot of difference. You are a minister; you should tell people these things.

DARSIE

And who listens?

MARY

What do you mean by that?

DARSIE

You are mistaken: this train is not bringing springtime back to us. It is only bringing what is already here, death and more death. In a few hours this street will be crowded with people to mourn the death of one remarkable human being. And then next week, she will slowly be forgotten, and the next year. . . like all of the other remarkable people that were once mourned. Like Daniel Boone near whom her remains will be laid. Like George Washington, and all the people who are remembered only by their names on the streets. She will be just one of the many, who were once welcomed by a silent and lonely night like this.

MARY

Please, you must stand over there. I am engaged.

DARSIE

I beg your pardon?

MARY

Just, that someone might see us. And misunderstand.

DARSIE

Misunderstand what? It is dark . . .

MARY

Precisely.

DARSIE

How can anyone see us, much less recognize us?

MARY

It's just that . . . people will talk.

DARSIE

So, you'd rather them see you standing alone? You, a young woman alone out on the street at night?

MARY

The street is over there. And I am to be a married woman.

DARSIE

Well, I am a married man!

MARY

Oh, and that is so much worse. Please . . .

DARSIE

[Exasperated, he complies.]

Hmm. All right. *[He crosses to the other side. There are only the stars to keep him company. He gazes up at the heavens.]* You sisters up there don't need to be spreading tales. Nor you, Hercules. And Serpens Caput. *[Chuckling to himself, he remembers a favorite story]* I knew a minister once who tied his horse in front of the tavern to visit a parishioner on the same street. A particular old lady saw his horse and told her friends. By mid-afternoon the story had spread that the minister had spent the morning at the tavern. So, that night, he took his horse and tied it to the hitching post and left it there . . . all night . . .in front of her house. *[SOJOURNER laughs]*

MARY

It is a wonder that he didn't have his horse stolen.

SOJOURNER

[After humming the tune]

You talk of Mrs. Tubman as though death were a stranger to her. As though she knew no sorrow.

MARY

She was always joy. Never *this.*

SOJOURNER

I was thinking of the third sister. The little one. Caroline America, they named her. *[She laughs]* "America."

MARY

Yes, a funny name. There is a silver spoon in the cutlery box with the initials C.A.T.

SOJOURNER

She married the doctor—Dr. John Duke. He treated the cholera victims in Paris, Kentucky. America grew sick and he closed his office to travel to New York in search of a cure. They returned on the funeral train within the year. To be buried. They died so young.

DARSIE

Here in Frankfort, over a hundred and fifty people died of the disease. It left many orphans. Mr. and Mrs. Tubman gave generously to help start an orphan school in Midway.

SOJOURNER

Then, on a mountain trail through Lincolnton, Mr. Tubman died of the typhoid fever. She gave him her promise there and there they said goodbye.

MARY

She would never speak of that trip.

SOJOURNER

She bore it always in her heart. No matter where she was, she was always at that mountain trail.

DARSIE

When she arrived here in Frankfort that Spring, she was his widow. A very rich widow. When she returned to Augusta, it was to nurse her brother Western who soon died from the yellow fever.

MARY

Mrs. Tubman built a house for Western's wife and children.

DARSIE

She was by her brother's side when he died. Her attorney, Mr. Cummings, put his hand on her shoulder while she wept and said, "Mrs. Tubman, I will be your brother."

SOJOURNER

Mr. Tubman requested in his will that Emily free his slaves.

DARSIE

Slaves could not be free in Georgia. His will bribed the state with money to build a university, but they refused it.

MARY

How did she free them?

DARSIE

Mrs. Tubman found a comrade in her guardian Henry Clay who was President of the American Colonization Society.

SOJOURNER

She gathered them together and offered them their freedom. *[That time has returned with EMILY appearing in her nightgown, carrying an unlit candle.]* Death was not new to Mrs. Tubman. It was not her enemy.

EMILY

[She opens a small pouch and examines three large shiny stones inside]

Dear Richard. We never had them cut, did we? I always thought we would do it later. This is the later, I guess, this time without you. *[She sighs]* All the while we were together there was this distant fear of losing you. Now you are gone, and although I am relieved of that fear, I am left with such loneliness. Like these rocks: uncut and useless. Oh, Richard, if I could only have you back for a day. An afternoon . . . a moment even. To tell you all the things I never said aloud. To see again all the things we once saw together but never really noticed. To touch you again, to feel your warmth, to smell your fragrance. Where are you now, Richard? Somewhere in the night? I am so desperately alone. You must hear me. *[RICHARD appears as he was before, in formal dress attire—the same as when they first met.]* Richard, what am I to do? I know you want our slaves freed . . . but a law must be passed. Nothing has changed since you tried. There is no law to allow slaves to be freed.

RICHARD

Then change the law.

EMILY

I rode to Washington D.C. with Henry Clay. They talk but they don't do anything. Nothing is happening with them. I have written to the Maryland Society—they promise a priest who will look after my people once they arrive in Liberia. But how can some of them go? They have family members who have been sold to other plantations—they can't leave them for another country. They will never see them again.

RICHARD

So, buy them.

EMILY

What if some of them don't want to go?

RICHARD

Let them choose.

EMILY

But how do we get them to Maryland without them being stopped and sold back into slavery?

RICHARD

Go with them.

EMILY

How will we run our plantations without them? And how will the ones who stay survive?

RICHARD

Hire them.

EMILY

You have an easy answer for everything, Richard. But it's not easy. It's dangerous. Very dangerous.

RICHARD

When I knew you in life, you could beat the devil with your fan! Diamonds aren't diamonds unless they shine . . . and they never shine unless they are cut. And diamonds are only made from pressure.

EMILY

It is different now, without you.

RICHARD

You have everything I had.

EMILY

I don't have you.

RICHARD

Don't you? Just as you clutch those stones, you hold me in your heart. You must believe in yourself.

EMILY

I believe in you. Will you always be there for me, Richard? To shine a light in the night?

RICHARD

I will be here.

ACT TWO

The same night, some time later. DARSIE and MARY stand waiting at the train station as before.

SOJOURNER

[Sitting, singing]

Same train, same train
Same train blowin' at the station
Same train be back tomorrow,
Same train, same train.

MARY

Must you keep singing that song? It is so morbid.

SOJOURNER

It is the song of my people. Of those who endured great sadness. Of the train of death that comes to rich and poor alike. A train of freedom.

DARSIE

Mrs. Tubman freed her slaves. Before the war. Years before.

SOJOURNER

Yes.

DARSIE

Some of them insisted on staying with her.

SOJOURNER

Yes. But most of them chose to go back to Africa.

DARSIE

But she continued to buy slaves–

SOJOURNER

To keep them together. She went to the auction blocks where they sold children away from parents, husbands away from wives. She bought them to keep the families together. Then she went with them by train to Charleston; Captain Robertson escorted them on to Baltimore by packet brig; from there they boarded the ship for Liberia.

MARY

You seem to know a lot about Mrs. Tubman.

SOJOURNER

Do I? I suppose I do. The jungles were hard and violent in Africa. Many of the people returned there could not endure that life and died. *[She laughs]* Oh, but not the Black Tubmans! No. Mrs. Tubman saw to it that they had been highly trained and prepared. And so, they were among the few that prospered. They built a town. Named after her.

MARY

I had a dream last night about the President.

DARSIE

Grover Cleveland?

MARY

Yes . . . and no. He was the President, but he was . . . . African.

DARSIE

The President?

MARY

Yes. Mrs. Tubman had been dead many years. I was in Aunt Louisa's house in Paris, Kentucky—but the house was owned by other people. Well, you know how dreams are.

DARSIE

What happened in the dream?

MARY

A man came to the door—he said he was Secretary to the President. He had come to learn about Aunt Emily. We gave him Mr. Tubman's prayer book. He said he'd take it to the President.

DARSIE

To President Cleveland in the White House?

MARY

The President's name wasn't Cleveland. It was Tubman.

DARSIE

Tubman?

MARY

Yes. The man who came to the door was a Black man, Secretary to the President of Liberia.

DARSIE

We spend half of our lifetime asleep. What a waste. I dream that someday we don't waste half a lifetime with our eyes closed.

SOJOURNER

[To MARY]

Perhaps it was a dream of the future.

DARSIE

The future. No . . .No, there is no future.

SOJOURNER

That is a deep sigh, from a very tired soul. Are you discouraged, pastor? Have faith.

DARSIE

Faith has died, I am afraid, and will be buried at sunrise. Up there where the cemetery is. Where they all sleep in their graves. Like the town and all that sleep in their beds. I wonder if they all dream tonight.

SOJOURNER

You haven't lost your faith. It is there. Maybe you have just misplaced it.

DARSIE

Somewhere in the night?

SOJOURNER

Sometimes the very thing we are looking for is staring us in the face.

MARY

They've changed the Sabbath and the pastor has lost his faith. When I was a child, the night was not such a stranger. We used to sit on the front porch, listen to the crickets, look at the stars, and tell stories. Where are the stories tonight? The night is silent. All the lightning bugs have died in their jars.

[SOJOURNER hums a bar of "Amazing Grace." She stops.]

DARSIE

It was closing time . . . And every night the man pushed his wheel barrow out the gate of the brick yard. A wheel barrow full of straw . . . Bricks had been missing now for some time and this man always pushes this wheelbarrow through the gate with straw in it. . . So, the foreman, determined to catch the thief, watched every night as the man made his way out of the gate pushing a wheelbarrow filled with straw. Always the same, night after night. Until one night he stopped him. "Stop there! Let me see what you are hiding under that straw!" And he looked . . .

MARY

. . . And? He found the bricks!

DARSIE

: . . .and there was nothing there. He let the man pass.

MARY

Ah! He wasn't stealing bricks after all.

DARSIE

No, he wasn't. He was stealing wheelbarrows.

SOJOURNER

[Laughs and then sings:]

Through many dangers, toils, and snares
I have already come.
Tis grace that brought me safe thus far
And grace will lead me home . . .

Sometimes the very thing we are looking for is staring us in the face.

MARY

In this night, there is nothing but darkness. Oh, come back Aunt Emily. Come back and light the lamps of this night for us! Listen! *[But there is no sound of the train]*

DARSIE

So, you are her . . . niece?

MARY

I am to marry her nephew. In October. Four and a half months away.

SOJOURNER

[Humming a bar of "Sweet Chariot," looking back to the heavens:]

Only the lamps of heaven are lit.

[Sings:]

I looked over Jordon and what did I see,
coming for to carry me home?
A band of angels comin' after me,
comin' for to carry me home....

MARY

Is there a heaven, do you think? Or have they changed that as well?

DARSIE

What do you think?

MARY

I think pastors are all the time saying, "What do you think?" Do we sleep in the ground until the trumpet sounds and we all awake? For Judgement. Or do we go straight to heaven?

DARSIE

The Bible says very little about heaven.

MARY

Surely Jesus said something about heaven?

DARSIE

He said not to be afraid. That there were many rooms and he would prepare a place for us. And meet us there.

MARY

Tell me he prepared a place for her. If anyone was deserving of going to heaven it would have to be her.

DARSIE

I don't know.

MARY

What do you mean you *don't know*? Pastors are supposed to know these things!

DARSIE

[Almost rudely]

I don't know.

MARY

[With a deep, deep sigh]

I don't want her to be dead. I still need her. Why was she taken from us? Why? Is God angry with us?

DARSIE

She was ninety-one years old.

MARY

I know how old she was.

SOJOURNER

[Sings:]

Behold the awful trumpet sounds,
The sleeping dead to raise,
And calls the nations underground:
O how the saints will praise!
Behold the Savior how he comes
Descending from his throne,
To burst asunder all our tombs,
And lead his children home..
The falling stars their orbits leave.,
The sun in darkness hide . . .

.

MARY

I've heard father Landon speak of the night the stars fell. People thought it was the end of the world. But it wasn't. Not then, anyway . . .

SOJOURNER

[Going through her bag]

Would you care for something to eat?

MARY

I could never eat again.

SOJOURNER

Come sit. You are weary.

DARSIE

[Looking up at the heavens]

Ah . . . the Serpents Head . . . and Tail.

MARY

[She looks at the constellations]

"The Serpent's Head . . ." Death is from the Fall of man, isn't it? Eve was tempted in the garden by the Serpent? And since then, all humanity has been cursed with death?

SOJOURNER

[Taking out an apple, she offers it to MARY]

The serpent represented wisdom.

MARY

It was evil!

SOJOURNER

Is wisdom evil? And ignorance good? It opened their eyes.

DARSIE

From knowledge comes truth. The early Greeks saw the body as evil, a prison of the soul. The Judeo-Christians saw the body and soul as one, and death as the intruder.

MARY

Now they've changed the Devil on us. It is the end of the world.

SOJOURNER

[Of the apple]

It is clean.

MARY

[She takes it and eats]

I am so confused.

SOJOURNER

Go get some rest . . . A young pretty girl like you should be in bed.

MARY

No, but thank you. Why don't you go and get some sleep? The Mansion House is a nice place to stay. They make everyone so kindly welcomed there.

SOJOURNER

Not everyone. *[Coloreds are not allowed there.]*

MARY

Oh.

DARSIE

Prejudice stems from ignorance. And ignorance from fear. That's why Mrs. Tubman believed so strongly that the clergy should be well educated. Brother Campbell was such a strong advocate of education that he turned his own home into a college and set up housekeeping in the cellar. Irish born and educated in Scotland, he came here with his father and became a great debater and reformer. When he toured the South, he was her house guest. In Alexander Campbell, she found a true comrade and friend.

[CAMPBELL, ANN Thomas, and EMILY appear, seated for after dinner conversation. They accompany the night with memory of Mrs. Tubman's home on Broad Street in Augusta.]

CAMPBELL

The Church throughout history had been like an *iron bedstead*. The early popes measured it by a man's stature at three feet. Then Martin Luther in the Reformation declared it to be four feet! John Calvin declared it five feet. A foolish attempt to make the deductions of some great minds the common measure of all Christians. The time has come for the Church to free itself of these man-made doctrines and creeds. If we would speak and hear the same things, there would be no Trinitarian, or Unitarian, or Episcopalian, or anything else but a "Christian." We would all be one in name.

ANN

This morning, Emily had such an unfortunate encounter with a Reverend from one of those churches. It was over the issue of a name. He argued long and learnedly that there was no importance in a name. She tried to explain to him that a church must have a biblical name. He told her, . . . Tell Brother Campbell what he told you, dear . . . He said, "A rose by any other name would smell as sweet!" Tell Brother Campbell what you did for the man that came for the money. She wrote him a check! He came asking for money and she wrote him a check, didn't you, and signed it.

EMILY

Mother . . .

CAMPBELL

I can understand. There was a fellow once worked for me in my winery. Hard working fellow, but with no name of substance. And he wanted to label his whiskey with it. I tried to be of help to him, but he would not listen. He had not the name for such a business.

ANN

Foolish man. Yes. Yes. *[She pauses]* What was his name?

CAMPBELL

"Jack Daniels."

ANN

Poor man. *[GUS brings in the coffee tray. ANN goes about serving]* We have some brandy if you would like.

CAMPBELL

No, thank you.

ANN

How silly of me to think that our good Brother would drink brandy! Where is my head! *[Having taken out a silver flask]* I prefer a bit of good Kentucky bourbon in mine. Would you?

EMILY

Mother—

CAMPBELL

No, thank you. I am of the opinion that to add a little alcohol to the pure water from the flinty rock so as to make it more refreshing is not unlike those who must rely upon instrumental music in worship. A prerequisite to fire up souls to animal devotion. To all spiritually-minded Christians, such aids would be as a cow bell in a concert.

EMILY

But what of the great organs in cathedrals throughout Europe?

CAMPBELL

Trust me, our souls are in greater danger from the smiles and allurements of the world than from its frowns.

ANN

But sometimes the water is not so pure. My youngest daughter died from drinking the water. And so did Emily's husband.

CAMPBELL

It is but a matter of opinion. We need not agree upon everything. Yet as Christians we can still come together at the Table in love. Every Sunday, on the first day of the week, The Lord's Day, as did the early disciples in the New Testament.

ANN

My daughter and I do not always agree upon everything. We disagree about card playing. She thinks it a *sin* to gamble. I disagree. I say it is a sin—a terrible sin—to *lose* at gambling.

CAMPBELL

Mrs. Campbell and I are astonished at the disrepair of the church buildings we find here in the South. The manners are more concerned with juleps, card playing and balls, races and round dances.

EMILY

But David danced before the ark in Jerusalem.

ANN

And in his underwear . . .

CAMPBELL

But he danced before the Lord. You have read in the Episcopal text, "Is anyone merry, let him dance." We read in by authority of King James: "Is any merry, let him sing praises." The Shaking Quakers dance to shake the devil out. Vain man he shakes the devil in! It is, as I have said. A matter of opinion. As for Mrs. Campbell and myself, we put away such things after our son drowned.

EMILY

Oh, Brother, I am sorry. How tragic.

CAMPBELL

Sadly, our son had not yet reached the age of accountability. I had warned him not to swim on the dog days of summer, before I left for Europe. While I was there, they accused me of slander during my debates against slavery. So, I found myself in jail. I had the most terrible dreams that night in the cell. The charges were dropped soon enough and immediately I made my way home. It took me forty-four days to cross the Atlanta. When

I returned, my dear wife, in her wisdom, to comfort my tears, did say to me: "Our Lord baptized him at his death."

ANN

Oh, to lose one's child! And you–imprisoned for speaking out against slavery!

CAMPBELL

The New Testament does not authorize a man to treat his servants as he treats his mules or his oxen; he must treat them as equals. "There is neither Jew nor Greek, there is neither slave nor free, there is no male and female, for you are all one in Christ Jesus."

ANN

Brother, my daughter and I must hold true to your teachings: Where the Scriptures speak, we speak, and where the Scriptures are silent, we are silent.

GUS

[Entering with a card]

Excuse me, Madam, but the man who was here earlier has returned. He says there is a slight problem. *[He hands her a card. EMILY reads it and excuses herself while handing the card off to her mother. EMILY leaves with GUS following behind. ANN reads the back of the card]*

CAMPELL

Is everything all right?

ANN

"Nothing in a name?" It seems that check she wrote the man, the bank refused to cash. *[She laughs]* She signed a phony name to it.

[At the train station the memory of Ann Thomas and Alexander Campbell disappears somewhere into the night]

MARY

I was never any good at names. When I meet someone, I say to myself "Remember this name." But when I am being introduced, I am so concerned about making a good impression—that I look all right and stand correctly—that I miss the name altogether when it is given. I have tried associating the names with their appearance, but it never works. I once met a Mr. Pigeon. I pictured the bird in my mind—[whispers:] he even resembled it. It was so easy. 'Came time to see him again, proud with my system of memory, I too quickly greeted him with the hearty handshake, "So good to see you again, **Mr. Peacock**!"

DARSIE

The Darsies were Irish. It means "Dark." Not at all suitable for me, do you think?

[SOJOURNER and MARY steal a glance at each other.]

MARY

The Flemings were Irish.

SOJOURNER

Mr. Alexander Campbell was anti-slavery. But he was also against the war.

DARSIE

Christians can never be reformers in any system which uses violence, recommends or expects it. He believed a date should be set when all Africans born would be free citizens and until that time the government should set aside money to assist them when it happened. Over a million dollars a year.

SOJOURNER

Some say the war cost that much per day.

MARY

It destroyed so many things.

DARSIE

Hemp was a major industry here in Kentucky until the Civil War. Now it's all white burley tobacco.

MARY

Hemp was used for rope when there were sailing ships.

SOJOURNER

When slavery came to an end, so did the collapse of the Southern hemp market. There were not enough hired hands to do the work.

MARY

Western's son was a General for the Confederacy. He was killed in the war. And on Valentine's Day.

SOJOURNER

The blockade kept her from fulfilling her promise. If her brother, Landon, in the North were to have her in his home, his penalty would be death for assisting a Southerner. She was unable to make the summer trips. *[She hums "My Old Kentucky Home."]*

DARSIE

Her plantations were supplied with hired labor before the Emancipation Act—that was how she survived while so many others collapsed.

SOJOURNER

The march of Sherman should have destroyed Augusta. But it didn't.

MARY

Don't mention his name. What is it with little boys wanting to play with fire! In Augusta, our men wanted to burn all the bales of cotton, before Sherman got to it, and they would have too, were it not for Mrs. Tubman and the ladies of our town who put up a fight. It would have burned down the town.

SOJOURNER

You were a child then . . . *[She continues to hum the song.]*

MARY

I remember the soldiers marching, . . .Refugees poured into Augusta. The women nursed the wounded in the churches. Mrs. Tubman paid for an ice machine to help the suffering soldiers; Captain I. P. Girardy saw it through the blockade. Later, it became an important industry for the South.

DARSIE

Think about it. Sherman left Atlanta following the path of the railroad–Augusta was right in his path to Savannah and the sea.

MARY

An easy target to destroy, too, as it was home to the Confederate Powder works. Sherman gathered some sixty thousand of his troops and headed toward Augusta. Outside the city they waited and watched for days. And then, at last, . . . a silence. . . *[SOJOURNER stops humming.]* Thanksgiving Day. And suddenly, the troops were gone. Augusta was spared.

DARSIE

It's always been a mystery.

SOJOURNER

The legend is that Sherman loved a widowed lady from the North, who owned much land in Augusta, and at her request his troops retreated.

DARSIE

Here in Frankfort, riots were rampant before the end of the war. General Burbridge was appointed commander of the Kentucky militia by his good friend the Governor. Whenever a Union citizen was killed, he would just go down to the jail, drag out four or five Confederate soldiers and have them shot to death. One need not tell ghost stories on dark wicked nights like this: the true stores are chilling enough.

[SOJOURNER hums a bar of "My Old Kentucky Home" and stops.]

MARY

Oh, don't stop. It was so pretty. 'Stephen Foster, isn't it? Sing the words.

SOJOURNER

[Sings]

The head must bow and the back will have to bend
wherever the darky may go.
A few more days and the trouble all will end
in the field where sugar-canes may grow.
A few more days for to tote the weary load,
no matter, 'twill never be light.
A few more days 'till we totter on the road,
then my old Kentucky home, good night.

MARY

"Totter on the road?" You mean . . .

SOJOURNER

To die. Those are the words of Mr. Foster.

MARY

Are you sure?

SOJOURNER

I'm sure.

MARY

Well, I'll have to look them up . . . later.

DARSIE

[Laughs to himself]

You have a lot to look up later.

MARY

That is a terrible song.

SOJOURNER

A father taken from his children, a husband taken from his wife, taken from the land familiar to him and sold down the river. Slavery was brutal to him. His only joy the memory of that home. His only hope was death.

[There is a silence.]

MARY

Well, that song will never be popular! *[To SOJOURNER]* Did you know Mrs. Tubman?

SOJOURNER

Have you been beaten?

MARY

Yes. *[Sadly]* In croquet. Just last week.

SOJOURNER

And you, Brother?

DARSIE

Yes. By life. By hypocrisy. By lack of commitment . . . need I go on?

SOJOURNER

I am thinking of a young girl. A girl who was beaten. An innocent child who worked as a slave. Five times she cleaned the room and every time her work met with a whip from her master's wife. Why? Because each time, after the cleaning, somehow there was dust on the furniture. She cleaned the room again, and this time, the lash did not strike her. A lady—a relative visiting from the South–had caught the tail of the whip, and threatened to leave if her master's wife did not stop whipping her—threatened to whip her herself. She asked the master's wife to leave them; then asked the girl to show her how she had done the work. For the seventh time she moved the furniture into the middle of the room, swept, –but the moment she picked up the dust rag, the lady said to her, "Now, stop there. Go away now and do your other work and I will call you when it is time to dust." When the time came, she called the girl and explained to her how the dust had settled, and that if she were to wipe it off now, the furniture would remain clean. The girl thanked her. The lady smiled and said, "You may call me 'Miss Emily.'"[1]

MARY

Were you that young girl?

SOJOURNER

There was another young girl named "Minnie."

MARY

Minnie?

SOJOURNER

Just a name. Another little girl.

MARY

"You've beaten me again."

SOJOURNER

Burned out of her home. All her toys and ribbons gone . . .

MARY

"What are you doing? Come back here. You're trespassing." *[MARY walks away from the Depot and into the time when she was a young girl called "Minnie." She is playing with her sister, KATE, who joins her.]*

SOJOURNER

You were different then. And the world saw you as different, and it has forever shunned that which it would not know.

KATE

Animal, vegetable, mineral?

---

[1] Sarah H. Bradford, *Scenes in the life of Harriet Tubman*, (Auburn: W. J. Moses, 1869), pp. 10-12.

MINNIE

All right. *[She takes a deep sigh]* Vegetable.

KATE

The pink myrtle?

MINNIE

No.

KATE

Azalea?

MINNIE

No.

KATE

Magnolia?

MINNIE

No. The house.

KATE

Minnie! That was only three! I have ten guesses!

MINNIE

Sorry. I wish I had a book to read.

KATE

The house? The house is not a vegetable!

MINNIE

It has flowers in the yard.

KATE

The house is not the yard. The house is mineral: made out of brick.

MINNIE

Made out of brick and wood. Wood is a vegetable—oh, Kate, please, let's don't play this anymore, I'm just not good at it. You've beaten me again. What are you doing? Come back here. You're trespassing.

[A young boy enters, YOUNG LANDON JR. He sneaks behind MINNIE and steals the ribbon from her hair. Full of energy, he dances around her with it, yelping like an Indian. His teasing betrays his fondness for her.]

MINNIE

My ribbon. Give it back.

KATE

Bandit! Give it back. Give it back, boy!

MINNIE

Please. It is my only one. I have no others now.

KATE

I said, give it back, now!

MINNIE

Please—

KATE

Ignore him, Minnie. Just pretend that he's not here. He'll go away. I don't see a boy!

MINNIE

But I don't want him to go away with my ribbon.

KATE

He won't. Just ignore him. Isn't it a lovely day?

MINNIE

No, its cold and I don't have a sweater anymore. Are you sure this is working?

KATE

What would he want with a ribbon? Unless he wants to tie up his pretty little curls! *[She sticks her tongue out at him. YOUNG LANDON JR. sticks out his tongue at her. KATE grabs for the ribbon, misses]* Give it back or I'll tell!

YOUNG LANDON JR.

Tell who?

KATE

Uh . . . that man over there.

YOUNG LANDON JR.

That man is my aunt's butler.

KATE

Is not.

YOUNG LANDON JR.

Is too.

KATE

Liar, liar, pants on fire!

YOUNG LANDON JR.

[The Southern folk sound so funny when they talk. Mimicking:]

LAR! LAR! PYAnts on fAR!

KATE

Well, you **look** funnier when you talk!

YOUNG LANDON JR

[Of the butler]

Here he comes. *[Quickly to MINNIE]* Hold out your hand and close your eyes and I'll give it back. Quick, close them! *[The girls close their eyes;*

MINNIE holds out her hand. LANDON JR. drops the ribbon in her hand just as he steals a kiss from her lips. He rushes off yelping with joy.]

MINNIE

He kissed me.

KATE

What? What! How dare him! [*Crossing after him*] Come back here, you boy! You awful, cad boy! I'll beat you to a pulp. Come back here, sissy! *[To MINNIE]* Are you all right?

MINNIE

It was rather nice.

KATE

We will report him! Come on. Uh, oh . . . that man. He's coming this way. Hide! *[They run and hide behind the bench. GUS enters, neatly dressed in tie and tails. He sees them behind the bench, stops. Whispering to MINNIE]* Do you think he saw us?

GUS

Excuse me, Miss. *[The girls ignore him. He leans over and taps them on the shoulder. They look up at him. He gives them a wave. MINNIE waves back, but KATE pulls her down again.]* Which of you young ladies would be Miss Mary Fleming?

MINNIE

[Getting up]

I'm Mary Fleming. They call me Minnie. This is my sister, Kate.

KATE

[Curtseys]

'Charmed.

GUS

I have a letter for you, Miss Fleming. From Mrs. Tubman.

MINNIE

Have I done something wrong?

GUS

Only if you refuse this letter.

MINNIE

It wasn't his fault, sir. I wanted him to kiss me.

KATE

Minnie! For shame!

GUS

Well, now, that is quite interesting, I'm sure. *[He offers her the letter.]* Please . . .*[She carefully receives it.]* Mrs. Tubman wishes to send regards to your family. Good day to you, Miss. And that kiss—that will be our little secret. No need to mention it again.

MARY

Thank you, sir.

GUS

And good day to you too, Miss Minnie.

KATE

[Curtseys]

Good day to you too, I'm sure. *[GUS bows and exits. To MINNIE]* Open it, you ninny!

MINNIE

Who is Mrs. Tubman?

KATE

The lady of the house. Here. *[She opens the letter.]* Read it. I always make the habit of never reading another person's mail, it is rude and vulgar. Besides, it is addressed to you. "Miss Mary Fleming."

MINNIE

But how does she know me?

KATE

I'll read it. *[From reading the letter:]* It says she knows how hard it must be for young girls to have had everything burned, and she wants us to have this money to buy lace and ribbons and other things little girls enjoy. Look! Here's a *check.*

MINNIE

How thoughtful. But I've never had a check before. We'll give to Mama and Daddy to help with the house . . .

KATE

And break the old woman's heart? I think not. If she wants us to buy lace and ribbons, then we'll buy lace and ribbons. Follow me. Let's see. . . our first stop for other things that little girls enjoy: the candy kitchen. We are full of business today!

[MINNIE and KATE disappear as those moments fade away and the present train station returns to the night.]

SOJOURNER

You were Minnie then. Before the world got to you.

DARSIE

People can be so cruel. The church would be all right if it weren't for its people. It opens its doors to every broken, bitter soul that walks the street. One of the early church fathers compared it to Noah's Ark. "We could not endure the stench on the inside if it weren't for the storm on the outside."

SOJOURNER

Is every broken, bitter soul cruel?

DARSIE

They don't mean to be, if they are. Only God knows what got to them before He did.

MARY

I think some people are just mean.

SOJOURNER

I see.

[MARY's memories come back to the streets of the town. ELLEN, a beautiful woman, in exquisite dress stands at L; MINNIE enters, a mature woman now, dressed in homespun jacket, hat, and gloves. ELLEN speaks as though addressing a crowd of her lady friends.]

ELLEN

Yes, my husband donated a melodeon to the church. It was found this morning in the coal bin! Religious fanatics! They do not approve of instrumental music in the church. In the Church? The great cathedrals of Europe have organs! Since the War, those-who-have-not change their theology to be those-who-want-not and then to those-who-declare-not. How convenient for the poor. Yes, it is true that Emily—my husband's dear sister– is a strong advocate of the teachings of Alexander Campbell. Did you hear Brother Campbell when he debated in Lexington against Nathan Rice? He was so incredible, that the moderator, the Honorable Henry Clay, even forgot himself, and applauded!

MINNIE

Good afternoon, Mrs. Thomas. Ladies. I hope you are feeling better today.

ELLEN

[Ignoring her, and addressing the "Ladies"]

Yes, it is true that Alexander Campbell used to oppose organ music, but he came to change "his tune," shall we say. *[She laughs]* True, he went to his grave opposing dancing, God rest his soul. Yet he did not oppose all dancing, it was just round dancing that he found sinful: he loved to square dance. Maybe in heaven they cut off the corners and he sees it round after all. *[She laughs gaily again]*

MINNIE

I am Mary Fleming, the girl Landon brought to your house last night for dinner. He said you were sick and we would have to come another night. I hope you are feeling better.

ELLEN

I beg your pardon. I do not believe we have met—

MARY

I know, but it was I that came with Landon. I'm from Augusta, Georgia. Landon invited me to come–

ELLEN

With my little Landon? I think not. He is to have dinner this very evening with the Senator's daughter.

MARY

But he invited me to come here . . .

ELLEN

[Empathetic toward this strange girl from the South]

I am sorry to tell you, dear. Landon has a way with the girls. I do hope you'll have a chance to see our town before you return to the South. *[She quickly walks away from her. To her lady friends:]* Some unfortunate waif of the Confederacy. I thought for a moment it was one of our own . . . from the Craw. *[She is gone L but LANDON JR. appears R, finely dressed in coat, tie, and hat, an adult.]*

MARY

Landon, there you are. I thought I'd lost you.

LANDON JR.

Why did you think that? Are you ready?

MARY

Yes. *[They start to walk]* You have a lovely little town.

LANDON JR.

Not as big as Augusta, but Frankfort is the capital of the state. This street used to be named Market Street before the train came through. All the farmers would bring their crops and sell them here. People came from all around.

MARY

You love this little town, I can tell. *[She puts her arm through his and snuggles closer to him. Instantly we see a change in him as the burdens of the day melt away; for a moment we see a secure and warm friendship between these two young people.]*

LANDON JR.

That is Lewis Street, named after General Andrew Lewis. General Wilkerson bought this land and named the streets after his friends. He never really lived here—his wife was afraid of the Indians. But he named the street there Ann Street in honor of her. Montgomery Street after the General Montgomery—although it's more fashionable name now is "Main Street" . . .

MARY

And "Holmes Street?"

LANDON JR.

Mr. Holmes bought the town from Wilkinson.

MARY

He must have been very rich.

LANDON JR.

He was. It's amazing what you can do with the right amount of money. He paid to have Frankfort become the capital.

MARY

And the "Craw?"

LANDON JR.

[He pulls away from her.]

You wouldn't want to see that.

MARY

Why not? Your mother's from there.

LANDON JR.

[Suddenly angered]

How dare you speak of my mother like that!

MARY

[Surprised at his sudden outrage]

I only heard her speak of it—

LANDON JR.

Apologize at once! The very idea! I can't believe what you just said!

MARY

What? What? I'm sorry—I didn't know. *[She is trembling with fear of him]* I don't even know what it is. What is the Craw anyway?

LANDON JR

That's where the poor people live, down by the river, that's all. My mother has no associations there!

MARY

Of course not. I didn't know, Landon. I was mistaken, please, I'm sorry—

LANDON JR.

[Calming but stern]

Well, you should be.

MARY

Why is it called "Craw?"

LANDON JR.

Because of the crawdads. The land was cheap there after the War—cheap because it flooded. Some call it the "Bottom." It's a hotbed of vice and corruption.

MARY

I didn't know.

LANDON JR.

Let's just forget you ever mentioned it. Now, come along, I must stop in town after I see you to your hotel.

MARY

[Eagerly]

We can walk through town on the way. I can go with you. I'd like to see their hats—

LANDON JR.

No. There isn't time. We'll cut through Catfish Alley.

MARY

Is it true that you are seeing the Senator's daughter tonight?

LANDON JR

Where did you hear that?

MARY

From your Mother. Is it true?

LANDON JR

When did you see Mother?

MARY

Just a moment ago. She was here with her friends. . . . Feeling better, of course.

LANDON JR

I hope you were polite to her!

MARY

[Astonished at his change, she steps away from him.]

Are you seeing the Senator's daughter tonight?

LANDON JR

It's just one of those debutante things. She is friend of the family. It means nothing. Now, let's be going—I can't be late–

MARY

Then walk me down Montgomery Street in the full sunlight, and not around the backstreets of town. Or are you ashamed of me, Landon? You're not the same here. Not like you were in Augusta. *[Remembering]* You were Junior there and I was Minnie.

LANDON JR

We were children.

MARY

I came to visit Kentucky at your request. I had never ridden a train before, much less traveled alone. I guess in many ways, I'm still a child. *[She offers her hand]* I'll walk with you down the main street . . . *[LANDON JR drops his head]* Or shall I walk myself to Market Street?

LANDON JR

It's called "Broadway" now . . .

MARY

There is a train arriving soon. *[He is silent.]* Goodbye, Landon, . . .

[LANDON JR. disappears. That time is long gone somewhere in the night. Forgotten and forgiven, somewhere out in the dark. The lights return on MARY, as before, at the train station.]

It was so much easier when we were children. There were no memories then.

SOJOURNER

Even God can't change the past.

[MARY looks in the direction of the train. It will be arriving soon. She hopes. She knows.]

ACT THREE

The entire cast enters and fills the stage, filing into "pews," leaving a center aisle. All face front with open hymn books. It is a church worship service. Without instrumental music, everyone begins to sing "Wondrous Love" to Southern Harmony. Many savor the sound with their eyes closed while they sing:

"What wondrous love is this, oh! my soul! oh! my soul!
What wondrous love is this, oh! my soul!

What wondrous love is this!
That caused the Lord of bliss,
To bear the dreadful curse for my soul, for my soul,
To bear the dreadful curse for my soul."

An organ is rolled on and the organist sits at it very dramatically and accompanies the hymn. Everyone sings the hymn again along with the organ, but the singers at one side are discontent. On the third verse, the singers at one side find a different hymn from their hymnals and begin to sing without the organ:

"O God, our help in ages past, our hope for years to come,
Our shelter from the stormy blast, and our eternal home!"

As the first side sings the fourth verse of "Wondrous Love" with the organ, the other side sings "O God Our Help In Ages Past," without the organ. Everyone starts singing louder and louder. They sing the verses again, against each other, throwing hymnals, fighting, shouting, etc. Both sides come to the end of their respective hymn and the organ stops. Everyone returns to his/her pew, and although ragged and torn, proudly sings a most beautiful "AMEN."

The cast disappears to reveal again DARSIE, SOJOURNER, and MARY at the Frankfort Train Station.

DARSIE

So many hateful things are done in the name of religion. Churches battling over organ music, when we had just come from a war to settle the issue of human slavery.

SOJOURNER

Jeroboam Beauchamp killed a man in the name of *love.*

DARSIE

[Remembering]

Jeroboam Beauchamp. Now there is a ghost story for the dark of night. I can almost see the house down there, past the Capital, in the moonlight.

Madison Street. Solomon Sharp lived there. He was representative to the U.S. Congress. Jeroboam Beauchamp loved Anna Cooke, a society girl. She was much older and he was infatuated with her, but she would not marry him. Anna Cooke, you see, had a past. She had been *jilted*, so she claimed, by the politician Solomon Sharp.

MARY

Father Landon studied law under Solomon Sharp. His uncle had once owned the house.

DARSIE

[As though the night closes in to shadow the telling]

Anna Cooke gave birth to a child—Solomon Sharp's child, so she claimed. And the child was born dead. She agreed to marry Beauchamp under one condition.

MARY

What was that?

DARSIE

That he kill Solomon Sharp. *[There is an eerie stillness that creeps from Madison Street.]* On a dark November night, Beauchamp donned a black mask, knocked at the door, and stabbed Solomon Sharp to death in cold blood. He did it to avenge her honor: he did it "out of love" for her.

MARY

They caught him, didn't they?

DARSIE

And he confessed. He went to jail and Anna refused to leave his side. There he wrote his Confessions and his love ballads. Oh, the public ate it up! It was published in all the papers, made him a celebrity, and put Kentucky on the map around the world. The morning they were to be hanged, both of them drank poison. Then they each stabbed themselves. It took several men to hold him up and put the noose around his neck. And when he died, at that very moment—so they said—Anna Cooke fell dead. They buried them together in the same coffin, embraced in each other's arms. It was called, "The Kentucky Tragedy." Edgar Allen Poe wrote a play about it, but it was never finished.

MARY

So many hateful things are done in the name of love. Why does God allow such things to happen? If God is the God of love? Where was God that autumn night?

SOJOURNER

Where was God on that autumn night when the town caught fire, and your church burned to the ground?

[The stage turns red with the movement of flames. From her bedroom in the house on Washington Street, ELLEN enters dressed in red night robe and cap, carrying a lantern in one hand and a bucket in the other. The years have retreated into the autumn night of 1870]

ELLEN

Little Landon! Little Landon, wake up! The town is on fire! Look out the window! Wake up! We must go help them. Take this bucket . . .

LANDON JR

[Appearing in nightshirt. Of the red flames:]

It's beautiful . . .

ELLEN

Your father is bringing 'round the carriage; your brother is with him. Wake up your sisters—*[She hands him the bucket]*

LANDON JR.

You seem to have it under control. I'm going back to bed . . .

ELLEN

It could spread and come this way! Your father and your brother—

LANDON JR.

But I'm not my father or my brother.

ELLEN

Don't give me that. *[Shoving the bucket at him]* Take this!

LANDON JR.

Do you mind if I put my pants on first? *[He takes the bucket and exits. She carries on her parental and societal duties.]*

ELLEN

Fire! Girls, your father is waiting outside! *[She stops and peers at herself in a mirror]* I wonder if it is sinful to wear red to a fire. *[She dismisses the thought and exits.*

[PHILIP FALL appears amidst the burned ruin of the church on Ann Street, several weeks later. This recent hardship has deeply aged his once handsome face. He stoops down and picks up a burnt Bible. He opens it: the pages are clean. Only a memory now watched and remembered.]

SOJOURNER

Philip Fall. There is a good English name. He came to this country to offer women the same education as men and started the Female Eclectic Institute at Poplar Hill. After becoming a pastor, he too was influenced by the teachings of Alexander Campbell and organized a new congregation here with the Restoration ideas. They met in homes. Finally, they built a church. Two doors: men went in one on the left and women in the other on the right. Separated by a coal bin. Divided by instrumental music, melodeons, pipe organs. Some said that it took a fire to cleanse them. . .

LOUISA

[Now a widow in her seventies, dressed in coat and hat.]

Brother Fall.

FALL

Mrs. Keiningham.

LOUISA

Emily said she thought that was you. I told her it couldn't be, because you were in Nashville. But she was right. It is you. How are you, Brother Fall –*[She offers her hand, but before he can answer:]* What a stupid question, you couldn't be very good now could you– your old church 'burned to the ground. I am so sorry—*[Before he can answer:]* Not that it's your fault—no, it was some lady's stove that caught fire on the other side of town—God bless her. It was a spark that shot straight across the sky and landed on the cupola: the church burned from the top down. Yes, the top down, just as if it was God himself who burned it down—Had you been here this thing would not have happened—*[Before he can answer:]* I mean, the pastors they've had since you left—God bless them—Oh! They just don't stand up to you, Brother Fall. They come and go like the wind; I can't keep up with them. Brother Moore was a good preacher—God bless him–I loved his sermon about falling from grace—but he was gone all the time. No, it just wasn't the same after you left. After all, you were here how long?–*[Before he can answer:]* Twenty-five years, I believe. That's a long time. Frankly, I don't know how you did it. There was such dissension and so many factions—Landon kept me abreast about it all—You know that he gave a melodeon to the church and they threw it out in the coal bin! And I mean, an expensive one—not the coal bin, of course, but the melodeon. They've done nothing but bicker since you left. One faction here likes something over there but that faction there likes only something over here—Landon tells me all about it. Young people expelled from the church for dancing—God bless them. One young lady –a good strong worker –God bless her–was reproved for wearing bright dresses to church. Why, one sister—God bless her–washed the venetian blinds and was criticized for letting her mind dwell on material things–

EMILY

[A woman of seventy-six years, also in coat and hat]

Brother Fall.

LOUISA

You were right, Harvie. It is Brother Fall. He's been telling me all about the fire.

FALL

I came as soon as I heard. It must have been a terrible fire to see.

EMILY

So much of the town burned. Your beautiful church that you worked so hard to build. They were able to save some of the furniture.

FALL

It was plain . . . a family arrangement. The character of the church was more important than bringing in numbers. I always felt that if the church could be first what it should be, then increase would follow.

LOUISA

Everything you worked for is lost.

FALL

Burned, but not lost.

LOUISA

They won't build again. No, no, no. Not with the way things are after the War. People can barely make ends meet. Oh, Emily, the livery stable on the corner burned so fast they couldn't get the horses out. And when the church bell fell—it must have shattered into a million pieces.

EMILY

[With an effort to soften LOUISA's remarks, to FALL:]

How is Nancy . . . and the children? And your church in Nashville?

FALL

All are doing well. And growing. I am very grateful.

EMILY

I'm sure I would not recognize little Lizzy–

LOUISA

Brother Arnold is pastor now. I told Brother Fall that this would not have happened had he not left us for Tennessee.

EMILY

I'm sure Brother Arnold has had a fruitful ministry—

LOUISA

Like fruit flies! No, no, no. It is a catastrophe. With a capital K. You should have been here, Brother Fall, they needed you—

EMILY

Your presence here now is encouraging to us, Brother Fall—thank you for coming. You always inspired us with your heroic spirit, as you do now for your congregation in Nashville, I'm sure.

LOUISA

'Just a disaster. Hopeless. They will never build again. No, no, no.

EMILY

Louisa, would you keep our place there at the station? I will be along shortly and the train is soon to arrive.

LOUISA

Good to see you again, Brother Fall, I mean, not good to see you like this, of course.

FALL

I understand.

LOUISA

Do you? I sure don't. It has been such a waste, if you ask me.

EMILY

Louisa Ann . . .

LOUISA

[Whispering to EMILY]

Try and cheer him up—he won't listen to me. And he looks like Death—God bless him. *[LOUISA exits.]*

EMILY

Have you been back to your school at Poplar Hill? They are doing so well. They have to turn students away!

FALL

Yes. They come from all over the country now.

EMILY

When I was growing up here, there were no schools for girls. I would have gladly attended yours. The gardens are so lovely.

FALL

Nancy and I brought many of the flowers back from England. *[He looks around the ruin where there is no beauty.]* I was told before I came to Kentucky that Kentuckians in politics and religion go the "whole hog." They were right.

EMILY

You always faced every hardship with dignity and strength, Brother.

FALL

We are not here, sister, in the manner of the willow, to bend and break with every challenge in life. We are here planted like the oak. Strong and enduring. Our growth has always been in the manner of the oak, gradual and firm, but long. *[EMILY takes out the beaded purse that holds the uncut diamonds.]* I believe there will come a day, Sister Tubman, when all our hearts shall be filled with love toward one another, and in that moment, we shall see only the lofty peaks of our common faith. Our minor differences– those separating valleys– will be lost in the mountains of truth. Mountains that will overshadow everything everywhere . . . united in the extended horizons.

EMILY

This street was named after General Wilkinson's wife, Ann. He built a house for her, but she never lived here. Holmes Street there, is named after the man who gave the lumber so needed to build this town, and in return they chose Frankfort as the capital.

FALL

Money can do wondrous things. And money with faith can do wondrous love.

EMILY

Brother, I have a train to meet. Before my late husband Richard Tubman died, I made him a promise that I would spend the summers in Kentucky and the winters in Georgia. November is upon us and I must keep that promise. I wonder if you would do something for me while I am gone. *[She hands him an envelope, while holding to the beaded purse.]* You see, I know of an architect who needs a job. I have written down his name and address.

FALL

I will try.

EMILY

And I know of a builder—if it wouldn't be too much trouble—who is very capable and needs to support his wife and family.

FALL

Surely.

EMILY

And the lumber, it comes down river, and could help a business that struggles to sell it. You will find their names all there. And I wish to pay them.

FALL

Most certainly. I shall try to find them work.

EMILY

I mean for them to build. Here.

FALL

In town?

EMILY

Your church. I wish for them to rebuild your church. The money and all the information are there. Will you see that Brother Arnold gets it, please?

FALL

You wish to help build the church?

EMILY

No, Brother Fall. I wish to build the church. From its front steps to its steeple. From its tomb of ashes shall we call it out. Just as Mr. Holmes did with his little bit of lumber and ulterior motive.

FALL

'motive?

EMILY

It wouldn't do of much harm, would it, if my church included a beautiful pipe organ? The grandest organ this side of the Mason Dixon line? One that will take an army of men to haul into the coal bin, which incidentally will be in the cellar and not next to the pulpit.

FALL

Mrs. Tubman . . . *[He does not know what to say.]*

EMILY

But unlike General Wilkerson's wife, Ann, I intend for it to be lived in. Wouldn't you agree? Its doors open to the people of Washington Street to those in the Craw.

FALL

I don't know what to say . . .

EMILY

I am only a steward, Brother Fall, with what the Lord has entrusted me. It is my greatest pleasure to use it to advance His Kingdom. After all, it all belongs to Him. Will you see to it that Brother Arnold receives my gift?

FALL

Yes, of course.

EMILY

I must not miss that train. I will write to you. Better yet, I may send one of those fancy "telegrams." *[She starts to the train station.]*

FALL

But . . . Mrs. Tubman . . . . *[As if the envelope might contain a fallacy]*

EMILY

Yes, Brother Fall?

FALL

Mrs. Tubman . . . Is it possible . . . I mean, have you such resources . . .

EMILY

Probably not. But we walk in faith, don't we? In the manner of the oak. *[She starts again to the train station, then turns.]* Besides, . . . The old girl ain't broke yet.

[That November night fades away in the memories of the past.]

DARSIE

She built them a new church. Much larger and grander . . . and with its own pipe organ. 'Paid for the entire thing. From the bell in the steeple to the cushions on the pews.

SOJOURNER

Where was God in the burning?

DARSIE

You tell me.

MARY

In the generous gift of an old woman. I'm going to walk over there. *[She exits to visit the church]*

SOJOURNER

Because of that gift, Brother Tyler came as their pastor. And afterwards, they called you.

DARSIE

Are you suggesting that the fire brought me here?

SOJOURNER

They called you.

DARSIE

I'd hate to think that God destroys things to get our attention.

SOJOURNER

They sent you a letter . . .

DARSIE

Yes. *[Oh, how he remembers it! Oh, how he would like to forget it!]* It intimated that nobody could possibly fill Brother Tyler's place, but as the church had to have *somebody*, it wanted me to come and try. After all, I was better than nothing. Nothing.

SOJOURNER

'Must have been a lot of head-shaking over them calling a man up north of the Ohio River. A Yankee! *[She laughs]* Not everybody liked Brother Tyler, you know. His informal ways hurt many a feeling when he first came here. He'd say, "If they leave their feelings lying around like cat's tails, they might expect them to get stepped on!" *[She laughs again, but DARSIE is not amused.]* But before long, he kind of grew on them. And they grew to love him. Do you love them?

DARSIE

The people who come to this town come to serve the State Government. They are here until the Government moves them somewhere else or gets rid of them all together. They have no intention of staying, so they experience a divided allegiance.

SOJOURNER

They are afraid . . . to draw close. And you? Were you afraid they would not endure you?

DARSIE

[In his own defense:]

This region was measured by the highest standards of oratory—of such as Humphrey Marshall and Henry Clay–

SOJOURNER

What good is it for the sun to rise if we live in a shadow? You expect so much from others, and so you are hardest on yourself.

DARSIE

People like to see a church advancing by leaps and bounds. They love nothing more than a big, roaring, red-hot protracted meeting with scores of converts in a great wave of religious vehemence.

SOJOURNER

You never answered me. Do you love them?

DARSIE

What is your name?

SOJOURNER

Do you?

DARSIE

How can I know you unless you tell me your name? A woman alone out in the streets at night? On the run . . . You make me think of that woman they call "Moses." The one that helped slaves escape up North. Her name was Tubman. *[SOJOURNER smiles.]* She led so many slaves to freedom. Runaways . . . the "underground railroad."

SOJOURNER

Look there! *[She points ahead]* What do you see?

DARSIE

The towers of the Penitentiary?

SOJOURNER

Built to resemble the Warwick Towers of England. Do you know of the Reverend Lambert Young? The commonwealth's attorney summoned him there one night to reason with the mob that sought to kill an innocent Negro man. They would not listen to the Reverend Young no matter how hard he pleaded. They killed the man. In cold blood. And Father Young knew them. He knew them all, each one by name. And later in court, the good Father was asked to reveal their names. To tell the truth. But did he?

DARSIE

[Turning away]

He refused.

SOJOURNER

Why?

DARSIE

Because he thought to testify would "prostitute" his office and bring disgrace upon his character. He was afraid.

SOJOURNER

Afraid to draw too close. For if we get too close, . . .we . . . touch? *[DARSIE turns to her]* Surely, our Savior touched the disciples if indeed he . . .washed their feet. The Apostle Paul wrote that in Christ "there is neither slave nor free, male or female." In the night . . . we are all the same color, are we not?

DARSIE

[He remembers:]

"Come to me, ye who are weak and heavy laden . . ."

SOJOURNER

We keep Him at a distance. Because to "come," . . . to come is . . . to put on the yoke . . .

DARSIE

To be yoked together.

SOJOURNER

[Precisely]

'Can't get any closer than that! And we don't want that, do we?

DARSIE

Or maybe we do. Deep down inside it is the thing that we hunger for. But we are afraid.

MARY

[Returning]

Her church is so lovely in the moonlight, its tall steeple. She built the church in Augusta as well. And several others.

DARSIE

I know of literally hundreds of thousands of dollars she has given away to those in need. *[Of the church]* There we would see her winning smiles and receive her kindly greeting as she came and went. Ever the same serene, bright, cheery old lady whom all so fondly loved, and so deeply revered. Where has she gone?

SOJOURNER

The spire points the way.

DARSIE

[Noticing the house across the street]

There's a light in the window at Dr. Sawyier's house. He is up early. I wonder what it was like for them to have the train come through their front yard? *[He exits.]*

MARY

[Watching him]

I think he is wrestling with himself tonight. Look. He's not going to Dr. Sawyier's. He's headed to the church, also.

SOJOURNER

I believe he is wrestling with God.

MARY

They tell me that Dr. Sawyer did not want to be a doctor. He wanted to be an artist.

SOJOURNER

Why didn't he –become an artist? If that was his dream?

MARY

His father would not allow it. He had to make money: be *successful.* But he has seen to it that all of his own children are artists.

SOJOURNER

Are they successful?

MARY

They are doing what they love. I think that is success, don't you? Aunt Emily sent Frank Boggs to Paris to study art. He is a very successful artist. *[Of SOJOURNER]* Do I know your name? You seem so familiar to me.

SOJOURNER

I should.

MARY

You remind me so much of *Becky*. Aunt Emily's cook.

SOJOURNER

Rebecca.

MARY

Aunt Emily made arrangements for her and Gus in her will.

SOJOURNER

Did she?

MARY

Yes. She left them stock in the Railroad. Aunt Emily had always been there for her. She chose to stay with Aunt Emily after Mr. Tubman died. And Gus went to Africa and missed Becky so, that he wanted to come back. Aunt Emily understood that: she paid for his return and met him in New York.

SOJOURNER

Life was safe with her?

MARY

Yes. And through the War. Aunt Emily has been that strong thread through it all. When the thread is broken, everything unravels. *[She tries to see through the veil]* Is that who you are? Is that your name? Dear sweet Becky? You needn't be afraid. She has you in her will. You must claim your inheritance.

SOJOURNER

Claim your inheritance . . . Look there! *[She points.]* What do you see?

MARY

The tunnel?

SOJOURNER

The site of a murder. A young Irish woman–her body thrown down that hill. Above the tunnel. They accused a Negro; his name was Jim Macklin . . . On New Year's Eve, a mob of Irishmen broke into the jail and took him by force. Their priest pleaded with them, but they pushed him aside, and dragged poor Jimmy to that very hillside and hanged him. Thirteen Irishmen went to court for the lynching. The priest refused to identify the mob, out of respect for his priestly office. He was sent to jail and there fell ill. The murderers were dismissed by the judge.

MARY

Why . . . *[She starts to cry]* Why must people be so cruel? *[She turns in such a fury, looking for the train, that she falls to the ground.]* Where is Aunt Emily! *[She sobs. All of the grief and anger she has stored away comes to surface. SOJOURNER goes to her and holds her.]* There is good in the world! Help me find it again! You sing the train a train of freedom. I want on it. I want on it!

SOJOURNER

The price of the ticket is high. You must surrender all that you have, and all that you have been.

[The winds of the night blow in the years just previous where an adult LANDON JR. sits behind his desk. EMILY enters. It is an office at the King's Mill in Augusta.]

EMILY

Knock, knock . . .

LANDON, JR

Aunt Emily! *[He goes to her and they embrace.]*

EMILY

I came as soon as I got your telegram. I can't believe it.

LANDON JR.

[He indicates a chair, and she sits.]

What all have you heard?

EMILY

Enough to say the least. That Bill Roberts tried to kill himself and they have him for grand larceny.

LANDON JR.

That's only half of it. The Enterprise has failed. Roberts and O'Donnell & Burke have declared bankruptcy, and the Bank of Augusta has closed its doors.

EMILY

Good heavens!

LANDON JR.

George Jackson has embezzled over a quarter of a million dollars.

EMILY

[She has heard rumor of this.]

So, it is true. *[LANDON JR sits in a chair next to her]* He was such a good man. 'Captain of the Augusta Volunteers during the War.

LANDON JR.

I know.

EMILY

Will he go to prison? *[LANDON, JR. nods. EMILY covers her face. For a moment they are silent, aware of that which they have no power.]* When I invited you to Augusta, business was constant. There was an air of secure success. With the Canal built, no cotton factory in the South gave brighter promise. *[The reason for her coming:]* I have a business proposition for you.

LANDON JR.

[He retreats to sit at the chair behind his desk, opposite her.]

If you are suggesting a lay-off, I've already given notice to some of my finest workers. I fear a strike: it could happen with the Knights of Labor union—and if so, we will have to shut down. *[Before she can speak:]* I don't blame them. The conditions are horrible. The pay is too small—people can't feed their families on what we give them. I hope there is a strike. I think the unions are the best things that have happened to us here. I wouldn't be surprised if they don't call for a national boycott of all our products.

EMILY

You are talking a lockdown.

LANDON JR

If it comes to that, yes. It's a different world, Aunt Emily.

EMILY

Every time I come back to my house, I find all my things just as I had left them—but the world outside never the same. I had always dreamed that you would one day be president of this Mill.

LANDON JR.

I am sorry to be such a disappointment.

EMILY

That remains to be seen. *[She takes out the beaded purse that holds the uncut diamonds.]* I understand that you are to be engaged.

LANDON JR.

I've never thought of leaving. Running is not the answer—

EMILY

They told me of the young girl. She is expecting a ring.

LANDON

Oh. *[A different "engagement." Sensing a conspiracy, he turns away from her.]*

EMILY

People in town find you to be a very handsome pair. Her father has a promising future in politics. My late husband gave me these. *[She opens the purse, and the stones pour out onto the desk. They glisten in the light.]* They are diamonds. They have never been cut. *[She heaves a heavy sigh]* I would like to make a little business proposition with you. I will give you these stones. I give them to you in exchange that you have rings made for *the girl you love.*

LANDON JR.

They must cost a fortune . . .

EMILY

The stakes are high. It is a business venture. *[LANDON JR. leans over his desk and gazes at the stones.]*

LANDON JR.

You would give these to me? If I marry her? Such precious stones?

EMILY

Love is the most precious possession of the heart. Your family gives you their approval. And I give you these stones. It is as simple as that. *[He reaches for the stones, picks them up, and weighs them in his hands. He drops them. Overcome with emotion, LANDON JR drops his head upon the desk and buries his face in his hands. Leaving the purse and stones on the desk, EMILY goes to him and puts her hand upon his head. He leans upon her and she holds him as a mother would hold her child. All of the emotion he has held for so long, afraid to show anyone, he releases in her arms.]* Oh, Landon. Dear Landon. Love is not easy. Mother knew that. I had to learn it, and now you. It comes with a price. But it is always worth that price.

LANDON JR.

It's too late. There is no hope.

EMILY

Where there is God, there is hope.

LANDON JR.

And where is that?

EMILY

[Touching his heart]

In here.

LANDON JR.

[Clutching the hand on his heart]

I'm dying in here.

EMILY

And that's because you need her, like you need the air that you breathe.

[LANDON JR. reaches for his handkerchief and wipes his face. EMILY returns slowly to her chair as he rises and goes to the window, his back to her. He shakes his head, as if to say, "You don't understand." It is his turn to heave a sigh. A sigh of stress but once released, of relief.]

LANDON JR.

It wouldn't be right. It wouldn't be . . . true. *[He laughs at himself, pacing behind the desk.]* You know, I was about to go through with it all. I really think I was. To please them. To buckle under . . . until just now. *[Describing it:]* I kind of turned around and . . . bumped into . . . *[With full conviction:]* No. *[Has she heard him correctly?]* No, . . . my answer is no. *[EMILY smiles.]* No. Thank you. Business is down these days, to be sure, Aunt Emily.

EMILY

Do you love this girl? *[LANDON JR. hesitates.]* This girl, Mary. *[But he is confused.]* The one for whom I give you these stones. To have rings made for Mary. "The girl you love"—isn't that what I said?

LANDON JR

You know Mary?

EMILY

Yes, Mary Fleming. Minnie. *[Humorously but adamantly:]* Is there another girl you love?

LANDON JR

I thought you meant—

EMILY

Mary Fleming. Minnie. Who else are we talking about?

LANDON JR.

But . . . Investigations have been made and she has been found . . . unworthy.

EMILY

Well, I have made a few investigations of my own of this Mary Fleming and her family; and everything I have discovered indicates that she is very fine. *[Has he heard her correctly?]* I said, all of my inquiries of Miss Fleming indicate that she is very fine.

LANDON, JR.

[A deep breath]

Oh?

EMILY

Her people are teachers. They have worked hard for the education of the poor. When I was a little girl, a great lady in our town, Mrs. Margaretta Brown, gave me a book and its teaching have always stayed with me. It was about procrastination. *[She puts the rocks back into their pouch where they have waited through the years.]* Don't waste any time, Landon. If she will marry you, have these made into a ring for her. *[She offers him the purse.]* Sometimes life is left unfinished, undone for us, just so that we can make our mark. Move in faith. Take it out for a good walk, and let it breathe a bit. There is a diamond inside of all of us just waiting to be cut.

LANDON JR

The cutting is painful.

EMILY

Landon, if Richard Tubman and I had waited for approval, we might never have been married. Why, I'd have suitors knocking at my door still . . . although, now, I'd probably have to open the door for them. *[He shows a bit of a smile.]* They would have said he was too old for me. *[She extends the purse again.]*

LANDON JR.

[He falls into the chair.]

I can't believe you know of Mary. *[Of the purse.]* I cannot accept such a gift.

EMILY

Of course not. I said it was a business proposition. And like every good business deal it is vitally important to weigh the odds. You marry this society girl in Kentucky and please your mother and all of society there—the whole world–and guarantee your life success and fame and money. Or you take these stones and marry out of love. *[He nods with understanding]* I give them to you and in return you are to marry Mary Fleming. That is, if she will have you. *[Humorously:]* For I doubt if she will.

LANDON JR

[Taking the purse.]

Aunt Emily . . .

EMILY

[She takes his hands with the purse]

Oh, Landon, do noble things, don't just dream them. Make life and death and that great forever one grand sweet song.

[Those days fade away as MARY walks down from the train station and slowly takes off a glove revealing a very large diamond engagement ring.]

MARY

I planned never to take it off. *[Slowly she surrenders the ring from her finger. There is a huge burden lifted from her when she takes it off, although she feels naked and vulnerable.]*

SOJOURNER

So important it is to remember from whence we came. Equally important it is to know how we got where we are. *[For MARY there is no choice in the matter, and she knows this. She hands the ring to DARSIE.]*

MARY

[Offering the ring]

Give it to him, will you, when you see him?

DARSIE

[Seeing the size of the stones:]

My goodness.

MARY

Will you?

DARSIE

[Shackled by duty and obligation to his higher calling, he accepts it.]

Are you sure?

MARY

[Surprised at the freedom of his remark, she laughs]

Yes. Oh, yes! Because I love him so. Look, it's starting to get light.

SOJOURNER

It always gets light before the sun rises.

DARSIE

[Noticing that they are out of ear shot from SOJOURNER. To MARY:]

The Thomas family left immediately from here and went to Augusta for the funeral. Landon Sr. and his daughter went in the night first. His wife, Ellen, and the rest followed. Soon they will be arriving back from Augusta on the train with the body. But you are not on the train with them?

MARY

[Looking down]

No. *[DARSIE looks at her for an explanation, also aware that he deserves none. He is silent.]* I had to leave.

DARSIE

You left Augusta all by yourself?

MARY

Yes. *[Of her family]* You don't know what it was like. *[She starts to explain, explain how isolated she felt when the family arrived in Augusta and gathered for the funeral, how she felt left out and set aside and forgotten, dismissed, discarded, how the funeral plans replaced her wedding plans; but she does not bother to explain.]* During the night, I left a note and took the train here. *[With another thought, and an unfortunate but truthful one]* I doubt they even noticed that I had left. Or that I had even been there.

DARSIE

You missed her funeral in Augusta?

MARY

I had nowhere else to go but here.

DARSIE

To the Thomas house?

MARY

No. It is empty. The clocks are stopped. The drapes drawn. The mirrors covered. The doors locked. *[DARSIE looks at the ring with its beautiful large stones.]*

SOJOURNER

Death is the night to this worried day that we call life.

DARSIE

[Remembering, reciting]

Like the globe on which we turn, part of this day cannot receive light, so that the other part will not be delivered into darkness.

MARY

Paul and Virginia?

DARSIE

Have you read it?

MARY

Yes. About the two children that grow up together on the island. *[Remembering it]* I didn't like the ending.

SOJOURNER

How does it end?

MARY

She leaves the island to become a lady in society. But her heart is with Paul and the island and she chooses to go back. There is a shipwreck. She can save herself if she will only take off her gown and swim. But, now that she is a lady, she cannot disrobe. Her dress weighs her down. And Paul, watching the shipwreck from the shore, cannot swim to her in time. And she drowns.

DARSIE

The priest is there to console him. He tells him all the right things about God; things that should set things right. But all that Paul wants to do is die.

MARY

There is nothing left for him but this terrible ache.

DARSIE

[He is silent. Uncertain now what to say. Afraid of being like the priest in story giving all the right answers but not certain of knowing the true questions]

Fear is like a demon that comes to visit and stays. Stays because we cannot let it go. It becomes our companion and shuts out the light of any other.

SOJOURNER

So dark, that we cannot see the stars.

MARY

[Secretly to DARSIE]

I have some money, money I've saved. *[It is a new idea suddenly, and a good one. To DARSIE]* We could go together.

DARSIE

[Repeating the idea]

Go together. Yes. Start all over, yes. Is it possible? There are always choices. If we choose . . .*[They look at one another and see each other.]*

MARY

Why have we never met before tonight?

DARSIE

You live in the South; I live in the North. I never noticed before. You are so lovely. *[She blushes]* No, I mean that in the best way. Landon is a lucky fellow. *[She smiles back at him. Sounds of the busy street coming alive awaken them both.]*

SOJOURNER

People are going to work.

[BOY appears hawking newspapers from a sack. DARSIE's eyes remain on MARY]

BOY

'Morning paper?

DARSIE

Yes, I'll have one. *[He finds a coin, pays the BOY, and slowly takes a paper. The BOY exits.]*

MARY

We are both runaways then, aren't we, Brother Darsie? Me from Landon and his family, and you from God. We both have our bags.

DARSIE

Where were you going?

MARY

Wherever the train takes me. I'll ride it till it stops. He is free from me now, don't you see? *[Holding back the tears, shakes her head]* While Aunt Emily was alive, we were to be married. But not now.

SOJOURNER

Our souls are weak and weary. Let them rest . . .

MARY

Those were her very words, before she died. "My soul is weak and weary, if it please Thee, let me rest." And then she was gone. And with her went everything. She held the keys to everything good in this life. She took them with her. And nothing is left . . . but this terrible ache.

SOJOURNER

Yes . . . that terrible ache.

MARY

Brother Darsie, where were you going?

DARSIE

[Reluctantly]

There is a church in Boston looking for a pastor. I thought I would go and interview with them. Brother Fall will give the prayer at the grave . . . They don't need me. *[He opens the newspaper; it is as good a place to hide as any.]*

MARY

Is he really that fine a speaker?

DARSIE

Oh, no. Better. *[With great admiration]* The sound of his voice is like music from heaven. *[He appreciates her support, and smiles. Then his eyes fall back to the newspaper.]* Ah! Here it is. *[From The Frankfort Roundabout he reads:]* "The remains of Mrs. E. H. Tubman are expected here this morning."

MARY

Is there no sadder news? Read the rest.

DARSIE

"One of the city hogs was run over and killed yesterday morning by an ice wagon."

PORTER

[Entering in a friendly manner]

Good morning. *[As he passes by, they greet him. He exits.]*

MARY

The whole town is waking up, coming alive again. Look. The pigeons have lined up on the pitch of the Capitol Hotel roof. All in a row. They must know the crowds are coming . . . and they've come early to get the best seats . . . *[To DARSIE]* I would hate to see you leave this town.

DARSIE

Well, the winds seem to be blowing that direction. There is no future for me here.

SOJOURNER

[To DARSIE]

I see another train. Farther down the track. It too will bring great sadness. There is scarcely a home in which the loss is not felt. *[She looks knowingly at DARSIE, and her words send a chill through him for he knows of whom she speaks]* Every race and religion is counted among the hundreds who will come to show their last respects. The bells of the court house and the engine house will toll, and business houses will be closed as a mark of respect to his memory. "You will best honor his memory by continuing and enlarging his work. In doing so, we shall honor Him whose we are and whom we serve."

DARSIE

So, you are a soothsayer as well? *[She looks at him with a smile, and begins humming "Beautiful Dreamer."]*

MARY

I pray that those winds will blow you back to us someday.

DARSIE

Don't make me sound like Jonah. I'd rather not be swallowed by a whale.

SOJOURNER

It was the great fish that saved him.

DARSIE

[Putting down the paper. With deep realization.]

Yes, that's right.

SOJOURNER

[She sings:]

Beautiful dreamer, wake unto me
Starlight and dewdrops are waiting for thee;
Sounds of the rude world heard in the day,
Lulled by the moonlight have all passed away.

[It is a moment of tenderness. Of contentment with each other]

DARSIE

The sun is beginning to rise. Perhaps the train should not come after all.

MARY

But the sun doesn't rise . . . does it? It never moves. The earth moves around it.

DARSIE

[Nodding with realization]

We are the ones that rise . . .

[Memory returns us to an older EMILY in her Augusta home preparing for the annual spring train ride to Kentucky. She wears her black travel clothes, and stops before a mirror. RICHARD of years before arrives in her remembrances.]

EMILY

When I was young, a painter came to our town and begged to do my portrait. Strange how people see us: it looked nothing like me. Now photography is the most fascinating of fashion. I've had my photograph taken . . . I keep having it taken, but the pictures look nothing like me. The camera will not lie. Every time, I'm older. I've turned into an old woman, but you . . . *[She looks to RICHARD who is still young and dressed as the first night they met.]* You are always the same.

RICHARD

You look the same to me. As beautiful as the first time I laid eyes on you at the ball at Colonel Ware's mansion. When the suitors were fighting to dance with you.

EMILY

I'm not that girl anymore, Richard. The years have changed me. And I want to welcome what is ahead. Not stumble into the future backing up from the past.

RICHARD

[Stringed instruments are heard playing a minuet.]

Ah, the minuet. *[He offers her his hand.]* Shall we? *[She reaches for his hand and they begin the dance, but it is interrupted by the arrival of LANDON JR and RICHARD fades away as the memory. LANDON JR is dressed in overcoat and hat, preparing for the annual spring journey to Kentucky.]*

LANDON JR

We are packed and ready to go, Aunt Emily. The train leaves within the hour.

EMILY

Promises are meant to be kept.

LANDON JR

I think you've kept it every year.

EMILY

Not during the War. It was too dangerous.

LANDON JR

I couldn't help but notice you doing a little step or two in here. They tell me you danced the minuet when General Lafayette came to town.

EMILY

They tell a lot of nonsense.

LANDON JR

I knew it couldn't be true. You being such a dancer—

EMILY

I'll have you know that I was a fine dancer.

LANDON JR.

Is that so?

EMILY

Yes, that's so. *[Once again, we hear the music of "Beautiful Dreamer."]*

LANDON JR.

The minuet.

EMILY

Landon Thomas Jr. I shall never dance the minuet again. Not with General Lafayette, not with my late husband, not even with you. So, don't ask me. Everyone knows the waltz is all the fashion now.

[She bows to him. Waiting for him to do the same, and after a stern stare, he obediently, but reluctantly, follows suit. She offers her hand, he takes it, and carefully puts his other hand around her waist as though thinking she might break. But as she leads him in the dance, it is clear that there is nothing fragile in her step. She leads him, eyeing him to see if he knows the steps as well as she. They laugh at this triumph.

[WE HEAR THE TRAIN WHISTLE FROM A DISTANCE. The memories fade away. A crowd gathers as the train station is once again in the company of MARY, DARSIE, and SOJOURNER.]

SOJOURNER

You need not welcome the train. Let the others.

DARSIE

When the soul rests, it doesn't mean that it dies . . . When the leaves fall in the autumn; it doesn't mean that the tree is dead—

[WE HEAR THE TRAIN WHISTLE AGAIN, AS IT APPROACHES THE TUNNEL.]

SOJOURNER

You have waited long enough—

DARSIE

This night is not about Mrs. Tubman at all, is it? *[To MARY]* It's about you and me.

MARY

[She reaches for her heart, of the terrible ache:]

Is there no way to stop this?!

SOJOURNER

Of course, there's a way. *[She has drawn their attention away from the train.]*

DARSIE

Are you a witch as well?

MARY

You can take away this ache? Why didn't you say so!

SOJOURNER

You never asked.

MARY

Please. Please!

SOJOURNER

It is so simple. So very simple. Pray that it returns.

MARY

What?

SOJOURNER

Just ask. Ask for it to be taken away.

MARY

The train?

DARSIE

[But he understands]

No, not the train . . .

[We hear the train's final whistle, coming upon us into town. Loud, strong, demanding. DARSIE, awakened, stares back at the SOJOURNER who smiles knowingly. Sounds of the train. Smoke. The crowd ascends upon it, enveloping them. The passengers descend from the train. The train brings a loud confusing mix of expressions. There is excitement and cheerful greetings and there are forlorn whispers of sadness. Each ignoring the other. Noise.]

SOJOURNER

[To MARY]

Mary, isn't that Mrs. Landon Thomas, Ellen, your Landon's mother? *[ELLEN stands at L, dressed in black, looking very sad.]*

MARY

[To herself]

Oh, no. It's Ellen.

SOJOURNER

Leave her be. Don't think of going to her–

MARY

No, I couldn't.

SOJOURNER

That's right. And you shouldn't. She doesn't deserve it.

MARY

She will never come to me.

SOJOURNER

Wish it away. That ache that you spoke. Now is the time.

MARY

[MARY looks at her gloved left hand, concealing the loss of the ring.]

But if you take away that ache . . . I will have no more connection to Aunt Emily.

SOJOURNER

That's the price.

[MARY crosses to ELLEN. ELLEN sees here. They stand at a distance from each other]

ELLEN

You left us.

MARY

Yes, I am sorry . . .

ELLEN

Landon was sick with worry. You left him at the time he needed you most.

MARY

I'm sorry.

ELLEN

It was thoughtless and cruel of you.

MARY

Yes . . .

ELLEN

And to travel by yourself, an unmarried woman without her fiancé . . . completely un-chaperoned; not only was it indecent, it was foolish and dangerous. Do we understand each other?

MARY

Yes.

ELLEN

Good. Why, if anything had happened to you . . . *[ELLEN reaches out her hand. MARY slowly walks towards her and takes it.]* . . . I would never forgive myself. We only have each other now. Promise me, that you will be there for Landon, always. *[With deep emotion:]* And me.

MARY

I promise. I will be here.

ELLEN

[To DARSIE]

Brother Darsie, you know that my son Landon is on the Board of Directors of the King's Mill in Augusta, Georgia? This is his fiancée, Mary. My daughter. She cared for Aunt Emily until her death. I am very proud of her.

DARSIE

[To MARY]

I'm not sure we were ever properly introduced. I am George Darsie.

MARY

[Offering her hand, as he takes it]

A ***handsome*** name.

ELLEN

You will be receiving an invitation, Brother. The North and South will be joined in this one.

SOJOURNER

Brother Darsie, isn't that Brother Philip Fall? *[FALL stands at R]* The pioneer of faith in this town. He looks so old and frail—I thought him younger. He has lived a long, hard life. Leave him be. Don't think of going to him.

DARSIE

No, I couldn't.

SOJOURNER

And you shouldn't. Brother Fall can take the internment. They would rather hear him than you. He doesn't need you to help lead the procession and the crowds of people following it.

DARSIE

Me? *[With a forced laugh]* It is not my place.

SOJOURNER

Of course not. If we fail to accept our call, someone else will carry on for us, don't you think? Don't bother to ask him, for he could never need you. The way is easy . . .

DARSIE

No . . .

SOJOURNER

So very easy to remove that ache of which we spoke. Wish it away. It is not too late. Now is the time. You would probably forget to signal the church bell anyway.

DARSIE

[Crossing to FALL]

Brother Fall! Good morning. Please accept my condolences at the loss of your good friend.

FALL

[Moving slowly and with confusion. In a whisper to DARSIE, not fearful that the others might hear him]

Where is God in this, George?

DARSIE

[Startled by this strangeness in FALL]

I've wondered the same thing . . . all night. But wherever Mrs. Tubman was, God was at work. *[He notices that FALL is attempting to weep, and quickly thinks to move them both away from the crowd. He wonders if Brother Fall is well.]*

FALL

But she is gone. Where?

DARSIE

To God, of course.

FALL

But we need her here.

DARSIE

And she will be—if we continue in that work; her name will never perish from our hearts–

FALL

Who will we lean on now, Brother? *[He breaks down and cries, puts his head in DARSIE's chest. DARSIE holds him]*

DARSIE

The same One she leaned on. You forget the source of strength you were *to her.* She always said so. *[Aware that the crowd is waiting.]* Brother Fall, perhaps you should call the pallbearers?

FALL

[Lost in his memories]

The church burned. To the ground. There was nothing. And she came. She came and built it for us. All of it.

DARSIE

Brother Fall, the pallbearers . . Someone has to lead them—

FALL

She just gave it all to us. As a gift . . .*[He covers his face. The memory is too much for him. It has all come home to him here. Caved in upon him.]*

DARSIE

[Looking to SOJOURNER]

Don't worry, Brother Fall. I will be here. *[He calls out:]* May I have the pallbearers?! We must continue now to the wagon! All pallbearers! Yes. Yes. Good morning. Are you all here? Good. Thank you—

ELLEN

Who will lead the procession? *[There is a pause]*

DARSIE

[Courageously]

Who? Why Brother Fall, of course. *[He puts his arm around FALL and helps him forward.]* Now, follow us. And have them ring the church bell, for we are ready. *[DARSIE passes MARY and they share a final glance. It is the look of two people who have arrived safely from a long journey together and become better for it. He discreetly hands her the engagement ring and tips his hat.]* I have a sermon to rewrite tonight. *[MARY nods and lowers her veil, clutching the ring in her fist. DARSIE leaves her behind as he leads the crowd off L]*

SOJOURNER

[To PORTER]

Excuse me? Do you know the Thomas House on Washington Street? Will you kindly deliver this bag there? *[The PORTER gathers MARY's luggage bag.]* And do you know the parsonage of the Christian Church? Would you be so kind as to deliver his bag there . . . for the time being, anyway. *[The PORTER takes DARSIE's bag; he gestures to SOJOURNER's bag.]* No. I have a train to catch. And many more to meet. *[She exits R as the crowd exits L]*

LANDON JR.

[Pushing through the crowd]

Mary!

MARY

Landon! *[She sees him and runs to him. They embrace.]* Forgive me. Forgive me for leaving–

LANDON JR

Shh . . . there is nothing to forgive–

MARY

I know how much you loved her–

LANDON JR.

Mary! How I've missed you.

MARY

[She is afraid to ask it. Afraid she has not heard it.]

Have you, Landon? *[Afraid to hear his answer.]*

LANDON JR.

Have I? *[He takes her hands but her fist opens to reveal the ring. Puzzled at first, he takes the ring, nods to her glove, she removes the glove and he places the ring on her finger.]* You silly goose . . . Don't you know, you are my life.

[MARY embraces LANDON, JR. She is happy and at peace at last. There is nothing more to say, nothing needed, only the secure holding of each another. The crowd has left them, they are alone together. The evening is gone, the train has arrived safely, and a new day and future awaits them. She looks around at the town and its streets that hold the memories she has loved so well.] I should have known I'd find you in this sweet old town. With its dear streets: Holmes Street, Ann Street–named after General Wilkinson's wife, and Mero Street named after the Spanish General, Market Street . . .

MARY

[Humorously]

They call it Broadway now.

LANDON JR

Yes, they do. The same old streets that she knew. The same old sky . . *[With deep sadness]* It's just that . . . all the stars have fallen. *[And then up into the heavens their eyes catch one lone star still shining in the early morning light, still clinging to the night that has passed.]*

MARY

Landon, look!

LANDON JR.

The last star of the night. *[They watch it together.]*

MARY

Ah, . . . *[The star disappears in the daylight.]* How quickly it is gone. And so quietly.

LANDON JR.

[The Church bell rings. He draws MARY closer to him, his eyes to the heavens:]

Welcome home, Aunt Emily!

CURTAIN

Figure 12

POSTSCRIPT

Emily Harvie Thomas Tubman of Kentucky
1794-1885

The first statehouse was being built in Kentucky when Emily Harvie Thomas was born to Edmund Pendleton Thomas and his wife Ann Chiles in Ashland, Virginia, on the 21st day of March in 1794. Kentucky had become its own state, just two years before, carved from the territory known as Virginia, and Frankfort had been chosen its capital. It was on the first floor of this new stone statehouse in Frankfort that Edmund Thomas set up office as the state's first land register; his brother John served as treasurer of the state.[1] In 1796, a land law was passed that supplied Edmund with $1,000 to go back to Ashland and appropriate military warrants, grants, surveys, and records for 10,000 land grants in Kentucky. When he returned, he brought his wife, Ann Chiles, and two-year-old daughter, Emily Harvie. Later he received a second grant of $3,000 to acquire land for the new state. The payment for his services was over 17,000 acres of land in Kentucky.[2]

---

[1] Carl E. Kramer, *Capital on the Kentucky*, (Historic Frankfort, Inc., 1986), p.41.

[2] Land Office/ Secretary of State, Frankfort, Kentucky. Jillson W. Rouse, Old Kentucky Entries and Deeds (Louisville: The Standard Printing Company, 1926), pp. 454–5.

In 1797, sixty-five residents owned land in Frankfort. Three years later the census recorded 628.[3] People were moving to the western territories where the land was cheap and the soil fertilized by limestone. Hemp, used for making rope and cloth, was the major component to Frankfort's agrarian economy with tobacco cultivation emerging. Edmund and Ann Thomas built a two-story log house covered in red painted clapboard on Market Street across from where the railroad depot would later be built.[4] They had five children: Emily Harvie born 1794, Western Berkley born 1799, Landon Addison born 1800, Louisa Ann born 1801, and Caroline America born 1802.

Figure 13 Emily Thomas by Jouett

In September of 1802, the family purchased land on Washington Street where Landon Thomas built his home in 1840. Father Edmund Thomas died suddenly in 1803, leaving his children under the guardianship of statesman Henry Clay. Clay was leader of the "War Hawks" of Congress, Secretary of State, and three times a candidate for the office of United States Presidency. His political duties might have made it impossible to oversee all of the children, whose parents named him to guardianship, and so it was that Emily and Western Thomas petitioned to the courts for attorney John Allen to replace Clay as their guardian.[5] Emily was fourteen at the time, Western

---

[3] Carl E. Kramer, *Capital.* p.41.

[4] Landon A. Thomas, *Recollections of Frankfort,* October 6, 1886, in vault at Kentucky Historical Society, Frankfort, Kentucky.

[5] Joseph Richard Bennett, *A Study of the Life and Contributions of Emily H. Tubman* (unpublished B.D. thesis, Butler University, 1958)

nine. Mr. Allen had been sworn into the Frankfort bar the year Emily had come to Kentucky.

United States Senator John Brown was friend to the Thomas family. His home, "Liberty Hall" was the finest in Frankfort, built between 1797 and 1803 from plans associated with Thomas Jefferson; Emily's playmates were the Brown children.
Mrs. Brown, with the help of a tutor, taught her children at Liberty Hall, and Emily may have been one of her students, for Margaretta, became a close friend to Emily and loaned her a book *The Dangers of Delay* in which Emily first learned the evils of procrastination.[6] As there were no established churches in Frankfort at the time, Margareta Brown and Elizabeth Love started the first Sunday School in 1810, to instruct children of Christianity; Emily at sixteen would have helped teach at this school.

The Brown's son, Mason, became close friends with Landon, and when Martin Hawkins tried selling his plan to the Legislature to improve the navigability of the Kentucky River (with a gratuity to himself of a saw and grist mill) he crafted an elaborate beeswax model of the River to demonstrate his ideas. Many in the town were on to the scheme, Landon and Mason especially, who broke in one night and chewed the wax model to bits.[7] The two boys continued their education together at Yale University where they rode off to study law and were not seen again in Kentucky until after they graduated. Landon wrote back of watching the first telegraph wires

---

[6]Emily H. Tubman, Letters to Philip S. Fall, Kentucky Historical Society Library, Frankfort, Kentucky.

[7] Ermina Jett Darnell, *Filling the Chinks* (Frankfort, Kentucky: Roberts Printing Co., 1966), *p: 36.*

being erected from Washington D.C. to Baltimore, and found it such a curiosity that he followed its entire construction by horseback.[8]

General James Wilkinson, who bought the land of Frankfort and platted its streets, built for himself a large log house but soon sold it to Major Thomas Love who named it "The Love House." Frequent entertainment and housing for legislators and local citizens took place in Frankfort at the "The Love House," Daniel Weisiger's Tavern, and the Mansion House of J.J. Marshall. At one of the Frankfort balls, when Emily was sixteen, she and her sister Louisa had their portraits painted by Kentucky artist Matthew Jouett. Emily did not find the painting flattering, rolled it up, and hid it in the attic, Mr. Jouett's technique of painting women's faces being very standard and too much so to suit her taste.[9] Louisa might have been more unhappy with her portrait for it has disappeared altogether.

The United States fought the British in a final battle for independence during the War of 1812. Lieut. Colonel John Allen, Emily's guardian, was massacred by the British and Native American Indians while commanding his regiment at the Battle of the River Raisin in Michigan.[10] Eight other Kentucky officers were killed, and the death toll of Kentuckians neared 400. Kentucky is said to have seen more casualties in the War than all other states combined.

Emily grew into womanhood, hesitant to accept the proposals of marriage, in a world that was rapidly changing. In later years, she would tell of the many prominent men who courted her, and she would laugh when retelling how one in particular had offered her

---

[8] Thomas, "*Recollections*"; Mrs. Emily T. Clay, Private Conversations with Russell R. Rechenbach, II, in her home, 939 Milledge Road, Augusta, Georgia, phone conversations and letters 1973-91.

[9] Clay, "Private Conversations."

[10] L.F. Johnson, *The History of Franklin County, Kentucky*, (Frankfort: Roberts Printing Co., 1912), p.56.

half of his estate in exchange for her hand.[11] Cities were growing as people left the rural areas in an Urban Revolution.

In the summer of 1818, while taking the waters at White Sulphur Springs, "Queen of the Watering Places," in the western part of the state of Virginia where elite families came to escape the Southern heat, the Thomas family met their cousins Colonel Nicholas Ware, his wife, and their niece and adopted daughter Mary Ariuton. The Wares invited Emily to spend the winter with them in Augusta, Georgia.[12] In Autumn of that year, Emily packed her winter dresses in saddlebags and with her brother Western as chaperon, rode horseback to Georgia.[13] Emily and Western stayed with the Ware's at their mansion which had become known as "Ware's Folly" due to its expense in construction, size, and grand oval staircases. Emily was pursued by many suitors there, but it was Richard C. Tubman of Maryland with whom she fell in love. Mr. Tubman was twenty-eight years her senior and a widower. As their winter trip came to its close, Mr. Tubman proposed marriage. Emily must have remembered the lessons in Margaretta Brown's book, for she foresaw the dangers of delay, accepted Mr. Tubman's proposal, and decided to marry immediately without written permission from her mother. They were married in Augusta on June 25, 1818. After their wedding,

Figure 14 Richard Tubman

[11] Clay, "Private Conversations."

[12] Bennett, "*A Study of the Life,*" p. 9.

[13] Clay, "Private Conversations."

Richard and Emily Tubman rode to Kentucky to share the news with Emily's mother and her family. It must have been quite a surprise to see the Tubman caravan travel down Market Street of Frankfort with their African enslaved persons.

It took Mr. and Mrs. Tubman a month to travel to New York by stage coach. Sixteen days by sailing vessel from Savannah. Mr. Tubman would have written to Newark to have a carriage made ready for them when needed. Emily remembers the water in New York being so brackish that it was undrinkable; carts labeled "tea water" drove around the streets selling fresh water from the country to be used for making tea.[14] This pilgrimage was the start of an annual tradition for Richard and Emily Tubman: they would spend their summers in Kentucky, possibly traveling up to Maryland, and return to their winter home in Augusta, Georgia, where they resided at 719 Broad Street. In her own words, she was "a young woman, full of life and spirit, newly married and having everything she ever wanted to make her life happy and comfortable"[15]

Figure 15 Richard Tubman Home,

[14] Dr. Ed Cashin, "Emily Tubman Remembers, Interview of March 15, 1885," *Richmond County History, Volume 29, No. 2 Winter, 1998*, Richmond County Historical Society, Augusta Georgia, p. 16. Interview first appeared in the Augusta Chronicle and Constitutionalist on March 15, 1885, given by Mrs. Tubman but at her request it appeared without the use of her name.
[15] Cashin, "Emily Tubman Remembers," p.14.

Mr. Tubman had come to Augusta at the age of twenty-seven from Baltimore, Maryland. He purchased several plantations in Augusta and exported from New York to Liverpool indigo, tobacco, and cotton. His partner in the cotton trade was George Hogarth of Savannah, Georgia. His brother Charles purchased land in Savannah and contracted yellow fever and died there.[16]

Mr. and Mrs. Richard Tubman were pillars of the Augusta community and its social life. Richard Tubman was a member of the Board of Directors that formed the Bank of Augusta in 1810. He managed the lottery that built the Catholic Church and served as chairman of the Board of Wardens in the building of St. Paul's Episcopal Church.[17] In 1825, when the French hero to America, General Lafayette, stopped at Augusta, Emily Tubman, with other ladies of the town, planned and decorated the banquet and reception at the Planter's Hotel. Fine furnishings were brought to the hotel for the event, and Mrs. Tubman furnished his bed with a handsome coverlet from her house.[18] Family legend has it that she led the minuet with the French General that night, although her modest interview of 1885, only mentioned having had the honor of a special introduction and handshake.

On their trips to Kentucky, Mr. and Mrs. Tubman of Augusta society would stop and take the waters at the fashionable White Sulphur Springs and then pass through the Cumberland Gap that had brought the early pioneers such as Daniel Boone to Kentucky not too many years before.[19] Richard bought for his wife three large uncut diamonds that he intended to have made into a ring for her. There were no Mantua dress makers in Augusta when she moved there, so Mrs. Tubman would take orders from friends and buy

---

[16] Richard Tubman papers, 1753-1858, Duke University Library, Durham, North Carolina.

[17] Cashin, *The Story of Augusta*, (Spartanburg, South Carolina: The Reprint Company, Publishers, 1991, pp. 79, 85.

[18] Cashin, "Emily Tubman Remembers," pp.14-15.

[19] Edith Deen, *Great Women of the Christian Faith* (New York: Harper & Row, 1959), pp. 178-80.

for them in New York when she and Mr. Tubman traveled North by stage or sailing vessel from Savannah. One trip from Savannah to New York took sixteen days due to contrary winds.[20]

Mrs. Mary Willis Woodson wrote in her "Recollections of Frankfort,"

> "Adjoining lot was a large frame house owned by Mrs. Thomas to which the family retired after Mr. Thomas' term of office was over. The young ladies of the family were remarkable for their beauty, refined elegant manners, culture and amiable dispositions. All married well: they were Mrs. Tubman, Mrs. Keiningham, Mrs. Duke."[21]

Western had passed the Bar in 1817 and married Emiline Few of Augusta, Georgia. Louisa married Richard Keiningham a merchant in Paris, Kentucky, who was a native of Gloucester, Virginia. Caroline America married a medical doctor of Paris, John B. Duke. Upon Emily and Richard's departure from Frankfort, Kentucky in November of 1825, former U.S. Congressman Col. Solomon P. Sharp answered a call at his door in the middle of the night and was stabbed to death by a masked assailant. Solomon Sharp had been the attorney for Emily's uncle, John Thomas, Treasurer of the state of Kentucky when John Thomas had been removed from office for illegally loaning money out to the Legislature members. In payment for his services, Mr. Thomas had given Sharp the house on Madison Street where he met his death.[22] Landon Thomas studied law in the office of Hon. Sharp when Thomas returned from Yale. Because Sharp was candidate for the Relief party for the House of Representatives, a handsome young man and at the peak of his career, much suspicion spread that the murder was a conspiracy, until Glasgow attorney Jeroboam 0. Beauchamp confessed to the crime. Beauchamp had killed out

---

[20] Cashin, "Emily Tubman Remembers," p. 16.

[21] Mary Willis Woodson, "My Recollections of Frankfort," *Through the Portals of Glen Willis* (Frankfort: Franklin County Trust for Historic Preservation), pp. 19-20.

[22] Thomas, *"Recollections."*

of love. His wife, Ann Cook, had given birth to a child that she claimed had been fathered by Sharp; Sharp denied all such accusations of abandonment. Miss Cook agreed to marry Beauchamp if he would avenge her honor. Beauchamp murdered out of his love for her and wrote of it in a ballad. The whole murder-for-love-triangle became known as "The Kentucky Tragedy" of which songs and novels were written.[23] On July 1, 1826, while the Tubmans would have been visiting Kentucky, Landon Thomas watched on horseback as Jereboam Beauchamp was taken to the gallows in Frankfort and hanged. Mrs. Beauchamp had visited the cell the morning of the execution with a knife concealed in her dress and the two stabbed each other in the hopes of dying together. It took two men to hold the wounded Jereboam up on the gallows to put the noose around his neck. As he fell to his death, Ann Cook Beauchamp died in the cell.

In 1828, Emily and her mother were baptized in the Kentucky River by Baptist minister Silas Noel, but both refused to hold membership in the Baptist church.[24] The following year, a great fire swept through Augusta leaving many without homes or business, and Richard Tubman worked on the committee to care for the homeless. As Augusta started to rebuild in 1829, Western and his wife Emiline Few gave birth to Ann Thomas' first grandchild, and they named their firstborn son Richard Tubman Thomas. The following year while Mr. and Mrs. Tubman were in Kentucky, the child died.

A year later, November 19,1831, Dr. John B. Duke placed a notice in the Paris, Kentucky newspaper *The Western Citizen* that appeared in the Christmas Eve edition. The notice explained that due to "the health of a part of my family" it was necessary that he should go immediately to New York, and as this trip would take more money than he had collected, he politely urged his patients to pay their delinquent bills. Their accounts were placed with Richard Keiningham during his absence. But within the

[23] Kramer, "*Capital*" p. 96.

[24] James Lamar and George Darsie, "*In Memoriam. Mrs. Emily H. Tubman*," pamphlet of Memorial Service in the Christian Church at Frankfort, Kentucky, Sunday June 14, 1885.

year, both he and Caroline America were dead. It was a terrible tragedy for the Thomas family; while still in mourning the Thomas family and the Tubmans attended the preaching in Frankfort of "Raccoon" John Smith. Being winter, and all the churches closing their doors to Smith, it took Judge Owsely to open up the court house which included the Legislature's members in the meeting. Smith was preaching the theories of the frontier camp revivals: a reformation based on the New Testament, abolishing what he thought to be trappings of man-made creeds, banning no one from the Eucharist, encouraging denominations to cease and all come together in unity among diversity. Smith represented Alexander Campbell in Lexington when their movement joined hands with the Christian Church movement of Barton W. Stone from Cane Ridge. The preachings of Smith and Campbell nurtured Mrs. Tubman and spoke deeply to her own theology.[25]

Landon A. Thomas "saw the falling stars in 1832." This may have been the Leonid Meteor shower of November 10th & 12th in 1833, that created such terror for the early pioneers and much fervor in religion.[26] In Clark County, a judge recorded the effect it had on the members of Log Lick Church:

> "The people were struck with awe and thrown into great consternation and one of the effects of the remarkable occurrence was to awaken a pious feeling, causing a general religious revival throughout Christendom....The little church was crowded to overflowing day and night with an eager and earnest people, singing and asking for pardon for their many sins. Old feuds were reconciled, enemies were made friends . . ."[27]

---

[25] Clay, "Private Conversations."

[26] Thomas, "*Recollections*."

[27] Mark Littman, *The Heavens on Fire: The Great Leonidic Meteor Storms* (Cambridge: Cambridge University Press, 1998), p.8.

Cholera swept the country as an epidemic in 1833. Revivals brought great numbers in grief, so much so that as time calmed their fears Alexander Campbell is reported to have said, "The cholera converts, of whom there are too many in most places, were about being delivered from their panic-begotten faith." Campbell and Phillip Fall both disagreed with revivals, or "protracted meetings," and saw that they were too concerned with increase of members than the character of the churches. When Campbell came to Frankfort to preach in 1835, only Walter Carr Chiles, Ann's brother and Emily's uncle, was the sole convert.[28]

International commerce seems to have been responsible for the spread of cholera from Europe and Asia to America. The doctors, like Duke, were overworked and many died. When the epidemic cleared, there were reported in Frankfort at least 150 deaths.[29] At nearby Lexington, one-third of the residents had fled the town, leaving the dead unburied, and the press reported 500 deaths there.[30] In the house "Federal Hill" at Bardstown, where Rowan cousin Stephen Foster may have written his song "My Old Kentucky Home," eight members of Judge John Rowan's family died of the disease in one day.[31] Concerned for the numbers of children left without parents, the Tubmans helped finance the start of an orphan home and school in Midway, Kentucky that would later become Midway College.

Amidst the scars of cholera, life resumed. Western and Emiline gave birth to a daughter, whom they named after Emily: Emily Harvie Thomas. On November 9, 1835, they had son and named him Western Berkley Jr. But as Uncle Richard and Aunt Emily continued their summer trips to Kentucky, Richard fell ill with typhoid near Lincolnton, North Carolina, 1836. At seventy years of age, and aware of his approaching

---

[28] Ermina Jett Darnell, *After the Manner of the Oak, A Study of the Growth of The Frankfort Christian Church* (Frankfort, Kentucky 1935), pp.19-21.
[29]Johnson, *"History of Franklin County,"* p. 97.
[30] John D. Wright, Jr., *Transylvania; Tutor to The West*, (Lexington, Kentucky: Transylvania University, 1975) p. 130.
[31] My Old Kentucky Home house tours, Bardstown, Kentucky, 1994.

end, he made Emily promise to continue the yearly trips.[32] In such a way she would not only protect her health from the Georgian heat and diseases, but would keep his memory alive. He gave her a set of pistols to protect herself there in the mountains and a sack of three large uncut diamonds.[33] She and the Tubman servants buried his body there along the wayside, and from there went immediately to stay with her mother and brother in Frankfort. The experience changed her life. The body of Richard Tubman was removed to a crypt beneath St. Paul's Episcopal Church in Augusta and Emily corresponded to the church's priest disapproving of his request for a lavish monument. Later she gave permission for the vestry to erect a plaque as tribute to him.[34]

Only weeks later when she returned to Augusta, it was to nurse her brother Western who was sick with the yellow fever. He died at age thirty-seven while at his bedside stood his little daughter, infant son, wife Emiline, and widowed sister Emily Tubman.[35] It was Western's kindness and professional skill that had assisted Emily in the management of her business. Having lost her husband of seventeen years and now her closest brother, as James Lamar said in his memorial address of her, "overwhelmed with the feeling of helplessness she began to believe that God led her into darkness only to bring her closer to himself." Throughout her life, she told Brother Lamar, God had sent friends to assist her. Her attorney, Henry Cummings, stepped forward and took Western's place in her life. "From the fullness of his manly heart he said, "Mrs. Tubman, I will be your brother." And he was. With what watchful care and devotion he discharged the trust committed to him, and was remembered by her always with affectionate gratitude." This post in her life was later fulfilled, after Cummings' death, by William A. Watts, and after his death, by his son John W. Watts.

---

32 *Augusta Chronicle* Tuesday June 9, 1885.
33 Clay, "Private Conversations."
34 Edward E. Ford, letter dated from Morristown, New Jersey, September 2, 1836, Richard Tubman Letters, Duke University.
35 Clay, "Private Conversations."

In the will of Richard Tubman, it was his request that all of his enslaved persons be given freedom. Enslaved persons could not be free citizens in Georgia. Mr. Tubman provided $10,000 for them to be relocated as free citizens in the United States, and half of this he offered to the state of Georgia for a university if his enslaved persons would be allowed citizenship in Georgia.[36] Emily petitioned to the state Legislature but with no success. She was persuaded by her friend and former guardian Henry Clay, president of the American Colonization Society, to seek refuge for her servants in Liberia, Africa. She rode to Washington D.C. with him to hear him speak concerning colonization. But she grew weary with the slow pace of its progress. Again, knowing too well the evils of procrastination, she began corresponding with John Latrobe of the Maryland Colonization Society which had broken away from the national organization.
Mr. Latrobe promised a more immediate settlement in Cape Palmas, Liberia, and guaranteed that her servants would be looked after by an Episcopal missionary and personal friend.[37]

Mrs. Tubman chose the state organization over the national. She called her forty-eight enslaved persons together and gave them the choice of staying with her as paid servants or starting a home in the jungles of Liberia. Only six chose to stay.[38] In an effort to keep families together and please her servants, Mrs. Tubman bought from surrounding plantations four enslaved persons that were family members of the ones leaving for Liberia and added them aboard. The Tubman servants were highly skilled agriculturists, each with a second trade, intelligent, and of Christian character prepared to endure all adjustments in weather and location.

---

[36]James M. Gifford, *Georgia History, Vol. 59* (A75), "Emily Tubman and the African Colonization Movement in' Georgia," Vol. LIX No. 1, (Savannah: Georgia Historical Society; Athens: University of Georgia, Spring 1975), p. 12.

[37] Ibid, pp. 15-17.

[38] Emily H. Tubman To Ralph R. Gurley, March 20, 1837, American Colonization Society Archives, Letters Received, vol. 66, Library of Congress, Washington, D.C.

As the Maryland Society was afraid to transport the servants to Maryland, for fear that they might be sold back into slavery upon arrival, Mrs. Tubman transported them herself by rail to Charleston where they were escorted by Captain William Robertson to Baltimore by the packet brig "General Pinckney." And on May 17, 1837, the ship "Baltimore" carried forty-six black Tubmans of the fifty-five aboard to become immigrants to Liberia.[39] But for some, America had become their home, and when one of the immigrants changed his mind and asked to return home to America, Mrs. Tubman rode to New York City to meet him and brought him back to Augusta herself. She corresponded by mail with the black Tubmans in Liberia, very interested in their successes. While other plantations flourished with black slave labor, Mrs. Tubman managed to keep her plantations in operation with paid labor.

Living as a widow in Augusta, Mrs. Tubman faced the 1840 flood. Broad Street was like a river, and Mr. Edward Campfield rode into her front hall in a boat to evacuate her.[40] This was the same year that Landon built his house on Washington Street in Frankfort to escape the coming train that would come through their front yard. He served on the committee that brought back to Kentucky the bones of Daniel Boone and his wife Rebecca on September 13, 1845. Their remains were brought from Missouri and buried in the Frankfort Cemetery with much parade and celebration. Landon was Chief Assistant Marshal of the parade for the burial of the Kentuckians killed at the battle of Buena Vista in July 27, 1847. He served the House of Representatives of Kentucky from 1840-1850.[41] When he chose a wife, it was Ellen M. Polk. The Thomases had four children, Landon Jr., Anne, Emily, and Western.

Mrs. Tubman's trip to visit her family in Frankfort took two weeks by carriage, 500 miles. As a child slave, Laura Herrington accompanied Mrs. Tubman and her sister

---

39 Gifford, "*Georgia History,*" p. 16.

40 Cashin, "Emily Tubman Remembers," p. 15.

41 Johnson, *"History of Franklin County,"* p. 120.

Mrs. Keiningham in the carriage and told that she had never seen either of them allow their backs to touch the cushions. Mrs. Tubman invested heavily in the Georgia Railroad and later rode its trains to Kentucky in twenty-four hours.[42]

A wealthy widow, Mrs. Tubman became a shrewd businesswoman and a strong religious leader. She saw her resources as a trust with which to serve those in need. Alexander Campbell, theologian and debater of the "Disciples of Christ" reformation movement, visited with her in her home. She endowed the Tubman Chair for Modern Languages at Campbell's Bethany College in West Virginia. Her parlour was home to the birth of the Christian Church in Augusta, Georgia. Her faith was put into action by philanthropic deeds throughout the communities in which she lived, and she requested that recipients keep silent about the help she gave them. Because of this, few records remain. But her pastor in Augusta, James Lamar, said of her: "Very little, comparatively, was within my knowledge; but I know of hundreds of thousands of dollars given away by this blessed woman in pure benevolence."[43]

It was only the Civil War blockade that prevented her from making the trip to Kentucky. On Valentine's Day of 1863, her nephew Western Berkeley Thomas Jr. was wounded and died fighting for the Confederacy. She placed a stained-glass window in memory of his life in the Augusta Christian Church. That year, Emily imported from France through the blockade an ice machine to aid the wounded and sick Confederate soldiers who were crowded into St. Patrick's Catholic Church. This was the first ice machine reportedly brought to America and it began a new industry for Augusta patented by I.P. Girardey.[44] During this same year she wrote to Louisa at Paris, Kentucky, on May 5, 1863: "From Burnsides' Military Commander of Kentucky, it

---

[42] Mrs. Wade Whitley, told to and written down by Mrs. Newton B. Fowler, copy in possession of playwright; told by Mrs. Whitley to playwright; told by Mrs. Emily T. Clay to playwright.

[43] James Lamar and George Darsie, "*In Memoriam,*" p.8

[44] Florence Fleming Corley, *Confederate City, Augusta, Georgia, 1860-1865* (Columbia: University of South Carolina Press, 1960), p.47.

appends death is the penalty for any citizen extending protection, comfort, or aid to a Confederate. I fear to come, if this be true, lest I endanger Landon and yourself . . . I am willing to suffer many inconveniences, fatigue nay danger."[45]

Mrs. Tubman clothed a regiment of Confederate soldiers whose uniforms were threadbare; when asked how she could afford to support the Confederates, she responded humorously, "Well, the old girl aint broke yet." When the war ended, and family fortunes were destroyed without the help of slave labor, Mrs. Tubman who had ceased to rely upon such labor years before, saw her plantations prosper. The Union forces paid the Railroad investors to transport their soldiers home. Free transport was given to Confederate soldiers; Mrs. Tubman assisted the Confederate soldiers to return home to their families. [46]

Figure 16 First Frankfort Depot

[45] Mrs. Emily H. Tubman, Letters to her sister Louisa Keiningham, Paris, Kentucky. Philip Fall Memorial Library, First Christian Church, Frankfort, Kentucky. Excerpts from letters sent by Miss Ellen Thomas, great niece of Mrs. Tubman dated May 5, 1863 and May 18, 1864. Original in Richard Tubman papers, 1753-1858, Duke University Library, Durham, North Carolina.

[46] Clay, "Private Conversations."

Figure 17
Frankfort Christian Church

As Mrs. Tubman was leaving for Augusta in the fall of 1870, a single kitchen stove started a fire that destroyed much of Frankfort. The Christian Church, which the Thomases and Tubmans had attended and supported, caught fire in its cupola and burned to the ground. The congregation had no insurance and had not been without division. There had been much disagreement in the church over instrumental music as some interpreted the Scriptures to say that only human voices were necessary for music in worship; Landon Thomas had donated a melodeon to the church and the trustees had thrown it out into the coal bin. Dancing had caused members to be excluded from membership; young women had been reproved for wearing colorful dresses. One woman had been accused of being too materialistic when she had chosen to clean the church's window blinds.[47]

In June, after T. N. Arnold was called to the pulpit, there was a called meeting of the church members to renew their allegiance to the Church; and in September the congregation met with plans to erect a new building. November 2, brought the fire.[48] It was written in the Frankfort newspaper, that a person in the crowd watching the fire said of it, "It takes a fire to cleanse us." For weeks, the congregation tried to stay together by meeting in various community rooms, until

---

[47] Darnell, "*After the Manner of the Oak,*" p.26.

[48] Mrs. M. C. Darnell, *One Hundred Twenty-Fifth Anniversary of the First Christian Church, Frankfort, Kentucky,* 1957, "First Christian Church: Records of the Church of Jesus Christ at Frankfort," p. 47; Johnson, *"History of Franklin County,"* p.176.

Mrs. Tubman offered to build a new church and give it as a gift to the people. Her brother Landon wrote, "The church burned, and my sister, Mrs. Emily Tubman furnished some $27,000 to rebuild it. She also furnished seats, cushions, bell and all."[49] The church was dedicated on August 1, 1872, complete with pipe organ. After her death, Landon had her name engraved in the chancel window and on the church bell.

Mrs. Tubman built for the Augusta Church a new building as well with parsonage. The old building was given to the Tubman School which offered education to young women and was named after Mrs. Tubman because of her bequest. She supported the construction of the Hunter Street Church in Atlanta, and the Christian Church in Athens. In Kentucky she supported higher education through bequests to Transylvania University, Hiram College, and the Kentucky and Northwest Universities. She made significant contributions to the monument to Henry Clay after his death; and hers was the first donation that started the drive to restore Mt. Vernon, the home of George Washington who had been president at her birth. [50]

Ernest C. Moberly in "The Christian Standard" wrote a clever article about Mrs. Tubman entitled "Nothing in a Name." It told of how a minister had come to her needing money for his church that had burned. He argued with her that there was nothing important in the name of the Church. Mrs. Tubman believed it should have a Biblical name. Finally, after an exhausting debate, she gave in and wrote his check. But the bank refused to cash it. He returned to Mrs. Tubman and explained that she had made an error. She in turn explained how she had intentionally signed it with a name of one of her servants. Thus, she proved her point. And having learned his lesson, she issued a new check.[51]

---

49 Thomas, "*Recollections.*"

50 Clay, "Private Conversations;" Cashin, "*The Story of Augusta*," p.108.

51 Ernest C. Moberly, *The Christian Standard* (Cincinnati, Olio, v.35, No. 34, August 26, 1899) p. 1073.

Mrs. Tubman financed the education of artists, such as Frank Myers Boggs to Paris, France, and ministers, such as W. T. Moore to Bethany College. Trying to understand the ministerial calling of an Episcopal candidate for ministry that she wanted to support, but disagreeing with The Thirty-nine Articles of Religion of the

Figure 18 Frankfort Christian Church

Episcopal Church, she is reported to have said to him, "To become a priest, you will have to promise allegiance to all 39 articles; and can you honestly say you believe in all of them?' "Well, no, not all of them," had been his answer. She was astonished and pleaded, "But one seeking your priesthood must swear allegiance to them all! Do you not see a problem?" "Oh, not at all," had said the simply," one must only swear to them once."[52]

[52] Clay, "Private Conversations."

Mrs. Tubman was interested in photography and electricity. She owned a rare collection of bird prints by the Kentucky painter and naturalist John Audubon that were given to the Kentucky Historical Society after her death. She bought land in Harlem, New York in hopes that it would become profitable. Her plantations in Columbia County produced the most excellent wheat.[53] She became the co-founder of the John P. King Manufacturing Company and placed her nephew on its Board of Directors; later he would become its president. She built a church for the mill workers of the company to encourage church participation.

Figure 19 Mrs. Emily H. Tubman

When the Fleming home in the country burned and only a portrait and a Huguenot bible in French were saved, the family moved to town where their daughters, Mary and Kate, were presented with an envelope from Mrs. Tubman by her butler. The letter contained a note and a check. The note read that Mrs. Tubman knew how difficult it must be for young girls to have had everything burned and she wanted them to use the enclosed check to buy themselves some "lace and ribbons." Mary Fleming became intrigued with this kind woman and met and fell in love with her nephew, Landon Jr. Mrs. Tubman

---

[53] Ibid.; Darnell, "*After the Manner of the Oak*," p. 42.

gave her nephew the three uncut diamonds given to her by the late Richard Tubman to be fashioned into a wedding ring if Landon Jr. would take Mary Fleming as his wife. Mrs. Tubman had made inquiries about the girl and her family that indicated that she was very fine.[54]

On March 15, 1885, just before her 91st birthday, Mrs. Tubman gave an interview to the Augusta Chronicle affording a rare glimpse of Augusta as it was when she first came to the town during the early Nineteenth Century; however, her distaste for notoriety prevented the editor from printing her name. When June of 1885 arrived, Landon Jr. prepared three times for their trip to Kentucky, each time Mrs. Tubman's health prevented it; and on Tuesday June 9, at 3:30 a.m. she died. Her last words were, "Father, I am weak and weary; if it please thee let me rest." On Monday night, her brother Landon and his daughter Ann, having received a telegram, boarded the train from Frankfort but arrived in Augusta to find her passed. After a funeral service at First Christian Church in Augusta, her body was placed aboard the train for her last trip home. For almost fifty years she had fulfilled her promise to Richard Tubman by keeping this annual pilgrimage from Georgia to Kentucky. This final journey was a vigil to the two of them.

The funeral train of Mrs. Tubman arrived in Frankfort met by a very large crowd of mourners who followed in procession to the Frankfort cemetery where she was laid to rest next to her mother. A prayer was given by Philip S. Fall, former pastor of the church in Frankfort, and by its present pastor, George Darsie. Landon Thomas and Louisa Keiningham stood at the grave as the only living members of the family of Edmund Thomas and Ann Chiles, just yards away from the graves of Daniel and Rebecca Boone. Also, in attendance were Landon's wife Ellen and children Landon Jr., Anne, Emily, and Western Berkley III, Landon Jr.'s fiancée Mary Fleming of Augusta, and Western Sr.'s daughter Emily Harvie Thomas Chrystie.

[54] Mrs. Emily T. Clay, private letter to Russell R. Rechenbach, II, dated March 24, 1980.

Mrs. Tubman was very generous in her will. The value of her estate was "something like $800,000.00, the investments being in railroad, bank, state and factory bonds."[55] She endowed some $200,000 to various charitable causes. Of these, she gave over $30,000 to the Foreign Christian Missionary Society; $55,000 to the Female Orphan School of Midway, Kentucky; $5,000 to the Free School Society of Richmond County, Augusta, Georgia (the oldest high school in the United States); $5,000 to the Augusta Literary Society; $5,000 to the Widows House Society of Augusta; bequests to the various churches, and for the education and support of ministers; and generous bequeaths to family members and servants.[56] The day after her burial was Sunday. The bell—engraved with her name—rang in the steeple of the Frankfort Christian Church, assembling a large attendance for morning worship. Mrs. Tubman's pew, now empty, was draped in black cloth. The entire service centered around the life of Mrs. Tubman as servant of God. George Darsie said of her in his sermon:

> "Here, where so often she has sat in our midst, a devout and dearest worshiper, mingling her voice with ours in songs of praise, and sharing in all the acts of holy worship; here, where so often we have seen her winning smiles and received her kindly greeting as she came and went, ever the same serene, bright, cheery old lady whom all so fondly loved, and so deeply revered; here, where the walls themselves seem to speak her name, and the very air to suggest her presence; where the vacant pew, by its own emptiness asks, "Where is she who through all these years has been wont to return to us with each returning June?" And the spire without, heeding the question, makes reply, as forever pointing upward it says: "Gone, gone to the land of eternal rest." [57]

---

[55] *The Frankfort Roundabout*, Frankfort, Kentucky, June 27, 1885.

[56] Mrs. Tubman's Will of May 28, 1881 (Court of ordinary Richmond County, July 1885. Estate of Mrs. Emily H. Tubman. Will recorded in Book " E " pp. 442-464.)

[57] Lamar and Darsie, "*In Memoriam*," p. 19.

William Shadrach Tubman, a stone mason, was one of the 69 freed enslaved persons of Emily Tubman skilled and sent to Liberia to form a settlement named Tubman Hill. His son became a Methodist minister, general in the Liberian army, and a former Speaker of the House of Representatives in Liberia. But the Rev. Tubman's son,
William Vacanarat Shadrach Tubman (November 29, 1895 – July 23, 1971), grandson to the resettled William, became the 19th President of Liberia. President William Tubman sent his Methodist bishop to the United States on a pilgrimage of Emily Tubman. It led him to Paris, Kentucky, to see if the house of Mrs. Tubman's sister, Louisa Ann Thomas Keiningham, was still standing.
Mrs. Tubman would often be the guest of her sister on her visits to Kentucky after the death of Mr. Keiningham. Mrs. Anna Bruce McClure Hinton was living in the house at the time and welcomed the bishop, took him through the house, and sent by him a gift to President Tubman of Mr. Tubman's Anglican copy of the Book of Common Prayer which had remained in the house all those years.[58]

---

[58] Edna Talbott Whitley, private letter to Russell R. Rechenbach, II, Paris, Kentucky, dated October 29, 1979.

The Rev. George Darsie

Figure 20

George Darsie (1846-1904) was the son of Scottish born James Darsie. George received from Bethany College an A.B. degree in 1868, and an A.M. degree in 1873. He served churches in Baltimore, Maryland in 1868, Tuscola, Illinois 1869-71, and Ravenna, Ohio before accepting the call to the Frankfort Christian Church in 1876. But in the Capital city, he found the politics of Kentucky and short-term state servants to be a hindrance to committed membership in the Church. Frustrated by this and other problems, and devastated at the death of Mrs. Emily Tubman, Darsie said goodbye to Frankfort and in 1886 took a church in Boston.

But the memories of Frankfort and his call to the church there could not be denied and he returned the next year with a fierce determination. He found that the young men were still hanging around the outside of the church instead of coming inside for worship, but who could blame them? The architecture outside commissioned by Mrs. Tubman was beautiful, the trees along the streets were so pleasant, and there the boys could get the best view of the promenading pretty girls. So, Brother Darsie organized the Christian Endeavor Society, a youth group for young people, that brought the young men inside to get acquainted with the young ladies. To continue building churches, he raised five thousand dollars for Church Extension in 1891. In March of 1900, he established a "Living Link" for the Frankfort Church to Dr. W. E. Macklin, a medical missionary in China. Dr. Macklin accepted the field of China when a hospital was built there from the bequeath given by Mrs. Emily Tubman to the Foreign Christian Missionary Society. Much of Dr. Macklin's work in China was to help Chinese men overcome opium addictions.

Ermina Jett Darnell, local Frankfort writer and historian, remembered meeting Brother Darsie when she was a young girl. She had just recovered from an alarming illness and the pastor said to her, "My dear, we prayed for you, and here you are, a monument to our prayers." Grateful for those prayers and that ministry, she dedicated her little book *After the Manner of the Oak,* to the congregation of the Frankfort Christian Church.

Darsie served the Frankfort Church for twenty-seven years. His sudden death in 1904, at age fifty-eight, was a shock to almost every family in town. Hundreds from every race and religious affiliation came to show their respect as his body lay in state at the Church. During his funeral service, all businesses in Frankfort were closed and the bells in the court house and engine house were tolled.[59]

[59] Darnell, "*After the Manner of the Oak,*"pp. 39-46.

Mary "Minnie" Cecile Fleming

Figure 21

Mary Fleming was the daughter of Robert Porter Fleming and Catherine Bathsheba Moragne, born January 16, 1860, in Summerville, Richmond County, Georgia. She encountered Mrs. Tubman through presents gifted to her after a fire took the Fleming country home. She married Mrs. Tubman's nephew, Landon Thomas, Jr., of Frankfort, Kentucky on October 21, 1885, and together they had six children: Ellen, Western, Emily, Landon, Frank, and Anne. Landon Thomas, Jr. became President of the Kings Mill, in Augusta.

Mary's brother, William H. Fleming, championed many causes for social reform and education in Richmond County: served as the superintendent of the County schools, Speaker in the Georgia House of Representatives (1894-5), president of the Georgia State Bar Association (1895), a Democrat to the United States House of Representatives representing Georgia's 10th congressional district in the 55th, 56th, and 57th United States Congress (1897-1903)[60]

Mary was a loving wife and mother, an active member of Augusta society, and a great lover of fashion. She died February 9, 1923, and was buried in Augusta Georgia.

[60] *Biographical Directory of the United States Congress,* "William H. Fleming."

I began writing *Sabbath of the Soul* in the summer of 1972, when The Rev. Dr. John Chenault invited me to write some dramatic scenes for the Centennial Rededication of the First Christian Church in Frankfort, Kentucky. I wrote a play entitled *A Stepping Stone to Broader Fields* and directed it that following Spring, my Senior year of High School. That summer, on a pilgrimage to Augusta, Georgia, I discovered to my great surprise [by just going through a motel phone book] a Mrs. Emily Tubman Thomas Clay who just happened to be the great niece of Emily Tubman.

Emily Tubman Thomas had been born after the death of Emily Tubman, but grew up with stories of the great family benefactress from her parents Landon Jr. and Mary Fleming Thomas. She had been named after Mrs. Tubman. As a child, she had great fun ice skating with her grandfather, Landon Thomas, then in his nineties. She had excelled in tennis as a young woman. She had married into the prominent Clay family of Henry and Cassius Clay, a marriage that had ended in divorce after the birth of three sons. She had reared her sons in Augusta in her parents' house. President William Howard Taft had visited her on his frequent trips there; she told me of her embarrassment when her youngest son had playfully stabbed the President in his palm with a fountain pen. An unfortunate and heartbreaking division had happened later in life when she had become estranged from one son over family business matters and from her church. Years of gas lighting and coal stoves had darkened the interior walls of the Augusta Christian Church sanctuary, hiding much of the original rare wall paintings that Mrs. Tubman had commissioned; a faction from the church had insisted and succeeded in painting over the artwork to give the sanctuary a clean look of green paint. All against the protests of Mrs. Clay and her family. She never again went back to the church for worship. She lived in a house that she had built on her parents' estate. Somewhat reclusive in her eighties, she was full of fun and wit, and keeping up with the daily news, had strong political views and opinions.

Mrs. Clay and I started a friendship that lasted for many years. She reminded me so much of my grandmother Stella Rechenbach whom I had adored as a small child. I was thrilled to sit and listen to Mrs. Clay talk of her "great Aunt Emily" and discovered many things that we in Frankfort had not known. Mrs. Clay owned an oil painting by Matthew Jouett of Emily Tubman, painted during a ball at the Weisiger House in Frankfort—her mother Mary Fleming Thomas had fished it out of hiding in the attic [Mrs. Tubman had told Mary that she had never liked the painting, that it did not favor her]. Throughout our first visit, that painting of sixteen-year-old Emily Thomas smiled over us within a brilliant aqua background that had darkened with age, promising that there were three in the room.

Mrs. Clay had great Aunt Emily's books, and in the "big house" next door she toured me around showing me paintings that had belonged to Mrs. Tubman, the Tubmans' furniture, etched glass hurricane candle shades, and the matching portraits of Mr. and Mrs. Tubman. One extremely large oil painting portrayed a caravan through mountains, painted by Frank Myers Boggs, whose education in Paris, France, Mrs. Tubman had funded: in return for her kindness she had asked him to paint her one painting. A large colorful pillow had been embroidered by Mrs. Tubman, and Mrs. Clay was careful to turn it toward the sofa so the sunlight of the room would not fade it. I was in Tubman heaven, seeing relics I had only dreamed of. She told me how her aunt, Catherine Louise Fleming, had told the story of the check for "lace and ribbons" that Mrs. Tubman had sent them as girls when their country house outside of Augusta had burned, which must have been around the same time of the Frankfort fire that burned the church. She told me of the three uncut diamonds that Richard Tubman had given Emily, and how Mrs. Tubman years later had called her nephew Landon Thomas, Jr. [who would become Mrs. Clay's father] into her office to give him the stones to be made into a ring for Mary Fleming if Mary would marry him. When she spoke of her grandmother, Mrs. Ellen Thomas, wife to Emily Tubman's brother Landon, she called her "Amma."

On one visit to Mrs. Clay's house she had a Dr. Pepper poured for me in a crystal glass on a silver tray, explaining that she had heard that young people liked such drinks. Every Christmas I would send her a poinsettia and every Easter a lily. Her elegant stationery would always meet me at the mailbox, engraved with her name and address, and painstakingly typed on an old typewriter with her signature from a fountain pen and a word or two apologizing that her handwriting was so bad that she chose to type. On one visit to Augusta, and once again touring the large house with her, she came to the large sitting room fireplace and said with deep emotion, "I shall never forget that night. They took a large stack of letters and threw them into this fireplace. They were the letters of Mrs. Tubman. I said, "Father, Mother, please don't burn them!" They said to me, "These are things that should remain private."" Mrs. Clay could not say to what this referred.

Nancy Elliott Fowler devoted many years of her life researching and lecturing on the life of Mrs. Tubman. It was her quest to educate the world on the remarkable life of Mrs. Tubman that has been lost or forgotten. Many times, she would say to me, "We've got to get the word out about this wonderful woman!" At her death, Mrs. Fowler's papers and files on Emily Tubman were given to me.

Plays grow up like people. Under the title *Tubman*, the play went on to become my thesis for a Master of Divinity degree at Lexington Theological Seminary. Later, I rewrote the play with its current title and directed it for the 1990 Bicentennial of White Oak Pond Church, Christian Church (Disciples of Christ) in Richmond, Kentucky, where I would serve as pastor for twenty-five years; Raccoon John Smith and Alexander Campbell had both preached at the Pond Church. When the play was sadly over and put away, the cast came together to incorporate into a community theatre troupe that was named Richmond Area Theatre, that later moved to the Battlefield Park and became The Rose Barn Theatre, after Shakespeare's Rose Theatre.

BIBLIOGRAPHY

Augusta Chronicle. Tuesday June 9, 1885.

Bennett, Joseph Richard. "A Study of the Life and Contributions of Emily H. Tubman." Indianapolis, Indiana: Unpublished B.D. thesis, Butler University, 1958.

Biographical Directory of the United States Congress, William H. Fleming.

Bradford, Sarah H. *Scenes in the Life of Harriet.* Auburn: W. J. Moses, 1869 Tubman

Cashin, Dr. Ed. "Emily Tubman Remembers, Interview of March 15, 1885." *Richmond County History,* Volume 29, No. 2 Winter. Augusta, Georgia: Richmond County Historical Society, 1998.

Cashin, Edward J. *The Story of Augusta.* Spartanburg, South Carolina: The Reprint Company Publishers, 1991.

Clay, Mrs. Emily T. Private Conversations with Russell R. Rechenbach, II. Augusta, Georgia: in her home, 939 Milledge Road, phone conversations, and letters, 1973-91. Private letter to Russell R. Rechenbach, II. Augusta, Georgia: March 24, 1980.

Corley, Florence Fleming. *Confederate City, Augusta, Georgia, 1860-1865.* Columbia, South Carolina: University of South Carolina Press, 1960.

Darnell, Ermina Jett. *After the Manner of the Oak.* Frankfort, Kentucky: 1935.

Darnell, Ermina Jett. *Filling the Chinks.* Frankfort, Kentucky: Roberts Printing Co.,1966.

Darnell, Mrs. M. C., "First Christian Church: Records of the Church of Jesus Christ at Frankfort." *One Hundred Twenty-Fifth Anniversary of the First Christian Church, Frankfort, Kentucky.* Frankfort, Kentucky: First Christian Church, 1957.

Deen, Edith. *Great Women of the Christian Faith.* New York: Harper & Row, 1959.

Ford, Edward E.. Durham, North Carolina: Duke University, Richard Tubman Letters, Letter dated from Morristown, New Jersey, September 2, 1836.

Fowler, Nancy Elliott, Mrs. Newton B. Fowler. "A Georgia Disciple Pioneer: Emily Harvie Thomas Tubman," unpublished lecture, in possession of author. Atlanta, Georgia: 1825 Clifton Road, N.E. August 1985.

Gifford, James M. "Emily Tubman and the African Colonization Movement in' Georgia," Vol. LIX No. 1, Georgia History, Vol. 59 (A75). Savannah, Georgia: Georgia Historical Society; Athens, Georgia: University of Georgia, Spring 1975.

Johnson, L.F. *The History of Franklin County, Kentucky.* Frankfort: Kentucky: Roberts Printing Co., 1912.

Kramer, Carl E. Kramer. *Capital on the Kentucky.* Frankfort, Kentucky: Historic Frankfort, Inc., 1986.

Lamar, James and Darsie, George. "In Memoriam. Mrs. Emily H. Tubman." Frankfort, Kentucky: pamphlet of Memorial Service in the Christian Church Sunday June 14, 1885.

Littman, Mark. *The Heavens on Fire: The Great Leonidic Meteor Storms.* Cambridge: Cambridge University Press, 1998.

Moberly, Ernest C. *The Christian Standard.* v.35 Cincinnati, Ohio, August 26, 1899.

My Old Kentucky Home house tours. Bardstown, Kentucky, 1994.

Rouse, Jillson W. Land Office/ Secretary of State, Frankfort, Kentucky. Old Kentucky Entries and Deeds. Louisville, Kentucky: The Standard Printing Company, 1926.

The Frankfort Roundabout, Frankfort, Kentucky, June 27, 1885.

Thomas, Landon A.. "Recollections of Frankfort,", Frankfort, Kentucky: Kentucky Historical Society,. October 6, 1886.

Tubman, Emily H. Letter to Louisa Keiningham, Frankfort Kentucky: Philip Fall Memorial Library, First Christian Church.

Tubman, Emily H.. Letters to Philip S. Fall. Frankfort, Kentucky: Kentucky Historical Society Library..

Tubman, Emily H. Letter to Ralph R. Gurley. Washington, D.C.: Library of Congress. American Colonization Society Archives, Letters Received, vol. 66, March 20, 1837.

Tubman, Emily H. Mrs. Tubman's Will. Augusta, Georgia: Court of ordinary Richmond County, July 1885. Estate of Mrs. Emily H. Tubman. Will recorded in Book "E," May 28, 1881.

Tubman, Richard. Richard Tubman Papers. Durham, North Carolina: Duke University Library, 1753-1858.

Whitley Edna Talbott. Interview and private letter to Russell R. Rechenbach, II. Paris, Kentucky: October 29, 1979.

Woodson, Mary Willis. "My Recollections of Frankfort,"' *Through the Portals of Glen Willis.* Frankfort, Kentucky: Franklin County Trust for Historic Preservation.

Wright, John D. Jr. *Transylvania; Tutor To The West.* Lexington, Kentucky: Transylvania University, 1975.

Emma of Elmwood

Introduction

For over a century, the citizens of Richmond, Kentucky, the students of Eastern Kentucky University, and the many visitors to our town have admired the enigmatic home and estate across the street. Named "Elmwood" for all the elm trees that once stood on twenty acres of land, the nine thousand square foot house is a rare form of 19th Century Chateauesque architecture. It is also known as "The Watts House," named after its original owner William Watts; but also, in recognition of Miss Emma Watts, William's only child.

This play entreats a person to know more about the many mysteries and stories that surround the Watts' home place and its matron. *Emma of Elmwood* is a fictionalized love story tinged with, what seems to be on the surface, paranormal activity. Emma Watts, who has a strong filial attachment to the house, appears to an architect whom the University has employed to oversee the demolition of Elmwood and its replacement by a Student Center and parking garage. Hum, does that seem an all too familiar activity in our society. Preservation and tradition be damned! In one scene Emma appears to the architect and tells him, "I think you took this job to find yourself. And this old place is going to help you do that." In another scene one of Emma's childhood playmates astutely observes that, "Home is only as lovely as the friends who frequent it." Emma would heartily agree.

If only walls could talk! Yet, they do talk through Miss Emma in this marvelous play. Miss Emma ultimately succeeds. I welcome you to come to Richmond and visit our Eastern Kentucky University, a comprehensive university where students and learning come first, and to enjoy this informative, tantalizing, and entertaining play that was written years before our University acquired the property. See how Miss Emma's love for home place conquers all.

Charles Hay,
Archivist Emeritus, Eastern Kentucky University

Emma of Elmwood

Characters

CHILD, Young Emma Watts
Dr. Paul GERHARDT, commissioned architect
Dr. Charles O'NEIL, professor at the University, Trustee
Mrs. MERRITT, caretaker of Elmwood
EMMA Watts, first lady of Richmond
HARRIETT, Emma's childhood playmate
MARY Watts, Emma's mother
COMMITTEE MEMBERS, from the Board of the University
MISS HARRIETT, Harriett as adolescent
MRS. MCGAUGHEY, Harriett in her old age, at the Manor
CAVENDISH, Miss Watts' priest

Time: Around the turn of the 21st Century
Place: Elmwood, Richmond, Kentucky

ACT ONE

Scene One

A small child of eight years stands at Center in a spot of light. She is neatly dressed and very poised. She holds a letter and reads with the confidence of childhood innocence.

CHILD

S. Claus Esquire,
Chimneyland

Dear Santa Claus,

I know you can bring me anything I want without any trouble. Please give me a dollhouse that is inside and outside like the one I saw at the Turo Infirmary Fair. I want it to be like it inside and outside and to be completely furnished just like it and to have an upstairs like it with as many rooms as it has and I want it to be a perfect copy of the one I saw. –If you don't want me to have it please give me other things.–Answer my letter directly and tell me whether you want me to have the house or not.

Yours truly,
Emma Parkes Watts

[The CHILD disappears as the light fades away. A door buzzer rings. We hear the distant sound of "horseshoes" being played somewhere outside. Cheerful afternoon sunlight gleams brightly through brilliant autumn leaves outside the tall dominate clear glass window above an ornate Victorian oak staircase. Outside where the sound of the horse shoe game continues its ringing, the world is a dance in one of its last remembrances of warm weather, what is called "Indian Summer." The movement of the leaves on the trees, their brilliant orange color, taunts the silence and confined pristine stillness of the great Entrance Hall interior of Elmwood, in Richmond, Kentucky. On the damasked silk walls have hung large oil portraits in gold gilded frames. To one side is a Drawing Room with Georgian sofas and chairs with a door leading

to the Dining Room. At the other side is a large ornate oak fireplace mantle, the doors near it lead to the Library. The room rests as chairs and tables once did when they were stored against the walls, waiting, waiting to come alive again with purposeful hospitality for the entertaining of long awaited guests. Time has stopped at Elmwood. The pendulum of the great Hall clock has not moved as the years passed. A door buzzer rings again. After a short pause, Paul GERHARDT appears in silhouette. For a moment he stands motionless, like the room, but soon steps into the light that comes from the large staircase window. We see that he is a man in his fifties, dressed in a suit and tie, one hand carrying his briefcase. There is no one to welcome him. His countenance might remind us of one like Dante, midway the path of life in that darkening wood astray. GERHARDT walks across the room, the sound of his shoes against the wooden floor accompanying him. As if trying to remember something, something from his past long stored away, he lets the room bring it back to him and recites aloud as to himself:]

GERHARDT

"These are the days when birds come back,
a very few, a bird or two,
To take a backward look.
These are the days when skies put on
The old, old sophistries of June,–
A blue and gold mistake . . ."

[The words take on a new acquaintance for him as he retreats into them once again] "To take a backward look . . ." *[Amidst his puzzlement, the ringing sound of the game of horseshoes interrupts his recitation. Then keys unlocking doors, opening and closing. Charles O'NEIL enters from what is the back of the house.]*

O'NEIL

She loved poetry, too. And the arts. That was beautiful.

GERHARDT

What was? I—was just talking to myself . . .

O'NEIL

No, it was. It was beautiful. No, it was wonderful.

GERHARDT

What? You think I go around reciting poetry or something?

O'NEIL

Absolutely terrific! And you are! I hope to hear more from you. *[We see now that O'NEIL has been talking on his cell phone. GERHARDT laughs at his mistake.]* I'll call you later. Thanks. Bye, now. *[He puts away the cell phone and notices GERHARDT]*

O'NEIL

Oh! There you are, Jerry. *[Of his phone:]* Amazing things. I can get so much work done now with this. 2.5 G. One day everyone will have one—mark my word. And the more that have them the more they will come down in price. Just wait. Sorry. I see you found your way through the front door. We usually come in the back way.

GERHARDT

I thought you . . .

O'NEIL

No, no. You were right to come to the front doors. That's the way you should first see the house. *[Of his phone again:]* I tried calling you on your phone.

GERHARDT

[Taking out his older cell phone.]

I usually leave it turned off.

O'NEIL

Well, how is anyone supposed to reach you? That's an antique.

GERHARDT

They keep changing them.

O'NEIL

It works, doesn't it? Well, turn it on. This is the way of the 21st Century. *[GERHARDT turns his phone on. Of the house:]* It is a beautiful old place, isn't it?

GERHARDT

Yes.

O'NEIL

Named after the trees, of course. Great elms. Her father, William Watts, named it, built it.

GERHARDT

That explains the "WW" over the front entrance.

O'NEIL

Yes. He was the town magistrate and built the place for his wife and daughter. Elmwood. *[The sound of its name gives a haunting resonance throughout the house. Of the trees through the doorway:]* Beautiful trees, aren't they? Like going back in time. The weather is nice today!

GERHARDT

Indian summer. I noticed some massive branches lying on the grounds out there.

O'NEIL

They should have been cleared away by now.

GERHARDT

Was there a storm recently?

O'NEIL

Yes. We had a ferocious ice storm. *Last winter.*

GERHARDT

Where did William Watts get his money?

O'NEIL

Cattle ranches and cotton in Texas. *[GERHARDT continues to look around. He goes toward the staircase.]* Beautiful oak, isn't it?

GERHARDT

The window?

O'NEIL

[At the staircase]

The stained-glass window was taken out and stored up in the attic. The executor of her estate was afraid it was going to fall. That's why the clear glass. Otherwise, the house is much as she left it.

GERHARDT

She?

O'NEIL

Emma Watts. William's only child. She and the house were born the same year; she lived here alone after her parents were gone. She died here. All of the furnishings are her's or her parents'. Nothing has been changed. It's almost as if she has just stepped out of the house.

GERHARDT

Who has kept the place up?

O'NEIL

Emma Watts.

GERHARDT

I thought you said she was dead.

O'NEIL

She is.

GERHARDT

[Looking around the untouched room.]

Expecting her back anytime soon?

O'NEIL

. . . Her will. She made arrangements for the place to be cared for in her will.

GERHARDT

So, it's just been sitting here empty all these years?

O'NEIL

Maintained by her estate. But the trust was to be terminated at the death of her last cousin.

GERHARDT

I see. And now the money is running out. I guess that's where the sale comes in.

O'NEIL

No, Dr. Gerhardt. That's where you come in. *[Of the house:]* It needed the right man. The best architect. And you are that man. We have put our trust and faith in you.

GERHARDT

Thank you.

O'NEIL

They did the best they could with the money they had . . . Did you see the stained-glass window over the fireplace in the Dining Room? There is a similar one at the home of Mark Twain.

GERHARDT

What was she like?

O'NEIL

Miss Emma? She's kind of a mystery. I know she ran the cattle farms in Texas and oil. Here she dabbled in antiques . . . She wanted to preserve the way of life of a lady of society in Kentucky during the Nineteenth Century.

GERHARDT

Preserve? You mean embalm, don't you.

O'NEIL

[After careful thinking]

Mr. Gerhardt. It is the end of a long battle.

GERHARDT

Battle?

O'NEIL

I don't think that Miss Emma got on well with our University. She never wanted it to get its hands on her property. That's why the will.

GERHARDT

So, the money dwindled and the troops have surrendered?

O'NEIL

It is rather a sad story when you stop and think about it. *[His beeper vibrates, and he checks it. Of the beeper:]* These beepers will soon be a thing of the past. Mark my word . . .

GERHARDT

[Unaware that O'NEIL is responding to a call.]

As an outsider, it's to your benefit that I don't share the sentiment. I'm not interested in Miss Emma or her wishes, or this house for that matter. That's my job. That's what I do. You have hired me to make plans for progress. All of this will have to be leveled to make room for expansion.

O'NEIL

[Into his phone, unnoticed by GERHART]

Yes. Yes, I understand.

GERHARDT

[He walks up the stairs and peers through the tall window of autumn leaves.]

Students have to walk for miles to get to classes—isn't that what you told me? There's no adequate student parking? The University has to have this land if it is going to grow? This property is practically swallowed up by the University as it is? Richmond is the fastest growing city in the State?

O'NEIL

[Into his phone:]

That's right.

GERHARDT

When you see the final plans, you'll be pleased. Trust me. I'm going to take this run-down old place and bring vibrancy to the University that it has never seen. In spite of Miss Emma Watts. Maybe she's stood in the way long enough.

O'NEIL

[Into his phone:]

You're right. Mow her down.

GERHARDT

Believe me, every worthwhile piece of woodwork and stone will be salvaged and used somewhere else. Nothing will be wasted. In fact, this entire mantle will be the central focus of the foyer in the Principal Building.

O'NEIL

[Into the phone:]

I'd just get rid of it all. What about the trees?

GERHARDT

Everything has a life expectancy. Most of the trees have come to the end of theirs.

O'NEIL

[Into the phone:]

They can be replaced. I'd just get rid of them.

GERHARDT

I'm sure they were lovely . . . once.

O'NEIL

[Into the phone:]

We'll have a bottle of champagne and celebrate when it's all done.

GERHARDT

No, the drinks will be on me.

O'NEIL

[Into the phone:]

I could bring the bottle tonight . . .

GERHARDT

What about the Committee Members?

O'NEIL

Oh, they'll be in bed. Man, you are sexy when you get this way. *[Softer]* What do you say we turn on the hot tub and let you get into something more comfortable? Or maybe nothing at all.. . *[Jeanette MERRITT enters, an older African American woman, small and petite, wearing an apron.]* We've got a date? I love you, Sweetheart. *[This leaves GERHARDT stunned. MRS. MERRITT, not seeing the phone either and not knowing how to take this, turns and leaves. We only now fully realize that O'NEIL has been conversing on his phone.]* I'm sorry, Jerry. It was my wife—we're having some landscaping done at the house. What were you saying? Yes, your plans. We're all excited about seeing them.

GERHARDT

When do you think construction could start?

O'NEIL

Well, first we have to see the plans. I mean, we can't say.

GERHARDT

Your University owns the place; you can do whatever you want. *[No response.]* Right?

O'NEIL

That's just it—

GERHARDT

What? You do own it? Tell me, you own it. How can you build a Student Life Center here unless you own it—

O'NEIL

If the design is convincing, then we hope the university can take ownership. That's why we need you. To show us it is possible.

GERHARDT

"If it's convincing?" But you said the *university* wanted me to design the complex for the building of the Student–

O'NEIL

I said we wanted you to design it for *when* we build it. And *when* we built it depends upon when we get approval to sell it.

GERHARDT

Miss Watts did not give this house to the University?

O'NEIL

No.

GERHARDT

You don't have approval to buy this property?

O'NEIL

I'm saying that we have approval to buy it, of course. We just don't have approval to sell it.

GERHARDT

"We." "We . . ." That doesn't make any sense. Let's say you get it approved, then you *are* going to use my plans for the construction?

O'NEIL

It is possible.

GERHARDT

Possible? *[He shakes his head in frustration.]* I thought you were going to use my plans. Maybe . . . maybe you are not ready for me with this.

O'NEIL

Jerry, one step at a time. Please. I would think that your plans would absolutely be used after the approval, but I can't guarantee that, because I don't know what's going to happen.

GERHARDT

[With disappointment]

I see.

O'NEIL

That's what we are working toward. When I talked with you on the phone, the deal seemed done. Then there was some pulling out, and well– *[O'NEIL's phone rings]* It's my new Blackberry. I've got an email I need to attend to. Would you excuse me? Are you in a hurry?

GERHARDT

No, go right ahead. I set aside the whole afternoon. I don't have anything until tonight.

O'NEIL

Mrs. Merritt should be here any minute. She will be a great help to you–she remembers what the old place looked like in its heyday–*[He rushes off working with his phone]*

GERHARDT

Did you tell her I'm planning to tear the old place down? *[Once again GERHARDT is left alone in the company of the old house. He walks around, looking the place over, as one does after the proper introductions have been made when making an acquaintance. But something about the room insists upon being more than that to him. We hear the sound of a chain saw out in the garden. There is the sound of people playing "horseshoes"–the metal ringing against the pole. EMMA appears from the staircase. She is a tiny thing, dressed in pressed cotton and linen, Edwardian day dress. Her long dark hair is piled high upon her head. A young woman in her twenties. She is pretty yet plain, with a sad and lonely expression printed into her face. Her gloved hand caresses the banister and everything in the house that she touches, for she loves her house.]*

EMMA

You like my house?

GERHARDT

Dr. O'Neil says you know the place well. *[He examines the large oil painting of a man that hangs on the wall.]* So, who is this? William Watts, no doubt?

EMMA

Yes.

GERHARDT

[Of the other]

And what? His wife?

EMMA

[With a chuckle]

His mother. She lived here with him. That's his wife there.

GERHARDT

It's really rather good. Rather stern expression. I bet she was a lot of fun!

EMMA

Laszlo was the painter.

GERHARDT

You know . . . I know this style. If I'm not mistaken . . . No, it couldn't be . . .*[He looks closely for the signature]* My God! It is! It's Philip Laszlo.

EMMA

It was painted in Germany.

GERHARDT

These should be in a museum. Father, mother, grandmother . . . someone's missing. The daughter. I don't blame her. What a waste of time to sit and pose for a painting. Can you imagine?

EMMA

Have you ever posed for a painting?

GERHARDT

I'm afraid not.

EMMA

And why is that?

GERHARDT

You have to be someone important . . .

EMMA

And you are not? "Someone important?"

GERHARDT

[He laughs, but there is no joy in his laughter.]

Not yet, anyway. We have photographs now.

EMMA

They had photographs then. You've posed for a photograph?

GERHARDT

No, not recently. Who would want to look at it? *[There follows an uncomfortable silence]*

EMMA

When then?

GERHARDT

When?

EMMA

When will you deem yourself important?

GERHARDT

Maybe after this job. There will be some who will think me important enough then.

EMMA

What type of work do you do?

GERHARDT

I'm an architect. I've just been hired for the Strategic Planning. Of the University.

EMMA

The University?

GERHARDT

Yes.

EMMA

[With loathing]

I should have known. *[She crosses to the front doors. Her walk is slow and smooth, every movement delicate and graceful. She looks out on the porch.]* I remember when the University was little.

GERHARDT

Nothing can stand in the way of its dream.

EMMA

And what is its dream?

GERHARDT

Expansion. Growth. Success.

EMMA

And all the time I thought it was education. The dream of wanting something better for our children.

GERHARDT

That goes without saying, of course.

EMMA

In this State, where would you say that dream began?

GERHARDT

I . . . don't know.

EMMA

In the Spring of 1775, Captain William Twetty's small group of pioneers were ambushed and murdered, and from the moment that first drop of blood fell into the waters of Dreaming Creek, there has been such fighting and killing. Born of ignorance and greed. And those who fought against such violence did so with the dream of education

GERHARDT

"*Dreaming Creek*?"

EMMA

That is the water that runs through our town. Daniel Boone named it. He fell asleep by the creek and dreamed of an Indian attack. That dream woke him up and he prepared himself for battle. True to the dream, they did attack, but he was ready. And the dream saved his life.

GERHARDT

Where is this Dreaming Creek? I'd like to see it.

EMMA

They paved over it. Presbyterians dreamed up the first college West of the Allegheny Mountains in Lexington. Thomas Jefferson complained that if more schools were not established in Virginia their students would have to go to "Kentucky or Cambridge." Because of the churches, the State had more colleges after the War of 1812 than any State in the Union. In our town, along the bank of Dreaming Creek, the Madison Female Institute was a famous southern finishing school for girls. It attracted students from all over the South prior to the Civil War. During the Battle of Richmond in 1862, its teachers and students used the building to care for the wounded. *[She blushes, having gone on too long with a stranger, for fear of boring him.]* Forgive me . . .

GERHARDT

No, no. Go on. I find it interesting. I never knew anything much important went on here.

EMMA

After the War, Central University was founded on the sympathies of the Old South, favoring slavery. A missionary was brought here to establish an anti-caste school. The Rev. John Fee. Perhaps you have read of him?

GERHARDT

Never heard of him. He called his dream "Berea;" it became the first college showing equality to whites, Negroes, mountain people, and women. "Anti-slavery, anti-caste, anti-rum, anti-sin." He and his students were marched out of town at gunpoint. Harriet Beecher Stowe praised his achievements. Have you have heard of Harriett Beecher Stowe? She wrote "Uncle—

GERHARDT

[Suspicious of her sarcasm]

Yes . . . I've heard of Harriett Beecher Stowe.

EMMA

Her book was about Kentucky, a looking glass of education: mirroring prejudice and injustice. Your university sprang from a State Normal School in 1906, a school for teachers.

GERHARDT

You sure know your history well enough. Have you been here a long time? *[EMMA nods]* I imagined you much older . . .

EMMA

Thank you. You are not from Kentucky?

GERHARDT

Chicago.

EMMA

That is your home?

GERHARDT

Not really. I've been all over. Never one place.

EMMA

Where did you grow up?

GERHARDT

Michigan. California. New York. My family was military. The only school I went to for more than a year was graduate school.

EMMA

You would like to see the upstairs?

GERHARDT

Yes, please. *[She leads him up the staircase, he follows her, but she stops half way and looks down at the view.]*

EMMA

This house made a lovely home.

GERHARDT

If you say so. Maybe some people need that sort of thing.

EMMA

You have no one place to think of as your home?

GERHARDT

I never wear a hat. *[EMMA looks at him with puzzlement.]* If home is where you hang your hat.

EMMA

Perhaps you could think of this house as your home. And you never have to leave. Never. Spring, Summer, Winter, Fall . . . always here for you, always the same. Always your home. A place no one can take away from you. *[We hear the sounds of horseshoes playing outside.]*

GERHARDT

You messing with my head?

EMMA

Father always loved to play horseshoes. It was always so nice when Father was home. Although I had to put on my company manners. *[We hear the sound of the chain saw outside again]*

O'NEIL

[Entering now, finishing a call on his cell phone, he puts out his cigarette.]

Sorry about that. Thank you, though. These things are amazing: if I can just get it to cook dinner I'd be set. Now, then, where were we? I wonder what is taking Mrs. Merritt so long.

GERHARDT

She was just about to show me the upstairs– *[He turns but EMMA is gone]*

O'NEIL

She's gone around back then–that's where I told her to meet us.

GERHARDT

There's a back stairs, yes, . . . *[He stands on the stairs for a moment wondering if he should follow her.]* I hadn't expected someone so lovely. I think I'm going to enjoy working on this project . . .

O'NEIL

She's a saint. We probably owe her the credit for keeping the place up all these years.

GERHARDT

I expected her–I don't know–to be older or something . . .

O'NEIL

She and her husband came here fifty years ago–

GERHARDT

No way!

O'NEIL

They used to work for the Governor but chose to come here instead. Miss Watts treated them like family. She provided for them in her will. *[Heading toward the Dining Room and the back of the house.]* Shall we? *[GERHARDT comes back down the stairs and follows him.]* The president of the University came asking her how much she wanted for her little house. She looked him straight in the eye and said, "How much do you want for your little University?" From that day on she vowed that the University would not get her property.

GERHARDT

How old was she when she died?

O'NEIL

Eighties. Nineties. Mrs. Merritt would know. But you'll find you won't get much out of her. She had great respect for Miss Emma's privacy.

GERHARDT

I found her easy enough to talk to.

O'NEIL

[Of a framed photograph on the nearby table]

There she is out in the garden. With the collies. Her collies were like children to her. They are buried here on the grounds.

GERHARDT

She hasn't changed a bit.

O'NEIL

There she is. *[MERRITT enters with a big friendly smile.]* So, you have met our chosen architect for the renovation? Dr. Gerhardt was just admiring the house.

GERHARDT

Someone has done a great job taking care of it.

MERRITT

Miss Emma always wanted the place to look nice. That's the kind of person she was.

GERHARDT

How long have you worked with Mrs. Merritt? *[There is the silence of confusion.]*

O'NEIL

Jeanette worked for Miss Emma and her parents . . . for a long time.

MERRITT

I enjoyed every day of it.

GERHARDT

I'm sure Miss Watts would be very happy with both your efforts.

MERRITT

Thank you.

GERHARDT

I'm sure you did the best you could.

MERRITT

Miss Emma was very good to us. She was good to everybody. She loved this house. *[She makes a concerted effort:]* She really loved this house.

GERHARDT

[Taking a deep breath, he controls his thoughts.]

Yes.

MERRITT

Spent her whole life here.

GERHARDT

Yes.

MERRITT

She and the house were born the same year. They grew up together.

GERHARDT

So, I was told.

MERRITT

Kept the place up all these years . . . Still does.

GERHARDT

Uh hum . . .

MERRITT

She wouldn't want anything to happen to it, you know.

GERHARDT

[Patience wearing thin.]

Little late isn't it?

O'NEIL

Paul–

GERHARDT

Now, let's be honest. Slates are missing in the roof–it leaks, and there is no greater threat to an historic house than water. Stained-glass windows falling out . . . The carriage house is in great disrepair. The fish pond covered in, trees growing out of it. The smoke house roof has collapsed.

MERRITT

We were just getting ready to fix that roof–

GERHARDT

Really?

MERRITT

Yes, ten years ago.

GERHARDT

I'm glad you are so attentive. And if it were to stand for another ten years, before the earth shifts and a bearing wall gives way, . . . it will be for what purpose? What good is it doing?

MERRITT

I told them that the smokehouse needed a new roof . . .

GERHARDT

I'm sure you did. I'm sure you did. *[He calms down and is more sensitive]* I'm not saying it's your fault. Just don't say its mine. All right?

O'NEIL

[Interceding]

Jeannette, Dr. Gerhardt loves old homes like this. That's why he has dedicated his life to architecture. He is an expert—his books are bestsellers.

MERRITT

Do you love this place, Dr. Gerhardt?

GERHARDT

I've not been called here to love anything. That was not part of the job description. Believe me; I could have taken much better offers than this one.

MERRITT

Then why did you take this one?

GERHARDT

[He looks to O'NEIL who avoids his glare]

Most people have no idea what it costs to keep up a house much less a great house such as this. Why, when the Watts were living, they had servants working every day of the year keeping the place up, repairing this and replacing that. It was a golden era before Income Taxes. It sank with the Titanic.

MERRITT

I've lived here all of my life. I'll have no place to go . . . My husband is dead. *[GERHARDT looks to O'NEIL for support, but O'NEIL's phone rings.]*

O'NEIL

[Excited about the phone:]

You know they come with all kinds of ring tones now. It will even play music for you—Sorry, I'll put it on vibrate. The voice mail will get it. *[He works at his new phone.]*

GERHARDT

[To MERRITT]

If you've lived here, too, on the estate, well, I'm sorry. That is something you need to take up with the President of the University. That's who hired me.

MERRITT

Miss Emma hired me. Miss Emma wanted things to stay put . . . stay as they were.

GERHARDT

Well, in that respect, let's bring back the wilderness and Dreaming Creek. That's the way it was originally. Until the Watts demolished it. I'm sorry she did not make the proper preparations for you and Mrs. Merritt.

MERRITT

Miss Emma made provisions for me. Miss Emma said in her will that I could live here as long as I wanted . . . *[GERHARDT looks to O'NEIL who can only shrug his shoulders. Here again is a serious obstacle of which he was not informed. GERHARDT has no idea of a solution, nor does he desire to take on its responsibility.]*

GERHARDT

Wills are meant to be broken. Maybe you and Mrs. Merritt should take that up with the President.

O'NEIL

Mrs. Merritt?

GERHARDT

She was here a minute ago. She was going to show me upstairs . . .

O'NEIL

Jerry, this is Mrs. Merritt.

MERRITT

Oh, no, not upstairs.

O'NEIL

Mrs. Merritt avoids the stairs these days. But we could just show ourselves up there and–

GERHARDT

Well, the *other* Mrs. Merritt, then.

O'NEIL

There is only one Mrs. Merritt.

GERHARDT

I thought the other lady was . . .

O'NEIL

What other lady?

GERHARDT

"What other lady?"? *[With a turn of frustration, he signals to the framed photograph]* There . . . Mrs. Merritt. In the picture with the collies. *[There is a silence. The sound of horseshoe again.]*

MERRITT

Miss Emma?

O'NEIL

That's a picture of Miss Emma and her dogs.

GERHARDT

What?

MERRITT

Yes. *[With a dancing fondness now in her remembrance]* Miss Emma loved her dogs. They're all dead now. Buried out back. They've been gone now a long time.

GERHARDT

That's a picture of Emma Watts? I thought you said she was dead . . . *[Realizing]* Okay. What's the deal here? What's going on?

O'NEIL

Mrs. Merritt is the only caretaker. There is a gardener . . .*[GERHARDT goes to the stairs, looks up. Stops. Then laughs]*

GERHARDT

Of course. The gardener. I thought she was the–

O'NEIL

He. The gardener is a man. In fact, he is sawing up the branches that fell last winter . . . as we speak. *[We hear the sawing again]*

GERHARDT

[Comes to himself and laughs]

'A good resemblance. Yes, very. There must be a student dressed up like her. Yes! That's who I was speaking with. She's around here somewhere. Unless she went on to class . . .

MERRITT

The house has been locked, Dr. O'Neil. It's always locked. I'm the only one with a key.

GERHARDT

O'Neil . . .

MERRITT

Dr. O'Neil entrusts me with all the keys. I let him in.

O'NEIL

We were the only ones Mrs. Merritt let in.

GERHARDT

The front doors were unlocked. I came in that way, remember? *[Suddenly wondering if it is all a trick, if he should move cautiously.]* Of course.

O'NEIL

Paul, are you all right? You act like you've seen a ghost.

GERHARDT

It must be the house. It tends to wrap you up in it all. That's what it is . . . or an actress . . .

MERRITT

Will there be anything else? I've got some beaten biscuits on the stove. Miss Emma taught me to make beaten' biscuits and there aren't any beaten' biscuits like Miss Emma made. We used to make them and take them around to all her friends in the town–they'd all say, "There ain't no beaten' biscuits like Miss Emma's." No, sir. You all go on upstairs and see just how nice a house this place is, holler when you're done and I'll come lock up. Don't mind my dog, now. She barks a lot. But I wouldn't put my hand through the fence if I were you. No, sir. *[As she exits]* Yes, sir. You just see for yourself what a fine old place this place is. *[She remembers]* She would never sell this old house. The President of the University came over one day. He asked Miss Emma, "Miss Watts, what would you take for your house?" She said to the President, "Dr. Martin, what would you take for your University?" *[She laughs and laughs]* Yes, sir. "What would you take for your University?" she said! *[She exits, shaking her head, remembering, laughing to herself.]*

GERHARDT

Charles, I could have sworn . . . *[He picks up the picture from the table and examines it]* And this is Emma Watts?

O'NEIL

Yes. It's a beautiful picture, isn't it? The gardens behind here. The gate's long since gone.

GERHARDT

It's so clear. Like it was taken yesterday.

O'NEIL

[Watching him carefully]

Anyway, shall we go on upstairs and then we have some folks meeting us for lunch. If we hurry, we'll be right on time. 'Traffic through town and all.

GERHARDT

Sure. *[He puts the picture down]* Is there some kind of group trying to save this old house, Charles? I mean, a group who wouldn't stop at going to the trouble of having an actress try to mess with my conscience and all–because if there is, I'm telling you up front, I have no patience for that kind of thing. None.

O'NEIL

No, Paul.

GERHARDT

I mean it. I've got enough crap going on in my life without having to fight city hall of small-town America . . .

O'NEIL

We're all glad you're here. Everyone hates to see the house go, but we know you know best. I've done my research; you have a fine professional reputation.

GERHARDT

Good. I like to choose my battles, that's all. It's not my fault that Mrs. Watts did not like your university.

O'NEIL

"Miss" Watts. She never married. *[He takes out a cigarette and starts to light.]*

GERHARDT

Don't smoke. It gives me a headache.

O'NEIL

Uh . . ., okay. *[He puts away the cigarettes.]*

GERHARDT

Where are you from, Charles? 'You from here?

O'NEIL

California.

GERHARDT

'You grow up there? You call it "home?"

O'NEIL

Sure do.

GERHARDT

[With sad disappointment]

Oh. I guess some of us aren't as fortunate, that's all. *[He looks around the room]* Getting to stay in one place . . .

O'NEIL

[As they climb the stairs:]

Yeah, it was home all right. Grew up there. Went to college there. Then graduate school. Took up the family business there. Married my hometown sweetheart . . .

GERHARDT

Oh, . . . *[It is like rubbing salt into a wound; he wishes he'd never asked.]*

O'NEIL

Got divorced there. Filed bankruptcy there. Lost everything I had there– the house, the car, the kids, . . . Thought about jumping off the Golden Gate bridge there– *[They disappear upstairs. EMMA walks slowly in, goes to the picture, puts it back where it was. She adjusts its location to make sure it is exactly right. Then she slowly wanders away.]*

ACT ONE

Scene Two

GERHARDT enters dressed in white shirt and khaki trousers, very clean, very well pressed, with work boots that have been cared for. He wears a leather belt displaying his name engraved on a brass plate. With a measuring tape he begins measuring the house: the floor, the mantles, the staircase, etc. He whistles as he works. EMMA appears from the stairs; she is dressed as before. GERHARDT sees her and jumps with sudden surprise.

EMMA

Sorry. I didn't mean to scare you.

GERHARDT

[Imperiously]

I don't do scared. I just didn't know you were there.

EMMA

I hope everything is the right size.

GERHARDT

[He is reticent, suspicious of her. He continues his work]

Humm.

EMMA

You always work alone?

GERHARDT

Uh humm. *[He struggles to hold down the tape]*

EMMA

Let me help you. *[She takes the end and holds it for him while he extends the tape. He writes down the measurement.]* Twenty-seven feet, five and a half inches.

GERHARDT

How did you know that?

EMMA

I know every inch of this place. It is as much a part of me as . . . me.

GERHARDT

I am mad at you.

EMMA

At me? Why?

GERHARDT

You walked out on me. You said you were going to show me the upstairs and then you disappeared.

EMMA

I didn't disappear.

GERHARDT

Yes, you did.

EMMA

You went upstairs without me.

GERHARDT

You left me holding the bag . . . I think they thought I was crazy.

EMMA

You've been smoking.

GERHART

Not me. 'Charles. Dr. O'Neil.

EMMA

It leaves such a smell on everything, as thick as soot from the coal grates.

GERHART

I know what you mean.

EMMA

Always when they don't know us, people make terrible assumptions about us. Always when they watch us from a distance.

GERHARDT

You hurt my feelings.

EMMA

I'm sorry. I didn't mean to.

GERHARDT

[He smiles at her, stops measuring, and is very pleasant]

You know, you look just like her in the photograph.

EMMA

Is that right?

GERHARDT

Dead ringer. Are you a Theatre major? Or is this one of those Chautauqua things . . . ?

EMMA

Chautauqua brought the arts and education to town. We went once to see their production of *As You Like It. [Remembering]* Orlando doesn't recognize Rosalind. Most people in town had never seen a Shakespeare play. Henry Allen Lane organized a Colored Chautauqua for the county, but it was a little more religious.

GERHARDT

They said you were not the caretaker.

EMMA

What idiot would have thought I was the caretaker!

GERHARDT

Me. You said you were.

EMMA

I did not.

GERHARDT

Oh, but you did.

EMMA

You thought I was the caretaker–

GERHARDT

You led me into thinking you were the caretaker.

EMMA

Are you the architect?

GERHARDT

Yes, I am.

EMMA

Good then. One of us is right.

GERHARDT

[Not knowing what she means by that, the argument is dropped.]

Thank you. I think. *[He has measured again and begins to write down the measurement]*

EMMA

Twenty-feet, twenty inches. *[He looks at her]* And a quarter. Sorry.

GERHARDT

You really do know this place.

EMMA

I've walked it enough.

GERHARDT

You walked out on me.

EMMA

I was still here. You just did not notice me.

GERHARDT

Now! Aren't you the interesting one? I didn't notice you? Oh, I noticed you all right. *[He puts down the measuring tape]* We were not properly introduced. Paul Gerhardt is my name. But my close friends call me Jerry. *[He offers his hand. She looks down at it and smiles]* What's wrong?

EMMA

Is it polite now for a gentleman to offer his hand to a lady?

GERHARDT

[He puts his hand down.]

Sorry. *[There is a moment's pause. EMMA offers him her hand]*

EMMA

It is nice to meet you, Mr. Gerhardt.

GERHARDT

[Shaking her hand]

My close friends call me Jerry. *[She only smiles]* You do have a name, don't you?

EMMA

[Turning away from him]

Yes.

GERHARDT

And a very good one, I must add. Of course. *[Playing along with her.]* So, what's a nice girl like you doing in a place like this? How do you spend the hours . . . besides walking the earth to and fro . . .

EMMA

I like to read.

[The lights suddenly change. MARY Watts enters. A woman in her thirties dressed in a house dress of the early Twentieth Century. It is a memory of Emma's, haunting the house, unnoticed by GERHARDT. Something of the past, or is it?]

MARY

Emma! Emma!

CHILD

[Calling from a distance]

Yes, mother!

MARY

What are you doing, dear?

CHILD

I'm reading.

MARY

Not again. I thought you finished that book.

CHILD

I did. I've started a new one.

MARY

Emma, it can't be healthy for you to be sitting around all day reading. You'll do enough of that when the term starts again. You need to get outside and get some fresh air.

CHILD

Yes, mother.

MARY

Emma!

CHILD

Yes, mother.

MARY

Where are you?

EMMA

I'm on the porch. You told me to get some fresh air . . .

MARY

What are you doing on the porch?

EMMA

Reading.

MARY

I meant, Exercise!

CHILD

Yes, mother.

MARY

You need fresh air and exercise! Do you want to get sick and die?

CHILD

No, mother.

MARY

I'm going to write your father and ask him about getting you a tennis set. Would you like that?

CHILD

For you to write Father? Oh, yes, Mother.

MARY

No, I mean for him to buy you a tennis set.

CHILD

Yes, mother.

MARY

Yes! For the yard. I know of a good coach for you.

EMMA

Yes, mother.

[The lights change back as MARY Watts disappears. The remembrance has gone as quickly as it came. But EMMA wonders if it still is there, somewhere. And she suspects that it will return.]

GERHARDT

I'm sorry? I said, do you do anything around here?

EMMA

Yes, Mother–I mean . . . *[She laughs at herself]* Sorry. Yes. I used to play tennis.

GERHARDT

Are you any good?

EMMA

I started playing at five o'clock every morning–

GERHARDT

You're kidding, is the sun even up then?

EMMA

Barely. But it was the only time the coach was free. Then I was playing every day. The yard was always filled with people. I'm afraid I get a little too competitive. Until I'm the best.

GERHARDT

I'm like that with baseball. But I love tennis. Would you like to play sometime?

EMMA

You wouldn't get mad if I beat you?

GERHARDT

[He laughs]

I'm afraid I'd beat you.

EMMA

You needn't worry. *[GERHARDT looks at her. A little in shock. A little in admiration.]* Earle Combs was from here. 'Played baseball here and then for the New York Yankees. Have you heard of Earle Combs?

GERHARDT

Yes, I've heard of Earle Combs. He played for the Yankees. He played with Babe Ruth and Lou Gehrig–"Murderer's Row."

EMMA

He went to school here.

GERHARDT

At your university?

EMMA

Don't call it "mine." *[They both laugh.]*

[The lights change again. HARRIET and CHILD Emma Watts stand as in a spelling bee. This is again something of the past, lingering in the house; forever reacquainting itself with EMMA. Or is it happening for the first time?]

HARRIET

University. U-n-i-v-e-r-c-i-t-y. University. [A VOICE explains this is incorrect. CHILD stands and spells:]

CHILD

University. U-n-i-v-e-r-s-i-t-y. University. [The VOICE explains that the CHILD is the winner. There is much applause. HARRIETT runs and hugs the CHILD, Emma.]

HARRIET

Emma, you were so good! I am so glad you won! I should have known, there's no "city" in University! [The two girls laugh]

CHILD

Would you like to see my new doll house I got for Christmas? You haven't seen it yet.

HARRIET

Is it like the one at the Turo Infirmary Fair?

CHILD

It is a perfect copy. Inside and out. We'll pretend that we both live there! Just you and me.

HARRIETT

Oh, yes, let's pretend!

CHILD

"Pretend:"

HARRIETT and CHILD

P-R-E-T-E-N-D! Pretend! [The girls squeal with delight and go running off. The lights change back]

GERHARDT

You don't even pretend to like the university, do you?

EMMA

In the winters of my life I've looked out my window and its intruding presence blocked my view across the street. The summer leaves would at least hide it for me. But now it is autumn and those leaves will fall. And I must close the drapes again. I will not pretend to care for arrogance nor rudeness.

GERHARDT

Why not?

EMMA

Why not arrogance or why not rudeness?

GERHARDT

You are a piece of work. Tell me . . . do you have a . . . significant other? *[EMMA looks at him with confusion.]* Are you . . . seeing anyone? Engaged? Married?

EMMA

No.

GERHARDT

Is there a boyfriend?

EMMA

I should ask you the same things.

GERHARDT

Not married, and no boyfriend. *[She does not laugh]* But . . . I was married once. Divorced. Then I started seeing someone pretty seriously and we broke up–it was worse than the divorce!

EMMA

I am sorry.

GERHARDT

Has there ever been one that you really cared about? That really cared about you?

[The lights change again. We hear and see MARY, the same as before.]

EMMA

"Cares about me?"

MARY

Do you really think he cares about you? Why should you be any different? Listen to me, dear. He treats all his students the same. You are no different.

GERHARDT

[Completely unaware of the remembrance and sounds of MARY Watts.]

The difference between men and women is that you never hear men gossiping, never see them jealous, hysterical. Plotting. Listening to other men behind their backs. Having "the vapors." You always know where you stand with men. But women . . . Lately I've come to believe they're all bitches.

MARY

You are no different. Emma. Emma, are you listening to me? You are no different.

GERHARDT

But I don't know. You don't seem like that. You seem different.

[The voice of MARY becomes more distant. As though leaving the room, the house, and returning from where it emerged.]

MARY

You are no different!

GERHARDT

Miss . . . Miss . . . Are you all right?

EMMA

[Aware that her mother is gone, she takes on an offended countenance.]

Is it the custom from where you come to speak in such a manner?

GERHARDT

I'm sorry?

EMMA

Such vile language. I am . . . surprised . . . I thought you to be such an educated man . . .

GERHARDT

What did I say?

EMMA

[Moving away from him, now suddenly uncomfortable with his presence.]

That word. "That women were . . ."

GERHARDT

What? Bitc—*[The immediate forceful stare that EMMA gives him, silences him]*

EMMA

That type of language has never been permitted in this house!

GERHARDT

[Moving away from her now, like a small reprimanded child.]

Forgive me . . .

EMMA

It may be best for you to leave, Dr. Gerhardt. *[She moves to the door to show him out.]*

GERHARDT

What? For saying "bitch?"

EMMA

I am not a sailor, Dr. Gerhardt. I am a lady. I will show you out—

GERHARDT

No, please. Please. For surely a lady exercises forgiveness. I am sorry. *[But he has been given permission to inspect the house–she is the stranger. Isn't she?]* Who are you really?

EMMA

"To thine own self be true and thus as the day follows the night thou can'st not be false to any other man."

GERHARDT

Are you a student at the University?

EMMA

It has been years since I was in school, Dr. Gerhardt.

GERHARDT

I bet you never graduated from this University.

EMMA

You are correct.

GERHARDT

Ha! I thought as much!

EMMA

I attended Vassar.

GERHARDT

Oh. *[Now suddenly he is uncomfortable in her presence.]* With honors no doubt?

EMMA

Of course.

GERHARDT

You graduated Vassar. I should have known.

EMMA

Why would I graduate? For a woman at that time graduation was rather meaningless. Most girls went to college to find a husband. My parents had other plans.

GERHARDT

So, you returned here? To watch the university across your street grow. *[To test her:]* And when the university president asked you what you wanted for your house, you said, . . .?

EMMA

Bob Martin was a fine man. He brought national acclaim to your University.

GERHARDT

Oh. Now it's mine, is it?

EMMA

The truth is that not everyone can be bought with a price.

GERHARDT

Can't they?

EMMA

No.

GERHARDT

Everyone I know can.

EMMA

Maybe you need to get some fresh air and exercise. *[GERHARDT bursts into laughter]* What?

GERHARDT

I probably do need to get out more. But I just think everyone has his price.

EMMA

Men maybe. Maybe, too, that's where men and women are different? Not me. Especially when it comes to someone's home. I'm not selling.

GERHARDT

No. You're buying. The question now is, What price will you pay to buy off the destruction of your house?

EMMA

You can make a home. You cannot buy one.

GERHARDT

[He does not know now why she is so insistent]

I do not believe in ghosts.

EMMA

You didn't see my mother just a while ago?

GERHARDT

Did you?

EMMA

Yes. And you didn't hear her?

GERHARDT

No. Did you?

EMMA

[She wonders if he is telling the truth.]

Everyone must have their own ghosts then. But you see me.

GERHARDT

Yes. Why? Are you a ghost?

EMMA

No! Are you?

GERHARDT

No.

EMMA

Good. *[She walks around and gets her breath. We hear the sound of the horseshoes.]* You don't question that you see me?

GERHARDT

What is this all about? *[Horseshoes again]* Who is playing horseshoes?

EMMA

I'm just wondering why you see me. No one else does. *[She has not forgotten his question.]* No.

MARY

[Only her voice]

He doesn't see you. He may see your Father's money . . .

GERHARDT

No?

EMMA

No, there is no boyfriend.

GERHARDT

[His face ignites a smile that cannot be hidden.]

You infuriate me! *[He laughs]* I'm glad.

EMMA

And you were wrong about the photograph. Lots of people would say that you have every reason to have your portrait made.

GERHARDT

Ah, . . . what a kind remark. *[He looks at her now with affection]* And who are they? *[He is suddenly maudlin]*

EMMA

I can't give you their names.

GERHARDT

Ha!

EMMA

Save one.

GERHARDT

And who might that be?

EMMA

"Whom."

GERHARDT

[Playing along]

"Whom" then?

EMMA

Emma Watts.

GERHARDT

[Silent at first, then:]

Thank you.

EMMA

You're welcome.

GERHARDT

[With disappointment]

I'm so much older than you. Where were you twenty years ago when I was so young and green and eager to get married?

EMMA

I was here.

GERHARDT

[Disappointed that she insists on playing this game]

Yes, of course. Trapped behind these great walls. There is a world out there.

EMMA

I've seen the world.

GERHARDT

Oh, really?

EMMA

I've seen Europe. France. England. I attended a garden party at Buckingham Palace at invitation of the King.

GERHARDT

Is that right?

EMMA

Have you?

GERHARDT

Attended a garden party? *[He laughs at the idea.]* I left my parasol at the cleaners.

EMMA

You are making fun? You don't believe in garden parties?

GERHARDT

I believe in them. For women. Garden parties and tea parties.

EMMA

As many men were there.

GERHARDT

Oh, really? *[For what kind of men would attend such a thing?]*

EMMA

You are so strange.

GERHARDT

Really?

EMMA

I would have thought an architect would die to see Buckingham Palace. The Tower of London. St. Paul's . . . To my mind the English gardens are nearer perfection than those of any country.

GERHARDT

I wouldn't know. I've never been to Europe.

EMMA

I'll be jiggered.

GERHARDT

I haven't heard that expression in a while.

EMMA

You must see Florence.

GERHARDT

But I plan to . . .

EMMA

When?

GERHARDT

Someday.

EMMA

I hope you do. And when you do, you must see Venice!

GERHARDT

Perhaps you could go with me, show me around?

EMMA

I am an unmarried lady. It would not do to have a traveling companion. If it were a man, there would be great scandal in the community. And if it were a woman, there would be whispers.

GERHARDT

So, you travel alone. To please society?

EMMA

Yes. No, Mother and I traveled together. But . . .*[She remembers traveling alone. She is confused.]* Yes.

GERHARDT

When is it, do you think, that we stop living for society and start living for ourselves?

EMMA

I don't know. We must be accountable to someone.

GERHARDT

When did you start traveling abroad?

EMMA

With my parents.

GERHARDT

Where did you go?

EMMA

Switzerland, Germany . . .

GERHARDT

Germany?

EMMA

Before the War, of course.

GERHARDT

Before the Second World War. Of course!

EMMA

Don't be absurd. *[Pause]* The First War, of course.

GERHARDT

[He laughs]

Of course. The Great War. You are so different . . .

[We hear the voice of MARY Watts]

MARY

You are no different! No different . . .

EMMA

There. Didn't you hear that? *[We hear only the sound of the horseshoes again.]*

GERHARDT

What?

MARY

He doesn't love you. He is just using you. You're young and innocent. He's playing with you, don't you know?

EMMA

No! No! He loves me!

GERHARDT

Who? Who?

MARY

[Entering, bringing the night of EMMA's party]

Your Father and I have given you everything!

EMMA

Then why is he never home?

MARY

Because of the cattle farms in Texas. He can only manage them there.

EMMA

Mother, do you really think he just works the cattle there? [There is a frozen silence.]

MARY

We will talk no more of it. He's home now and he's waiting, and so is everyone else. Your Father has gone to a lot of trouble and expense on this party. And he's brought you back a beautiful new doll—although it's a surprise. [She fusses over Emma's dress.] Now then, I forgive you. You've never looked lovelier. White . . . Someday it will be your wedding dress, and we will stand here, and speak of more pleasant things.

EMMA

I am going to marry him, Mother!

MARY

Emma!

EMMA

You cannot stop me. I have my own money Grandmother left me. I will return to Germany-

MARY

I forbid it!

EMMA

Why can't you be happy for us! He loves me! Don't you understand? I know that I am no great beauty. But he makes me beautiful. He paints me beautiful. [She walks away from her, turns her back, as if at a mirror.] He sees ME.

MARY

He doesn't see you. He may see your Father's money. You have always been a faithful daughter!

EMMA

When I follow your orders, yes! When I do as I'm told! But when will my life be my own, Mother? When will I have a party for ME!! . . . [There is a knock at the door.]

MARY

I wanted to spare you this. But you might as well know now as later. Your artist friend will never marry you—

EMMA

He will!

MARY

Because he is already a married man. [A knock again at the door. In response:] Yes?

MISS HARRIETT

It's Harriett, Mrs. Watts.

MARY

[To EMMA]

I'm sorry. Harriett wishes to see you. Do you feel like seeing Harriett? Shall we let her in? [EMMA, her eyes filling with tears, can only nod her head. MARY affectionately touches her daughter's shoulder. EMMA holds to the hand and they share a moment between mother and daughter, woman to woman. EMMA struggles to speak:]

EMMA

Is the doll really pretty?

MARY

[Wiping her daughters tears]

Oh, yes. [Kisses her. To HARRIETT:] Come in, Harriett!

MISS HARRIETT

[Enters as a lovely teenage woman, dressed for the party. Wise for her years, she senses something is wrong]

I am sorry to disturb you–

MARY

That's quite all right, Harriett.

MISS HARRIETT

–but they are waiting for you, Emma.

MARY

Emma is just a little nervous, that's all. Perhaps you can help calm her spirits. [To EMMA] I am going down to join your Father and our friends. You know your entrance. The music–

EMMA

Yes, mother. I know my entrance. [MARY exits. EMMA runs to a sofa in tears]

MISS HARRIETT

Emma, Emma, don't cry.

EMMA

Harriett, I'm so miserable. I hate my life.

MISS HARRIETT

[Stroking her hair]

Oh, don't say that. This is your night. Every girl in town would die to be you. We would all just die! [She gives her a handkerchief to dry her eyes] You are so beautiful.

EMMA

Harriett, I am so in love it makes me sick.

MISS HARRIETT

Oh, Emma, I am so happy for you!

EMMA

Happy?

MISS HARRIETT

Yes. How wonderful for you!

EMMA

No, you don't understand. Mother and Father have forbidden me to see him–

MISS HARRIETT

No! How awful–how cruel!

EMMA

Dear, Harriett. You would not approve either.

MISS HARRIETT

Of course I–

EMMA

No . . . you don't understand. [MISS HARRIETT is silent] If I tell you, you will hate me, too.

MISS HARRIETT

Never, Emma. [Slowly and with great affection. There is a pure friendship here.] Never.

EMMA

[With nothing to lose]

He is older. And . . . [But she cannot bring herself to admit it. MISS HARRIETT cannot speak] But he loves me. [She bursts into emotion. As if at a mirror looking at herself:] He loves me! And I love him. I adore him!

MISS HARRIETT

Of course, you do . . . Of course, he does!

EMMA

[Falling into a chair, she has not the energy to fight what she knows is true]

He didn't want to hurt me.

MISS HARRIETT

[Nervously looks out the balcony window]

There. There. It's going to be all right. Your parents love you, Emma. They could only be thinking of what is best for you. That's all. They've just forgotten what it was like to be young.

EMMA

They smother me. I feel like a caged bird. I want to fly!

MISS HARRIETT

Now . . . it's a parent's job to smother us. What else would they do? [They start to chuckle]

EMMA

Do you hate me? I wouldn't blame you if you did. I hate myself!

MISS HARRIETT

For what? For following your heart? For falling in love? Do you know how rare that is!

EMMA

[She stands and takes a deep breath]

I know it can never be. But still, it hurts. It hurts ***so much****!*

MISS HARRIETT

They try and make us believe that love is easy. They lie to us when they tell us it is. But Emma, in spite of everything: how fortunate you are to have known it. I love you and shall always love you like my own sister! [The two girls embrace]

EMMA

But Harriette, I have to tell you—

MISS HARRIETT

[Looking deeply into her friend's eyes:]

Not me, you don't [The music starts]

MISS HARRIETT

The music . . . you must get ready.

EMMA

Yes, for display. "Self-reverence, Self-knowledge, Self-control," was our school motto; well, I'm a failure at that, too. I'll never be anything more than an old maid!

MISS HARRIETT

Oh, no. Don't you see? You'll never be an old maid, now. [She gives EMMA a wink and helps her up to the mirror] We're so flushed, your father will swear we're wearing rouge. Or that we've sampled the champagne! [She gets her to laugh] That's better. After all, you made a choice, and a good one. You're headed to Vassar, for Pete's sake! And I just bet, your special someone is out there—somewhere–thinking of you tonight. And, the poor fellow, with a broken heart, too, by gum!

EMMA

By gum!

MISS HARRIETT

You look lovely. Super! Oh! [She suddenly remembers and presents EMMA with her nosegay. EMMA exits with MISS HARRIETT behind her; she turns to look at her wise friend and then disappears onto the balcony.]

[MRS. MERRITT enters to find GERHADT by himself, EMMA's debutant evening a long-ago memory that has passed.]

MERRITT

I heard you talking; I thought someone else was in here with you.

GERHARDT

Yes, the . . . *[EMMA is gone. He is not quite sure when she left.]* Just talking to myself, . . . "by gum."

MERRITT

I brought you some beaten biscuits. *[She offers a mason glass jar filled with small beaten biscuits]*

GERHARDT

That was very nice of you. Thank you.

MERRITT

I'll just put them right here for you when you're ready. *[She places the jar on the table]* You holler if you need anything . .

GERHARDT

Yes, I will, thank you. Oh, come to think of it . . . I have a question. "Harriett." Who would that be?

MERRITT

"Harriett?" I don't know.

GERHARDT

There's not a Harriett Somebody living around here?

MERRITT

No. Not that I know. Miss Emma, she used to have a playmate Miss Harriett long ago.

GERHARDT

Is that so? Where is she?

MERRITT

Why she was over there at the nursing home. I think she's still living.

GERHARDT

Never mind.

MERRITT

[Starts to leave, turns. Laughs.]

For a minute I thought . . . I thought I heard Miss Emma in here. Sometimes . . . sometimes I think I hear Miss Emma a walkin' round the house. Just a walkin' like she used to.

GERHARDT

That's pretty scary.

MERRITT

Miss Emma? *[She bursts into laughter at the very thought of such an idea.]* Miss Emma? *[It must truly be the funniest thing she has heard in a long time. How could anyone find Miss Emma scary? She laughs again and then exits laughing].*

GERHARDT

I never knew I was such a comedian. *[To himself, looking at the jar.]* I guess it could have been fruitcake. *[He goes back to working. EMMA enters with a long roll of papers tied with ribbon].*

EMMA

These might be of help to you.

GERHARDT

Where did you go?

EMMA

You're as bad as Mother. She always had me call home after I had arrived. She wrote me every day when I was at Vassar. Always when I left and arrived there, she had me call home to let her know I was there and all right. We had a code. I would call and let it ring once, and then hang up. She would know I had arrived safely.

GERHARDT

You had me scared.

EMMA

Funny you should say that. Sometimes I think this place is haunted.

GERHARDT

You were talking to a "Harriett."

EMMA

Did you see her?

GERHARDT

No. Should I have? Who is she?

EMMA

A friend I had once. *[Of the roll of papers:]* Here, I want you to have these.

GERHARDT

[As he receives them]

What have we here? *[He goes to the center table and opens them]* These couldn't be . . . couldn't be . . . My God! *[He cannot believe his eyes. Can it be possible?]*

EMMA

Father's plans of the house.

GERHARDT

Bingo! Where did you get these? These are the house plans. They must be ancient! I can't believe it. Who gave these to you?

EMMA

They were hidden for years. I thought maybe they would help you.

GERHARDT

[We see a joy in him that he has not shown us before.]

Absolutely! But . . . you didn't steal them?

EMMA

[She laughs.]

No.

GERHARDT

Thank you. God Almighty! How can I ever thank you!

EMMA

I see that Mrs. Merritt has made my beaten biscuits. *[She opens the jar]* It is an old recipe. Did you try one?

GERHARDT

[Absorbed in the plans]

No thanks! I've had them before, thank you. I'd like to keep my teeth.

EMMA

You haven't tried one of mine.

GERHARDT

Yours. *[He laughs]* Yes, of course. Of course.

EMMA

Have you ever made beaten biscuits before?

GERHARDT

No, not me.

EMMA

Why is that?

GERHARDT

That's . . . you know, the kitchen. That's for women.

EMMA

Well, are you not into eating? *[She is calmly ferocious]* Here **try one.**

GERHARDT

[He looks at the papers again and figures:]

What the hell–*[Of his thoughtless profanity in her presence:]* –oh, excuse me. Sure, I'll try it. Haven't used the Dental Insurance in a while. *[He bites into one and is quickly surprised.]*
\

EMMA

They are good, aren't they?

GERHARDT

So light . . . fresh. So, this is a beaten biscuit. And your recipe?

EMMA

Yes. Mother taught me . . . I taught Jeanette. I'd be happy to teach you. You must start with the right weather. *[She realizes something about him.]* I think if you tried cooking, you might enjoy it. *[He turns away and forces himself back into the papers.]*

GERHARDT

What happens if the weather is not right?

EMMA

You wait until it is.

GERHARDT

Well, the weather has never been right for me.

EMMA

What does your house look like?

GERHARDT

I live in an apartment.

EMMA

It must be beautiful. As artistic as you must be.

GERHARDT

Actually, it's just a pile of books. And a path to get through.

EMMA

And the kitchen?

GERHARDT

I eat out a lot. I guess it does have a kitchen.

EMMA

[Laughs but with a sweet teasing]

I'm sure if you arranged a vase of flowers it would kill you. *[He does not look up from the papers]* I've always thought it important to have things around that spoke of one's personality. That encouraged feelings of oneself. I loved decorating my house. *[She remembers]* And cooking on autumn days like this. Canning. We would all be together in the kitchen . . . *[It was a happy memory, then saddened]* Of course, it isn't much fun cooking for one. Humans weren't meant to be alone, do you think?

GERHARDT

You were in love once?

EMMA

I am too transparent with you.

GERHARDT

You were hurt. I am sorry.

EMMA

It was a long time ago. He noticed me. He made me feel important. No one had ever done that before—in that way.

GERHARDT

He was an artist?

EMMA

Yes, and a very good one. It started out innocently enough. I had always painted, you see, and Mother insisted he see some of my work. So, I started taking lessons. We spent hours together, and sometimes alone. I don't know. If I had had a daughter, I would not have left her alone . . . And yet I hated my parents for interfering. Hated them for jerking us out of Germany, bringing me back here to the dolls in my dollhouse. It makes no sense.

GERHARDT

Love goes beyond the head. So, you never married.

EMMA

I am not an old maid. A spinster, maybe.

GERHARDT

Is there a difference?

EMMA

A spinster had a choice, but an old maid never had one.

GERHARDT

And you had a choice?

EMMA

If I were a writer, I would have written a happy ending. He was a painter, and he painted it.

GERHARDT

He painted you?

EMMA

We paint the masterpieces of our lives by the circumstances that surround us, often against our wills. Besides, he had a wife.

GERHARDT

Oh.

EMMA

And you? You said you had married. Was it out of love?

GERHARDT

Love . . . no, lust, maybe. I don't know. You have to really love yourself before you can love someone else. And I don't mean in a selfish, conceited way. . My therapist says I need to get in touch with my "feminine side." *[He laughs.]*

EMMA

What does that mean?

GERHARDT

It means I need to make beaten biscuits in the kitchen. And like it.

EMMA

I hope that someday you fall madly, passionately in love. And it doesn't destroy your world.

GERHARDT

Is that what happened? It destroyed your world?

EMMA

Yes. It was a fragile one, but the only one I knew.

GERHARDT

[Taking another biscuit from the jar]

These can be habit forming. So light . . .*[He takes a bottle of pills from his backpack, drowns a few down with a bottle of water]*

EMMA

What are those?

GERHARDT

Something for the nerves. I've had quite a time lately. Stress, I guess. The doctors prescribed a long rest. And what do I do? Take this job. *[Turning the pages of the plans.]* More fuel to the fire. But the extra bonus I could not afford to ignore.

EMMA

Money. I was always at work keeping it. Making sure there was enough to last . . . I suppose that was what Father was doing in Texas while Mother and I waited at home. It came with a heavy price.

GERHARDT

At least he came home. 'You ever wonder . . . *[He pauses]* . . . if there was someone in his life there . . . in Texas?

EMMA

I certainly hope so.

GERHARDT

Shame on you! *[But pleased]* You surprise me.

EMMA

Everyone is entitled to some happiness.

GERHARDT

[Of the plans:]

These are great. Such detail. *[Of her father:]* So, after his death, what became of the Texas farms and cattle?

EMMA

It was the year after we returned from Europe. Mother managed them. And the oil, what oil there was. And then it was my turn.

GERHARDT

I have an old flame from college from Texas. She's been hounding me about going to our reunion next week. She is cousin to the Johnsons. You know, Lyndon B. and all?

EMMA

Yes. He visited me here.

GERHARDT

At Elmwood?

EMMA

Yes. We had common interests in Texas and family ties.

GERHARDT

Well, aren't you just the little Yellow Rose of Texas?

EMMA

I love yellow roses. *[GERHARDT quickly busies himself with the papers.]* Don't you?

GERHARDT

[It is unburdening when he admits to her:]

Yes . . .

EMMA

It's all right. *[She laughs. He laughs.]*

GERHARDT

They are glorious!

EMMA

[Glowing with an appreciation for his interests.]

We have such beautiful roses in the garden. *[She stops herself to think and reflect.]* Have . . . had . . . *[She dismisses the confusion]* Why don't you go?

GERHARDT

[Suddenly hurt.]

You want me to leave?

EMMA

Of course not, you noodle. The college reunion! Why don't you go to it?

GERHARDT

I don't keep ties with the past.

EMMA

You should go. It would be great to see old friends.

GERHARDT

[He hesitates]

Would you go with me?

EMMA

Me?

GERHARDT

It's about five hours. We could go and have dinner, and I'd drive you back . . .*[She is silent]* And then, maybe not. Sorry. I get carried away. That's the way I am. I should have known you wouldn't want to go with me.

EMMA

No, no! It's not that I wouldn't want to go with you.

GERHARDT

What then?

EMMA

I just haven't been out of this house in so long. *[She stops]* Yet I've been to Europe. When was that?

GERHARDT

Not too long ago?

EMMA

No, I haven't been yet. And yet I have been, long ago. That doesn't make any sense, does it?

GERHARDT

No . . .

EMMA

Mother was here, and yet that was long ago. I've lived here without her, for a long time . . .

GERHARDT

[Of his pills]

Maybe you need a few of these. It helps cut the edge.

EMMA

Sometimes it seems like all of this is past. That I don't live here now at all, that I lived here long ago. What do you know about Emma Watts?

GERHARDT

She was a nice old lady who loved her big old house. They were the same age, she and the house.

EMMA

"*Old* lady?"

GERHARDT

She died years ago. Left a trust to keep the house up.

EMMA

Then I . . . *[She tries to comprehend it. When she does, she is not frightened, but almost relieved].* Then maybe that explains it. 'Explains a lot of things.

GERHARDT

What's that?

EMMA

I *am* a ghost.

GERHARDT

You convinced me.

EMMA

You still don't think I'm who I say I am, do you? And you say that who I think I am is long gone. One of us is lying and one of us is telling the truth.

GERHARDT

"I think she doth protest too much."

EMMA

What reason would I have to lie about who I am? I know who I am. I know my life–it gets played over and over again like a phonograph . . . that's it!

GERHARDT

We don't have phonographs anymore.

EMMA

Yes, of course. A record player.

GERHARDT

[Sarcastically]

Never mind.

EMMA

If I'm not who I say I am, how do you explain those plans? How did I know where they were?

GERHARDT

I don't know. How did you know?

EMMA

Father told me. Just last week . . . no, last– It has been, "a long time ago."

GERHARDT

Ghosts are scary, and you can see through them.

EMMA

Do I scare you?

GERHARDT

I told you, no.

EMMA

Can you see through me?

GERHARDT

Completely.

EMMA

Yes?

GERHARDT

I can see through the people-pleaser on the outside to the woman on the inside. Yes. To that person that you are afraid to share.

EMMA

You can, can't you? You can see right through me. And I can see right through you, Dr. Gerhardt.

GERHARDT

Oh, you can?

EMMA

I think you took this job to find yourself. And this old place is going to help you do that.

GERHARDT

What? So, I've "lost" myself? Is that it? My feminine side? I'm some sort of a lost soul? *[She says nothing, but sees right through him. And the longer her silence, the more the rage rises within him.]* What are you, a Psych major? I never should have told you about the pills. Now, that's between the two of us, understand? No one else needs to know that–

EMMA

I told you, I'm Emma Watts–

GERHARDT

Yeah, Yeah, and I'm Abe Lincoln. If you're up for the theatre tonight, perhaps we could get a BOOTH together–I'm sure I'd get a BANG out of it. *[He goes to the grandfather clock.]*

EMMA

You're trying to be funny again—*[To help him with the clock]* There are keys in the face. Just put them in and wind—

GERHARDT

I know how to do this, thank you! *[But he is clumsy with it and cannot figure it out. EMMA finds the key and winds the clock.]*

EMMA

Like this. It is really very easy.

GERHARDT

[With bristling anger]

If you're a ghost, why aren't you keeping people like me away?

EMMA

That sounds a little Noel Coward . . .

GERHARDT

[He moves the hands of the clock and lets them chime.]

Well, maybe we need a little Noel Coward. Yes, you should be moaning and groaning with chains and all–

EMMA

I might just do that.

GERHARDT

Come clean, will you? It's getting a little old.

EMMA

You said I was. Old. A little old lady. *[Of the clock:]* You are an hour behind.

GERHARDT

[Ignoring her]

We set the clocks back an hour this weekend. "Fall back, Spring forward." But you wouldn't know about that would you? For you it just stands still! *[He sets the pendulum in motion.]* Emma Watts is dead and buried in the town cemetery. Are you telling me that you are her?

EMMA

She. "Are you telling me that you are SHE?" Yes. And if there is anyone with reason to get angry it is not you.

GERHARDT

You are wrong. It is me!

EMMA

It is I!

GERHARDT

If you are Miss Emma, then what do you have to be angry about? You've been given everything you ever wanted on a silver platter!

EMMA

Silver platters tarnish easily.

GERHARDT

Good reason to keep it undercover, hidden away, in the dark. This old house of yours could use some airing out. What good is it doing anyone?

EMMA

And what good are you doing, Dr. Gerhardt? This old house is one of the finest houses in Richmond.

GERHARDT

WAS! No one has the money or interest to keep it up! Not even you, whoever you are! You know . . . *[He gets his breath]* You know, you really ought to thank me–

EMMA

Oh, really?

GERHARDT

Tearing this place down is the best thing that could happen to you, to any of us, to the whole town!

EMMA

"*Tearing down*?" *[She had never even entertained the possibility of this.]* You plan to . . .

GERHARDT

Yes. Before it falls down. *[He closes the clock.]* Oh! Get off it! You knew it all the time . . .

EMMA

I thought you said you were an architect. I thought architects built things . . . not tore things down. All this time I thought–you can't be serious. Tear down a house like this! Are you insane?

GERHARDT

Isn't that what they do around here: tear down old historic things? No one complains. Nobody cares about your damn house! It will make one hell of a parking lot!

EMMA

You are cruel!

GERHARDT

You are naive.

EMMA

I am not!

GERHARDT

[Rolling up the plans, he stuffs them in his backpack.]

I have a preliminary meeting in the morning, and I will present my plans for the new parking facility and Student Life Center. To be built where we stand right now.

EMMA

You will not get away with this!

GERHARDT

'You going to sic your collies on me? Who is going to stop me?

EMMA

Please . . .

GERHARDT

Who!

EMMA

Me!

GERHARDT

I'm scared. Good night, "Miss Emma." *[GERHARDT starts to exit but we hear O'NEIL. He stands to the side in the doorway.]*

O'NEIL

'You all right?

GERHARDT

Oh! It's you. Mad as hell, that's all. She infuriates me!

O'NEIL

Is everything all right?

GERHARDT

Oh, this young actress . . . *[He turns around but EMMA is gone]* . . . this . . . Not surprising. Ghosts just up and vanish when they want to, don't they?

O'NEIL

What do you mean?

GERHARDT

[Scratching his head again, sighs, laughs.]

Could all of this just be my subconscious?

O'NEIL

Let's face it. You are also a woman inside. God made you that way. Don't apologize. No one looks better in tights than you.

GERHARDT

What?

O'NEIL

[We see now that he has been talking on the phone.]

Hi, Jerry. I'll be right with you. *[Back on his phone.]* I'm pretty much free for a couple hours, what do you say we go downtown for a drink? No? All right. I'll call you later. 'Love you. *[He ends the call on his phone. To GERHARDT:]* What's up?

GERHARDT

She just infuriated me, that's all.

O'NEIL

Who?

GERHARDT

That girl I was telling you about yesterday. The one who keeps saying she's Emma Watts. The one who looks like her. I don't know what's wrong with me. I'm old enough to be her father. Her grandfather! Well, maybe. I never thought I'd be the type to fall for such a young woman—

O'NEIL

Paul, you sure you want to go through with this tomorrow? You know, we could wait a week or so. A month. It will be Christmas break soon and–

GERHARDT

What do you mean? Why would we want to wait? I'm ready for tomorrow, and with a few adjustments I'm all ready for the final presentation Monday morning.

O'NEIL

It's just . . . Paul, I might as well be honest with you. I did a little research– it's my job–and I found out about your problems . . .

GERHARDT

[This he did not need. He should have known it could not have been hidden]

What do you mean?

O'NEIL

I think you know. It's just between the two of us.

GERHARDT

Who else knows?

O'NEIL

Nobody else. And nobody needs to find out—

GERHARDT

It's just stress. The doctors said stress—

O'NEIL

Sure it is. And you've been under a lot of stress, we all have. And with your back-ground . . .

GERHARDT

Background?

O'NEIL

I had to do a mental health background search on your family–

GERHARDT

Good God! Not that . . .

O'NEIL

Jerry, the human psyche is my field. I'm one to believe genetics can be overridden. Now, I'm telling you, no one needs to know. I'm just concerned that you pace yourself carefully, that's all.

GERHARDT

You know about the breakdowns, then.

O'NEIL

And the suicide attempts.

GERHARDT

[Humiliated, he turns away to the staircase.]

I'm better now. I really am. I really did see that girl—

O'NEIL

It is not uncommon for the psyche to get shattered. Maybe she represents a part of you that is missing.

GERHARDT

Women have not been a success point in my life.

O'NEIL

And you will always be chasing after the wrong type until you come to terms with that stranger within you. Especially after the relationship you had with your mother.

GERHARDT

You really have done your research.

O'NEIL

Look, my intentions are completely selfish. I have a lot riding on this. We all need to succeed and you are our man.

GERHARDT

Thanks. Thanks, Charles. You are a good friend.

O'NEIL

What' you got there?

GERHARDT

These? *[Of the plans]* The original house plans.

O'NEIL

[This is a revelation to him.]

Where did you get them?

GERHARDT

Oh, . . . they must have been around here somewhere–

O'NEIL

[He is overjoyed. It is almost unbelievable.]

These are the original house plans.

GERHARDT

That's what I said.

O'NEIL

There are no original house plans.

GERHARDT

Sure, there are. There's bound to be copies–

O'NEIL

No. No, Paul, there's not. We've inventoried every inch of this place. They don't exist. Where did you get these?

GERHARDT

You'd never believe it.

O'NEIL

[Taking out his PalmPilot, he checks his schedule.]

Come go with me: we'll get a cup of coffee. This PalmPilot is a life saver. Let me check my calendar: I have about forty-five minutes tonight. I love this thing; I can write all my notes. 1024 KB. . . .

GERHARDT

Aren't you a little worried about all of these new devices?

O'NEIL

What do you mean?

GERHARDT

It reminds me of the radio and television. They became the norm, but also added expenses. Before you know it, everyone will have to have all of these new-fangled gadgets of yours and many can't afford them. Every parent will be sending their child to school with one, just to prove that their child can have it better than they did. *[A moment of ponder, then:]*

O'NEIL

Oh, that'll never happen. *[They start to exit but his cell phone rings.]* Oh, before I forget it, I need to get your E-mail address in my BlackBerry. *[Into the phone]* Yes, hello? Yes, Dr. Gerhardt is here with me right now. Yes. *[He looks to GERHARDT for reassurance]* Yes, everything is on schedule . . .

ACT TWO

Scene One

It is Saturday morning. The room is full of people wearing name tags, mingling around, sharing coffee: they are the COMMITTEE MEMBERS. GERHARDT stands next to the center table with a large covered drawing. Folding chairs have been set up. O'NEIL goes to the side of GERHARDT and greets the committee.

O'NEIL

I think we are all here. Shall we be seated, and we will begin. *[Everyone finds a seat. The room calms down and O'NEIL continues. The MEMBERS are eager and willing. They find every word enjoyable and exhilarating: nothing can go wrong.]* One great University. One great house. All of these years, they have resided just opposite each other as neighbors, divided by a simple road. We now begin to look at the possibility of bridging that gap. As many of you have already met Dr. Gerhardt, I believe a formal introduction does not seem necessary. Allow me to suffice in saying that we are all very pleased to have someone of Dr. Gerhardt's caliber and expertise helping us approach what at one time seemed an impossible development for our university. *[There is a jovial response from the crowd.]* Although it has been a very long time in coming, I think we are all glad that our wait has made available to us this brilliant professor of the New York Academy of the Architectural Arts–a wait worth waiting for. Without any more need for adornment than his reputation and body of work show for themselves, I welcome, to present to us a small preview of Monday's presentation: Dr. Paul Gerhardt. *[The COMMITTEE MEMBERS applaud. The excitement and congenial laughter in the crowd is beyond words or reason.]*

GERHARDT

Thank you, Dr. O'Neil. It is a pleasure to be with you in Kentucky. I've been told that Kentucky is known for its Bourbon, horses, and beautiful women. Dr. O'Neil had to of course twist my arm to come! *[Everyone laughs as a sign of acceptance and welcome.]* After months of careful study of this area and your university, I feel very good about the proposals that I bring to you. And although I know that this grand old house has been an austere place of beauty for your community, I am comforted to discover that Mr. Watt's plans were not complete in themselves but only in the foundation for what is to be built upon this land called "Elmwood." The realization of a dream. *[He unveils the drawing. It is of a large modern building. The sound of the game of horseshoes in the background. Then a strange, disturbing groan. Thinking it himself:]* Someone must have missed breakfast. *[Expecting raucous laughter, there is none. He continues:]* In this drawing you will see the magnificent edifice that will compliment your university. A student center of such advancement that you will be the envy of every university and college in the state. *[Another loud groan. The front doors fly open. The MEMBERS are oblivious to this, so he ignores it.]* A parking garage to make accessibility for all students much easier and more efficient. The appearance of which convinces the viewer that it has been there all along. *[O'NEIL gets up and closes the door. It flies open again, and he carefully shuts it once more. We hear the groan and loud clanging of chains]* In this next drawing you will see the preservation and restoration of . . . gothic architecture of the neoclassical—Ah . . . Are there questions that you would like for me to answer? *[The MEMBERS look at each other with puzzlement.]* I mean, I know that there has been great concern about the loss of this old house. With the exact measurements of this building from the original plans, I can now assure you that many prized pieces of the interior can be reused. In fact, I have chosen to keep the entire front mantel that you see here in this room intact and as the focal point in the lobby of our Center.

[EMMA enters with two brooms extended out and covered by a white sheet, shoes at the end of each broom handle, with her head leaning backwards she attempts the appearance of "floating" horizontally across the room.]

COMMITTEE MEMBER

[Oblivious to EMMA's comic presence, raises a hand]

I have a question.

GERHARDT

[Distracted by EMMA but attempting to control the meeting]

Yes . . . yes, go ahead, please.

COMMITTEE MEMBER

How have you addressed the issue of handicapped accessibility?

GERHARDT

Yes, of course. The codes must be met to the safety and convenience of all persons–

COMMITTEE MEMBER

The integrity of the appearance must be kept at all costs, but not to the detriment of students and their education. After all, that is our sole purpose. And there is nothing worse than these great ramps of concrete garnishing the lawns of historical sites—

COMMITTEE MEMBER

How can elevators be installed? They can't be visible to the exterior of the house. It will give the appearance of bastard architecture, piecemeal work!

[There is much agreement from the Committee. EMMA groans loudly, but the MEMBERS drown her out with approval of the suggestion. EMMA's sheet and brooms dismantle themselves to her frustration and she exits unseen by anyone. GERHARDT cannot believe that no one saw this.]

GERHARDT

[In a desperate whisper to O'NEIL]

Tell me they did not see that!

O'NEIL

See what?

GERHARDT

"See what?" That ridiculous display of theatrics!

O'NEIL

I just closed the door. I thought the wind–

GERHARDT

No, no. Her.

O'NEIL

[Very puzzled]

I didn't see anyone–

GERHARDT

Thank God–*[EMMA enters, takes GERHARDT's cell phone from the table and exits examining it. GERHARDT has tried to retrieve it but misses. He points to EMMA for O'Neil to see. Heavily whispering:]* There! She took my phone! *[He looks to O'NEIL who has seen nothing]* Are you blind?

O'NEIL

[Now worried]

Are you all right?

COMMITTEE MEMBER:

Have you thought about the great garden in the back of the house? Could it not provide an arboretum for the University? *[There is much debate between the MEMBERS. Suddenly a cell phone rings a particular melody, another rings, and then another joins in, etc. until there is a symphony of phone ringing and MEMBERS answering them, turning them off, etc. The tunes include "Ode To Joy," "The William Tell Overture," and for one very prim and proper little spinster, "The Stripper."*

[EMMA appears again with a long silk scarf that she floats around the face of GERHARDT who fights the distraction. He grabs the scarf, pretending to use it in the presentation.]

COMMITTEE MEMBER:

Dr. Gerhardt? The entrances? Will the main entrance be from Lancaster? And if not, from where? And handicapped accessibilities . . .

GERHARDT

As you know, the original entrance of traffic to the house–although never paved,– *[Against his will, he uses the scarf to demonstrate the curving of the road, and several find this amusing and laugh]* –was from the Lancaster Avenue. Keeping with that tradition, the flow of traffic will continue straight from University Drive–*[There is much approval of this. But GERHARDT keeps looking at O'NEIL who gives him no awareness of EMMA's presence]* University Drive . . . Uh, yes, now, where was I?

O'NEIL

The traffic flows from University Drive . . .

GERHARDT

Yes, with entrances from Barnes Mill as you can see in the drawing here–*[EMMA has taken the drawing, and begins floating it up and down, GERHARDT fights to hold on to it. The MEMBERS find this funny and laugh; GERHARDT tries to cover up with humorous gestures as well.]* And ah, all of our assumptions about this have been up and down, up and down over the years, yes? Uh, *[As he tries to point]* –and there is a pedestrian overpass–*[The COMMITTEE is very pleased with this. A problem for years is now resolved.]*

COMMITTEE MEMBER

But the trees. Are you taking all the old trees down?

COMMITTEE MEMBER

The trees need to go! They have been a hazard for years, just crying out for a lawsuit. We don't need those old limbs falling on students in wheelchairs, professors on the way to class–

[EMMA takes a pitcher of water from the table]

GERHARDT

[To EMMA]

Oh, no you don't! *[He leaps over the table and as it turns over with him, he passes out from the strain and falls on his back].*

O'NEIL

[As others attend GERHARDT, he goes to his phone.]

No need for alarm. I'll call 911!

[The lights fade out. We hear the town clock strike. The grandfather clock strikes. There is the forever sound of horseshoes being played. The day has passed. It is dark outside. Night. When the lights fade up again, we see GERHARDT sitting on the floor stage center with a glass and bottle of Scotch. He takes out a pocket knife and cuts the hospital bracelet from his wrist. EMMA enters.]

EMMA

Are you mad at me? *[GERHARDT does not answer.]* I wouldn't blame you for not talking to me–*[GERHARDT tries to ignore her.]*–For never talking to me again. *[No response]* Do you hate me?

GERHARDT

We can't see you. Can't hear you. *[He takes a deep breath and then a drink.]*

EMMA

Do you hate me? Do you? Say something.

GERHARDT

[He explodes]

YES! I hate you and I'm mad as hell with you!

EMMA

There's no need to get emotional. If it makes you feel any better, I'm very ashamed of myself.

GERHARDT

And you should be! *[He takes another breath and another drink]* Your behavior was inexcusable!

EMMA

I know. I'm sorry.

GERHARDT

It was stupid. It was childish! You who pride yourself on being the best, you can't even be a good ghost! It was not even funny!

EMMA

Okay. I said I was sorry.

GERHARDT

They all think I'm crazy now. I will probably lose my job. Lose my career! I have never been so humiliated. It was inexcusable. And what's worse it was so . . . so damn <u>uncreative</u>! *[He is exhausted from the encounter]* Yes, I'm mad at you. *[He calms down. Thinks. Then:]* 'Mad at you for being a ghost.

EMMA

I told you I was.

GERHARDT

I know. I know. What do you expect me to think?

EMMA

You? What about me? I've just come to realize it, too. After all these years.

GERHARDT

What? So, you are saying, what? That it's more exasperating for you? You've always got to be the best. The better. Got to win! Is that it!?

EMMA

No. I never wanted to be a ghost. I don't know how.

GERHARDT

That, my dear, is most obvious. But you are a ghost. Or I have gone off the deep end. Off. Jumped off. *[He makes the sound of diving into water]* No life jacket. Dead. Dead crazy. Lunatic. One way ticket to the Funny Farm, do not pass Go . . . Just like my . . .

EMMA

Just like . . . ?

GERHARDT

My grandmother. My mother. God, I loved them. But they were crazy as loons. No kidding. And I've got their genes. It comes honestly.

EMMA

So you have ghosts in your closet as well.

GERHARDT

Don't EVEN go there . . .

EMMA

Your father . . . How was he? *[GERHARDT does not answer.]* You have his genes, too, don't you?

GERHARDT

That's not much consolation, but thank you. *[There is a silence]* He left us when I was a kid. Never heard from him again. No, I never had anybody at home to call when I arrived safely someplace. *[He takes another drink]* What's it like? On the other side? If there is another side . . . I mean, I can see you. You look real to me. Alive enough. You look–

[HARRIETT appears. She is older now. An attractive young woman. In a suit and gloves. The lights change]

HARRIETT

Emma! Emma! Over here. It's me. Harriett. Harriett McGaughey. Do you remember me?

EMMA

Harriett. Why, hello.

HARRIETT

They told me you had come home–

GERHARDT

You look–

HARRIETT

Great! You look great. I've been keeping up on you through the papers–I've cut out every article. Every one and pasted them in my scrapbook. I am so proud of all your awards. I'm so proud to know you, Emma.

EMMA

Thank you, Harriett. Thank you for that lovely card, and all the letters. I've been meaning to send one to you, too, and congratulate you. You graduated from here at the Teacher's School–

HARRIETT

That's all right–

EMMA

I can't believe how fast the last four years have gone–I kept meaning to write back, but I just never did find the time–

HARRIETT

I understand. How could you with all you were accomplishing. It was silly of me to write you so often, anyway. But you look great. Just super. You're such an accomplished lady. –My family's getting together for a picnic this evening; I'd love for you to join us. Can you? Would you?

EMMA

Oh, I'd love to, but we'll be at the races. . . [We hear friends calling EMMA away]

HARRIETT

[Disappointed but gracious.]

I understand.

EMMA

We simply must get together this summer–

HARRIETT

Yes, of course.

EMMA

Goodbye, Harriett.

HARRIETT

Goodbye, Emma. It was so good to see you. Goodbye.

[HARRIETT disappears and the lights come back. The memory returns to the shadows. Not forgotten; always there.]

GERHARDT

It is so good to see you.

EMMA

I don't know when I've changed this dress. *[She sighs.]* I am a horrible person. Spoiled, yes. And lonely.

GERHARDT

What of your friends?

EMMA

Most of them are dead. *[This does not seem right at first. Her friends are young—but then she remembers.]* Yes . . . that' right.

GERHARDT

What of the others?

EMMA

There was one. But we were in different social circles, and I neglected her. And then when we were older and we needed each other, . . . it was too late.

GERHARDT

So, you just stay inside your house?

EMMA

Yes.

GERHARDT

Don't you find that strange?

EMMA

[After a moment]

Yes.

GERHARDT

I thought your kind went on to heaven. You know: that **big house** in the sky. A home better than this old place.

EMMA

Yes . . . I can't deny that.

GERHARDT

And I can't believe any of it. *[They sit in silence. We hear the horseshoes.]* Do they never stop playing? Listen. *[We hear them again]* A lot of these old Victorian houses on the street rent to fraternities. They must be out in their yards drinking beer and playing. At all hours. You want a drink?

EMMA

I don't drink. Although I had a martini once. *[GERHARDT starts to laugh. EMMA laughs. They laugh together. He refers to the meeting earlier and her antics:]*

GERHARDT

That was one hell of a groan! *[They laugh]* Of course, they were just oblivious to everything. Not one of them could see you. Not even Charles. Where did you learn that trick with the brooms?

EMMA

I saw it in one of the talkies at the Opera house.

GERHARDT

[He stops to get his breath]

God, you are lovely.

EMMA

You embarrass me.

GERHARDT

No, you are. As lovely as . . . the *moonlight sliding down the stair* . . . *[He laughs at himself]* I'm drunk. And you're beautiful.

EMMA

I'm not beautiful.

GERHARDT

Well, I think you are.

EMMA

If so, then you make me that way.

GERHARDT

Thank you. That was a nice thing to say.

EMMA

You're welcome.

GERHARDT

I thought that perhaps you were some plot to throw me off. To sabotage the project. Tamper with my mind–drive me crazy. Humm. Too late. Got there first.

EMMA

"I met a lady in the meads . . ."

GERHARDT

"Full beautiful, a faery's child; Her hair was long, her foot was light, And her eyes were wild . . ."

EMMA

You love poetry, too.

GERHARDT

I once tried to memorize all the sonnets of Shakespeare. *[Suddenly afraid of his careless honestly:]* Now, don't let that out. *[Sarcastically:]* 'Must be my *feminine side coming out.* It's just—*[Referring to the alcohol]* –the spirits. *[He laughs at his choice of words.]* God, I'm an idiot. *[He drinks.]*

EMMA

Mr. Crossfield used to say that it was not a disgrace to be a milkmaid, but it was a disgrace to make bad butter. Why are you so afraid to be who you are? You are an artist, and a good one. Stop worrying about what other people think. If your friends don't like it, well, then they are not the kind of friends worth having. *[MRS. MERRICK enters and sets the table with candles, silverware, napkins, crystal glasses, and returns with two plates of food, and a decanter of wine.]* I thought your drawings were very good.

GERHARDT

How can you say that? Knowing what they will cost you?

MRS. MERRICK

[With a strange look to GERHARDT]

It's none of my business. Uh-uh. None of my business. *[She carries things to the table. Puzzled, GERHARDT laughs it off and drinks.]*

EMMA

"Was it the mat that winked, Or a nervous star? The *moon slides down the stair* to see who's there . . ." You spoke it a few moments ago.

GERHARDT

Emily Dickinson. *[With uneasy thought]* Don't tell me she was a friend of yours?

EMMA

No!

GERHARDT

What? Not in your social class?

EMMA

I didn't know her. I didn't know the Bronte sisters either. I wasn't even born.

GERHARDT

Oh . . . Besides, she never went out of the house *[He looks to EMMA]* . . . too.

EMMA

[Reciting from memory "Returning"]

> "I years had been from home, And now, before the door,
> I dared not open, lest a face I never saw before
> Stare vacant into mine and ask my business there.
> My business,–just a life I left, Was such still dwelling there?
> I fumbled at my nerve, I scanned the windows near;
> The silence like an ocean rolled, and broke against my ear.
> I laughed a wooden laugh that I could fear a door,

Who danger and the dead had faced, But never quaked before.
I fitted to the latch My hand,

[GERHARDT now recites it with her:]

with trembling care, lest back the awful door should spring,
And leave me standing there. I moved my fingers off
As cautiously as glass, And held my ears, and like a thief
Fled gasping from the house."

EMMA

When you can write like that, why go out of the house?

GERHARDT

[Of the poem, he holds his bottle high:]

To all the cowards who couldn't open the door! *[He drinks]*

EMMA

You should eat something. *[She goes to the table and puts some food on a plate.]* How long have you been sitting here?

GERHARDT

All day? Since the meeting. What time is it?

EMMA

The clock struck seven. Or was it eleven? Is there any difference? The clock always strikes. Thank you for setting it again.

GERHARDT

You're welcome. *[He takes another drink]* The clock has struck all day.

EMMA

So, what have you been doing all this time?

GERHARDT

Drinking and thinking. I'm afraid to sleep. I might dream. Indians, you know. *[He winks and drinks.]* Trouble is, I never seem to wake up from the dreams. *[He sighs heavily and runs his fingers through his hair, rolls his head to release the tension in his neck. EMMA moves behind him and rubs his neck; it offers great relief. But he pulls away suddenly. EMMA looks at him for an explanation.]* All we need now is some John Barry music. *[He laughs, but she does not understand.]* Perhaps I'm showing *my* age. But this old place stays the same, doesn't it. Always been here. Elmwood.

EMMA

Not always. Colonel Caperton built a log house here. That was after Patrick Henry chartered the county with Milford as the county seat. John Miller's son bought the log house that stood here and tore it down. And he built for himself a nice brick Federal house.

GERHARDT

What became of that house?

EMMA

Father tore it down to build Elmwood.

GERHARDT

History repeats itself.

EMMA

Come on. *[She helps him up. MRS. MERRICK has left]* I've got supper for you. *[She lights the candles, sits down to the table, and bows her head in silence and prays.*

GERHARDT

[As he eats]

I'm starved. And this looks delicious.

EMMA

I remember cooking in the kitchen. And then I remember it being many years ago. And it's all in the same moment.

GERHARDT

[Of her silent prayer:]

I don't believe in anything.

EMMA

No? I believe in you. You can't keep my house?

GERHARDT

Don't worry. The minute I open my mouth and suggest it come down, they'll tar and feather me and run me out of town. But you know, the next person they get will suggest the same thing. This house has got to come down sooner or later.

EMMA

If anyone is going to take it, I'd rather it be you. *[He is overcome with emotion from this and does not know how to respond. He can barely swallow his food now.]* What's wrong?

GERHARDT

[After a moment, he recovers himself. He smiles.]

I've gone crazy, lost my job, my reputation, but I'm having the greatest meal, in the greatest house, with the most wonderful woman I've ever known. And when she speaks, its poetry.

EMMA

Now the drink is talking.

GERHARDT

Drink will always bring out the truth in a man.

EMMA

[She pours the last drop from the decanter into his glass].

You know what that means?

GERHARDT

No.

EMMA

The last drop is saved for the one you love the most. *[He drinks and eats.]* I want you to do something for me, Jerry. Will you?

GERHARDT

I'll try.

EMMA

Two things. *[She presents an envelope]* Take this to the Manor Nursing Home to Harriett McGaughey. Then I want you to have my priest perform the Eucharist here in the house.

GERHARDT

Your priest? Is he still living?

EMMA

If you ask him, he'll understand. *[She laughs to herself]* He was a very young man then. And he never seemed to age. Have him come and perform the Eucharist. *[She gets up and goes to the phonograph, winds it, and puts the needle down. It plays a lively tune.]* Will you dance with me?

GERHARDT

You? Dance? Oh–don't tell me. You have trophies . . .

EMMA

It's the Cha-cha-cha. You know it. It's very new . . . and very old. *[She laughs.]* See what I mean? It doesn't make any sense. But just the same– *[She dances the steps. Slowly he follows. They dance together. It is fun. They laugh and turn, and move together in the rhythm. As he pulls her close for a turn, they stop. They are caught in each other's stare. She moves away to one side of the table. He moves to the other. He picks up the decanter and pours, a remaining drop, into her glass. A clock strikes midnight.]*

GERHARDT

Are you an illusion? A shadow of a time that was? Or a shadow of *me*, that got lost in the darkness of things? Don't leave me tonight. Please.

EMMA

Jerry . . .

GERHARDT

I have waited all afternoon for you. Just hoping to see you again. Dying to be with you. Hear your voice. Be near you. I'd lost it. Love. I'd forgotten what it felt like. You've brought it back to me. *[He closes his eyes and drinks in the feeling. When he opens them again, he is startled that EMMA is still there, but very pleased and relieved for it.]* Just look at us. From too different times, yet this hidden soul of harmony?

[Reciting Milton from memory]

"And ever against eating Cares,
Lap me in soft Lydian Airs,
Married to immortal verse
Such as the meeting soul may pierce
In notes, with many a winding bout
Of linked sweetness long drawn out."

[He kisses her. When they pull away, they then look at each other for a long time. She puts a hand behind one of the candles and blows out its flame, then takes the other and his hand to lead him up the stairs.]

GERHARDT

[Stopping her half way up the stairs]

I don't want to rush you. Not if you're not ready.

EMMA

It's been a hundred years, believe me, I'm ready. *[She leads him up the stairs with the candlestick guiding the way. The light follows them out.]*

ACT TWO

Scene Two

It is early Sunday afternoon, the next day. O'NEIL enters from the back of the house and calls for GERHARDT. MRS. MERRICK follows him into the room.

O'NEIL

Jerry! Jerry! Dr. Gerhardt!

MRS. MERRICK

Was your dinner all right last night?

O'NEIL

[To MERRICK, confused]

Ah, yes . . . thank you. Jerry!

MRS. MERRICK

Good. 'Course, it's none of my business.

O'NEIL

What?

MRS. MERRICK

Nope. Nope. None of my business. *[As she exits]* This old world has changed. I'm not one to question. No, sirree. No, as long as you folks are happy . . . 'none of my business. Not enough happiness around. Although, you missed church. *[She is gone. GERHARDT appears from the top of the stairs. He is in wrinkled unbuttoned white shirt, with the shirt tail out, and khaki trousers, barefoot, and his hair is tussled. But his face is aglow. Never has he been so happy and at peace. We might not even recognize him.]*

GERHARDT

[In a joyous state]

Good morning, Charles!

O'NEIL

Morning? It's afternoon. We were to have lunch. Where were you?

GERHARDT

Isn't it a wonderful day! *[He stands looking out the window at the landing of the stairs.]* Why did they take the stained-glass window out? It must have been brilliant when the sun came through here.

O'NEIL

I saw your car out front; I thought you might be in here. Where were you last night? You didn't . . . you didn't stay here?

GERHARDT

Actually, Charles I did. How else could I truly get a feel for this place?

You know: that *sense of home.*

O'NEIL

Mrs. Merrick said the police were here last night. That you were digging in the garden?

GERHARDT

They were the nicest young boys. I told them not to worry about it. They didn't know who I was.

O'NEIL

What were you looking for in the middle of the night out there?

GERHARDT

Oh, I am sorry. OH! Yes, after yesterday's meeting. Yes. I am truly sorry, Charles. I guess I've let the trouble of the house coming down and all that get to me. It is a beautiful place. Well, I will see you in the morning. Nine o'clock. I'm sure you have things you need to be doing–*[He ushers O'NEIL to the door.]*

O'NEIL

No, I'm fine. Are you expecting someone?

GERHARDT

No, of course not. Of course not. It's just . . . Perhaps you have a phone call, or messages you haven't checked? You should be playing golf while the weather is nice–

O'NEIL

We were to have played golf right after church.

GERHARDT

Out of the question. Something has come up. You go ahead–

O'NEIL

But–

GERHARDT

[Frantically looking around. To himself:]

Damn it, Charles, she won't show up while you're here!–

O'NEIL

Who? *[GERHARDT looks at him with deep excitement. Finally:]*

GERHARDT

Miss Emma.

O'NEIL

What? *[GERHARDT can only explain with his catlike expression. O'NEIL takes out a pack of cigarettes to light.]* Jerry, you've been working too hard—

GERHARDT

Please, don't smoke.

O'NEIL

Why? "Miss Emma" wouldn't mind.

GERHARDT

Yes, she does.

O'NEIL

Miss Emma smoked.

GERHARDT

No, she didn't.

O'NEIL

I know for a fact that she did. She smoked like a chimney.

GERHARDT

[To himself]

That can't be.

O'NEIL

What?

GERHARDT

[Quick to cover himself:]

Oh, Charles! Don't you know when someone is pulling your leg!

O'NEIL

Oh?

GERHARDT

Please, enjoy your day. I'm fine. I'm just trying to get everything ready for tomorrow.

O'NEIL

I thought you had everything finished–

GERHARDT

Yes, well, I've had an inspiration. I just need some private time to get it all in order. I'm sure you will be pleased. Now, PLEASE, GO!

O'NEIL

You sure you're okay?

GERHARDT

[Pushing him out the door. Quickly:]

I've never been better. I feel great. GO! NO! Wait! *[He grabs him by his tie and pulls him back, producing the letter].* I've got to deliver this. To the Nursing Home. Will you go with me—'help me find it?

O'NEIL

Yeah . . . Sure. But let me drive you . . .

GERHARDT

[Embracing him]

Thank you!

MRS. MERRICK

[Entering from the front doors and sees them embraced.]

Uh-uh, none of my business . . . *[She turns back around and exits. The men look at each other. The lights fade out with the sound of organ music.*

[As the lights come up again, we see MRS. MCGAUGHEY, a frail old woman neatly dressed, playing a small organ. GERHARDT comes and sits in a chair

beside her, and O'NEIL stands. She finishes playing. They applaud politely. It is a room in the Nursing Home.]

O'NEIL

That was lovely. Mrs. McGaughey, you knew my grandmother Lizzie–

MCGAUGHEY

I should say so. Little Charlie . . . Your daddy moved off to California. You grew up there. I remember when they called your daddy "Little Charlie," before he moved off to California. Your grandpa was "Big Charlie." Of course, they're dead now.

O'NEIL

That's right . . . I'm Charlie. Little Charlie.

MCGAUGHEY

No . . .

O'NEIL

Yes—

MCGAUGHEY

No . . . no, no ….*[It dawns upon O'NEIL that perhaps dementia has set in. Sadly, he looks to GERHARDT. Perhaps they are not alone in the room: Alzheimer's?]* Teeny! They called your daddy Little Charlie. They called you "Teeny!"

O'NEIL

[In front of GERHARDT, he is suddenly embarrassed.]

That's right.

GERHARDT

Really?

MCGAUGHEY

You was a teeny itty bitty thing. I remember you. Teeny O'Neil.

GERHARDT

[Holding back the laughter]

They didn't call you Teeny O'Neil?

MCGAUGHEY

They did! *[They laugh together. Only O'NEIL is not amused.]*

O'NEIL

[Explaining to GERHARDT]

I'm the third. Charles III.

MCGAUGHEY

Little Teeny. Why, it's so good to see you. And you all grown up.

O'NEIL

It's good to see you, too. Mrs. McGaughey, I brought a friend with me.

He's been hired by the University. Dr. Paul Gerhardt. He'd like to give you something.

MCGAUGHEY

Give me something? Why, dear, you don't have to give me something. I don't know of anything I need. But thank you just the same. Just having you here is enough. You all grown up. *[To GERHARDT] Teeny's* grandmother and I played for the Episcopal Church. I played the organ and sometimes she'd play the piano.

GERHARDT

Is that right? You were the organist?

MCGAUGHEY

I should say I was. For fifty years. I was the organist of the church. And you are working at the University?

GERHARDT

Yes, I am.

MCGAUGHEY

I went to that University. Back when it was the "Normal School." For school teachers. I graduated from that University. It was a long time ago. There were lots of us became teachers. But they're all dead now.

O'NEIL

I'm sorry.

MCGAUGHEY

No need to be sorry. That's what we're supposed to do, isn't it? After we've lived a good life? But then, some of them went mighty early: the boys in the War . . .

O'NEIL

Paul has brought you a letter—

MCGAUGHEY

[Remembering the War:]

Everyday there would be fewer and fewer in class. Until we closed.

O'NEIL

–from one of your friends.

MCGAUGHEY

Honey, I'm a hundred years old. All my friends are dead.

O'NEIL

Surely not . . .

MCGAUGHEY

Oh, yes. All the people from my time are gone. Governor McCreary, Laura Clay, President Roosevelt, I remember them, all before your time. Before your time.

O'NEIL

Emma Watts . . .

MCGAUGHEY

She's dead, too. Vice President Johnson visited her, you know, and he's dead too. Dr. Martin wanted to buy her house for the university. Did you know that? Yes. *[She laughs]* "How much do you want for your house?" he asked her. She just looked at him and said, "How much you want for your university?" *[She laughs, then]* Yes, he's dead too. He was a big man.

O'NEIL

He was tall—

MCGAUGHEY

Tall and fat! Yes. Mary Pickford. Clark Gable. Irene Dunn . . . there're all dead. Now, Rosemary Clooney of Maysville . . .

O'NEIL

[Agreeing with her]

George Burns. Bette Davis–

MCGAUGHEY

Bette Davis?

O'NEIL

Yes.

MCGAUGHEY

No! Bette Davis is dead? Thank goodness. They should have buried her long ago. They're all dead. Everybody's dead.

GERHARDT

[He looks around.]

You have a lovely house. *[He does not say "room," for he knows this is her home now.]*

MCGAUGHEY

A house is only as lovely as the friends who frequent it.

GERHARDT

Yes, that's true. *[Now then:]* Mrs. McGaughey, I have a letter from Miss Watts.

MCGAUGHEY

Emma? Bless her soul *[Her countenance changes. GERHARDT hands the envelope to her. She takes out the letter and looks at it]* A letter, yes. *[Softly]* Bless her soul. I don't have my reading glasses. We used to call them "cheaters."

GERHARDT

Would you like for me to read it to you?

MRS. MCGAUGHEY

Would you?

GERHARDT

Sure. *[He takes the letter and kneels beside her. Reading from the letter:]*

S. Claus Esquire,
Chimneyland

Dear Santa Claus,

[He is confused. Is this the right letter? He looks to O'NEIL who has no answers. Cautiously he continues to read:] "I know you can bring me anything I want without any trouble. Please give me a dollhouse that is inside and outside like the one I saw at the T—"

MCGAUGHEY

the Turo Infirmary Fair . . .

GERHARDT

Yes . . . I guess it is . . . *[He continues to read:]* "I want it to be like it, inside and outside, and to be completely furnished just like it and to have an upstairs like it with as many rooms as it has and I want it to be a perfect copy of the one I saw. –If you don't want me to have it please give me other things.–Answer my letter directly and tell me whether you want me to have the house or not.

Yours truly,
Emma Parkes Watts
[He folds up the letter, and with it a longing deep inside him.]

MCGAUGHEY

Thank you.

GERHARDT

I'm sorry, but I thought she had written you a letter . . . but she couldn't have, could she? *[Puzzled]* And this is a letter of a child . . .Mrs. McGaughey, you and Miss Watts may not have been very close as you grew older, but I want you to know that she regretted that. Your social circles may have kept you apart–

O'NEIL

Jerry . . .

MCGAUGHEY

Emma was always my best friend.

GERHARDT

When you were little, but she may have ignored you as she got older–

MCGAUGHEY

No. No. Emma was always . . .always my friend.

GERHARDT

Yes, but–

MCGAUGHEY

[With insistence; she sounds like a school teacher now:]

She was always my friend.

GERHARDT

Yes, ma'am.

MCGAUGHEY

Thank you for coming to see me.

GERHARDT

Here's my card. *[He hands her his card.]* I'll leave one at the desk with the Nurse, too, so you can always get in touch with me.

MCGAUGHEY

That would be nice. Now, if you'll excuse me, I've got to get ready.

GERHARDT

Get ready?

MCGAUGHEY

Oh, yes. You just missed her, you know. She was here right before you came.

GERHARDT

Who? *[He pauses]*

MCGAUGHEY

Yes. She said you'd bring the letter.

GERHARDT

You saw her? *[He looks at O'NEIL but continues with MCGAUGHEY:]* You saw her, too?

MCGAUGHEY

I should say so. She promised to call on me tonight. We are going out. Together.

GERHARDT

Really? Where?

MCGAUGHEY

Out on the town, where else? *[With a clever wit]* Now, sir, I'm not about to tell you all the secrets us girls share. But we're going to have a good time. Just the two of us.

GERHARDT

Yes, you used to pretend–*[Somehow it makes sense to him. Somehow it is true.]* Just don't stay out too late.

MCGAUGHEY

[She whispers with a smile]

Don't you wait up for us. *[As GERHARDT moves to the door]* So, you are an architect? *[But GERHARDT doesn't recall having mentioned this.]* Build something that will last.

GERHARDT

[He nods.]

Good bye, then.

O'NEIL

Good-bye, Mrs. McGaughey. *[He kisses her on the cheek.]*

MCGAUGHEY

Good-bye, Teeny. Thank you for coming to see me. *[MRS. MCGAUGHEY slowly stands up after they are gone. She carefully moves to the door and feels to be sure the door is shut. We only now realize that she is completely blind. The lights fade out.]*

ACT THREE

Scene One

Elmwood, sunset, Sunday evening. We hear the sound of horseshoes being played. The door buzzer. CAVENDISH sweeps into the room like a charming storm, his arms loaded down with robe, stole, Prayer Book, and Communion kit. He is dressed for the event in coat and tie, a handsome man, very tan, who looks younger than his years, and is energetic and friendly.

GERHARDT

You were her priest?

CAVENDISH

My God, the place has not changed a bit.

GERHARDT

I'm sorry, but . . . Tell me again why you are here?

CAVENDISH

Mrs. Merrick called me. 'Said you wanted to see me. *[GERHARDT is still perplexed]* To perform the Eucharist?

GERHARDT

[Now remembering]

Yes! That's right. You're the young priest. Well . . . I mean you were. *[He is not gray, and at his age.]*

CAVENDISH

It's amazing what a little color will do, huh? *[He stops and throws him a grin.]* I meant the *suntan*—I've had a week in Florida.

GERHARDT

[He laughs and feels as though he has known this man all his life.]

Yes. Yes. *[He leads CAVENDISH into the house.]* It's like time has stood still?

CAVENDISH

Yes. Shall I set up here on this table?

GERHARDT

Please do. May I help you?

CAVENDISH

[He unloads the items onto the table. GERHARDT awkwardly tries to help.]

I understand you're the architect commissioned by the University . . . for the new complex? What a challenge they've given you.

GERHARDT

I could be hired, if they like my ideas.

CAVENDISH

[He finds this strange but is not surprised.]

I'd have thought they would have hired you from the start. I understand that you have spent time in California–

GERHARDT

Forgive me, but I'm in a hurry. I mean, I don't want to appear ungrateful or irreverent or anything, but I'm so looking forward to seeing . . . a particular lady . . . if you understand?

CAVENDISH

Sure. *[As he sets everything in place]* Will she join us?

GERHARDT

I don't know. Who?

CAVENDISH

Mrs. Merrick, of course. *[He puts on the robe and stole, opens the kit to take out the chalice, paten, Host box, wine bottle, linens, and candles.]*

GERHARDT

Oh. I don't think so.

CAVENDISH

'Anyone else going to join us?

GERHARDT

No, no. Just the two of us.

CAVENDISH

"Where two are gathered . . ." Let us begin then, shall we? *[He searches for matches and lights the candles.]* I sometimes would bring Miss Watts the Eucharist to this house. It seems like yesterday. *[He laughs]* And there was this one time—

GERHARDT

[Impatiently]

Please–if you don't mind?

CAVENDISH

Yes. Of course. *[Back to the present. He searches for something. GERHARDT grows more impatient.]* Now, where are my glasses? I have the hardest time keeping—*[GERHARDT sighs ferociously]* Surely, I didn't go off without them? Damnit!

GERHARDT

In your pocket, there!

CAVENDISH

[Finding them]

Yes. *[He opens the Prayer Book immediately to the place marked. Calmly, with great ease.]* Shall we begin with the "Our Father?"

[The lights change to spot only CAVENDISH and at the other side of the room, an older EMMA, seated by herself, now in her later years holding a cane.]. . . And lead us not into temptation but deliver us from evil. Amen.

EMMA

Would you like a martini?

CAVENDISH

No, but thank you . . .

EMMA

I thought you liked martinis?

CAVENDISH

Yes, I do . . . but we're not finished.

EMMA

But you said, "Amen." I thought that meant the end.

CAVENDISH

Well, yes, usually it does. But we've just started.

EMMA

Funny how they start off with an "AMEN," isn't it?

[The lights change back to only GERHARDT and CAVENDISH]

CAVENDISH

I believe in one God the Father Almighty, Maker of heaven and earth, And of all things visible and invisible; and in one Lord Jesus Christ . . .

[The lights change to the CAVENDISH and EMMA]

. . . And I look for the Resurrection of the dead, and the life of the world to come. AMEN.

EMMA

I've asked Mrs. Merrick to bring us some martinis.

CAVENDISH

[With good humor]

We're almost there–

EMMA

There are a lot of Amens.

[Lights change back to GERHARDT and CAVENDISH]

CAVENDISH

The Body of our Lord Jesus Christ which was given for thee, preserve thy body and soul unto everlasting life. Take and eat this in remembrance that Christ died for thee, and feed on him in thy heart by faith, with thanksgiving. *[CAVENDISH eats of the bread, then offers bread to GERHARDT.]*

GERHARDT

No, thank you.

CAVENDISH

But I must have a communicate–in order to celebrate the Eucharist.

GERHARDT

No, but thank you—*[He pauses.]* Oh, all right. I guess . . . *[He partakes awkwardly. CAVENDISH pours from the bottle the last drop into the cup. This catches GERHARDT's attention as he remembers the night before.]*

CAVENDISH

[Holding the cup]

The Blood of our Lord Jesus Christ, which was shed for thee, preserve thy body and soul unto everlasting life. Drink this in remembrance that Christ's Blood was shed for thee, and be thankful. *[CAVENDISH drinks of it and then offers it to GERHARDT, who does the same.]*

[The lights change to CAVENDISH and EMMA. There is a silence.]

CAVENDISH

–to whom with thee and the Holy Ghost, be all honour and glory, world without end. AMEN. *[He waits]* That was the final AMEN.

EMMA

Then, let's have our martinis!

[The lights change back to GERHARDT and CAVENDISH who is putting away the Communion set]

CAVENDISH

I had come to celebrate with her. Afterwards she served us martinis. *[He laughs remembering]* She was very much a lady. Very kind. Very alone. A very proud woman, but very generous. She paid the tuition for several young girls to go to Vassar. And she gave our church the house next door for the college students to meet.

GERHARDT

Next door? I must see it–

CAVENDISH

The University tore it down after her death. For a parking lot.

GERHARDT

Paradise always makes for a good parking lot. Were you with her when she died?

CAVENDISH

No. I was moved by then. When they move you from a parish it's expected that you stay away. *[He starts to the door]*

GERHARDT

Reverend, someone said you once taught Psychology at the University?

CAVENDISH

Yes, I did. And history.

GERHARDT

I was told that we all have a female part to us . . .

CAVENDISH

Freud and Jung thought so.

GERHARDT

And if we are out of touch with one or the other . . . our reality is out of whack, so to speak? Oh . . . never mind. *[He ushers him to the door, then he stops:]* Reverend, do you believe in ghosts? *[CAVENDISH turns and looks at him.]* Do you believe that a person can be so attached to their place in life that they become imprisoned by it, and can't move on?

CAVENDISH

That characterizes rather well more than half the people I know . . . Yes. I think you have made a wise point. And Freud and Jung would concur.

GERHARDT

Yes. Yes. Thank you for coming today.

CAVENDISH

I'm glad I could be of help. Is there something more I can help you with?

GERHARDT

Not now. But, yes, sometime, if I could give you a call . . .

CAVENDISH

Call me anytime. I'd be glad to hear from you.

GERHARDT

Thank you. *[He shows CAVENDISH to the door, then:]* Reverend, . . . Can I tell you something? I've got to tell someone, someone who might understand.

CAVENDISH

Sure . . .

GERHARDT

I've seen her. Miss. Watts. Here. Not only have I seen her, I've spent most every hour of the last few days with her. And . . . I love her.

CAVENDISH

[After a silence.]

You are a fortunate man.

GERHARDT

Yes. *[But he does not know why]* Why's that?

CAVENDISH

You have discovered that you *can love.* And that's worth more than you know.

GERHARDT

Yes. Thank you.

CAVENDISH

[Stopping to look back at the great hall of the house]

This is a grand old place. She was a grand lady. Tell her I said that, if you see her again. And, *[He chuckles]* ask her about the martinis. *[He smiles knowingly and is gone. The lights go out on the scene.]*

ACT THREE
Scene Two

It is Monday morning. The Entrance Hall of Elmwood. The COMMITTEE is seated once again in folding chairs. GERHARDT is finishing his presentation with projections, new plans of Elmwood.

GERHARDT

It looks just like Elmwood from the exterior: the trees, the house intact, just as it looked over a hundred years ago. A beautiful accent to our community. But as you draw closer, you see an Elmwood restored to its brilliance that even its own architect, in his greatest moments of inspiration, could not have imagined. And behind the house, the new complex in complete splendor–with easy access from the North and the South. Handicapped accessible. Low maintenance. Beautifully landscaped. A much needed parking garage where the old orchards used to be. Sixty percent of the green space preserved with seventy-five percent of its trees. Its doors opened to welcome visitors, town and gown, students and education dignitaries, in the warmest spirit of Kentucky hospitality. The home, unsurpassed, and fitting . . . for our University President. *[Music, "My Old Kentucky Home" is played in the background from the computer.]* A home on campus that preserves the privacy of his own house and family off campus. But here hospitality is in our neighborhood, just across the street, just a knock on the door to make you part of the family. Some of these trees have stood since the days of the Abolitionist Cassius Marcellus Clay, the composer Stephen Foster–trees that take hundreds of years to grow. It is their shade that creates the pastoral ambiance that helps bring about peace and tranquility in a world where students are sometimes stretched beyond their limits. Elmwood. Built just above "Dreaming Creek," named by pioneer explorer Daniel Boone himself, where our dreams of today prepare us for our future. Here we find our President and family, in the heart of our University, an institution supporting the educational needs of students across the country. Linking the path of yesterday to a thoroughfare of tomorrow. And still a place of beauty, dignity, and hospitality, with the charm of a Southern lady of Kentucky.

[GERHARDT turns on the lights and shuts down the projector. To a room of silence. You can hear a pin if it were to drop. Then: Thunderous applause. The COMMITTEE MEMBERS stand. Something inside of GERHARDT breaks, and if there were ever a separation between him and this old house, it is gone. They are one. The COMMITTEE MEMBERS gather around him and congratulate him and one another. It is the solution they could not imagine, but the very one they have dreamed.]

COMMITTEE MEMBER

A brilliant concept! This way he and his children don't have the university invading upon their space; that's been a problem with some of our Presidents. You know, when she was living, the President back then made a call on her here and he asked her, "Mrs. Watts, what will you take for your house?" And she looked him straight in the eye and said—

GERHARDT

I don't give a damn.

O'NEIL

[With the COMMITTEE MEMBER left stunned, O'NEIL interrupts:]

Dr. Gerhardt, you are–

GERHARDT

I know. I'm fired.

O'NEIL

[Grabbing GERHARDT, he kisses him on the cheek.]

–*AMAZING*!

MRS. MERRICK

[Who just happens to be standing there.]

None of my business. Uh-uh . . . *[She kisses him also!]* You've saved this old house and I still have a home. *[To O'NEIL]* Kiss him again! *[They all laugh. O'NEIL's phone rings]*

O'NEIL

[On his cell phone]

Yes. The plans will be delivered this afternoon. And it sounds like we are going ahead with Dr. Gerhardt's proposals.–Oh, excuse me, I've got a call coming in. Would you mind holding? Thanks. *[He pushes a button]* Yes? Yes, he's here. *[To the others present:]* This "Call Waiting" is just the best– *[But the news is sad.]* Oh? Oh. I'm sorry. Yes, I'll tell him. Yes. Thank you. *[To GERHARDT:]* 'The nursing home. Mrs. McGaughey expired last night. They wanted to make sure you knew. They said they tried to call you but your phone's not working. *[GERHARDT's phone rings. He answers it. O'NEIL pushes a button on his own phone]* Yes, I'm here. Thanks for holding . . . Everyone is very pleased. Dr. Gerhardt did remarkable work. He solved several old problems with one fell swoop. Yes, he's a genius–

GERHARDT

[On his own phone]

Hello? Hello? Humm. *[He reads the phone:]* "Out of the Area." *[He laughs to himself. He nods, knowing that EMMA has made it home, and has called to tell him she has arrived safely.]* Humm. *[He dials]* Battery has run down. *[To O'NEIL:]* Sorry, old man . . . *[He takes O'NEIL's phone from him and speaks into it:]* Would it be a terrible bother if Dr. O'Neil were to call you back in just a minute? No? Thank you so much. I've got to tend to a very important matter and my phone's out—*[He dials. To O'NEIL:]* Thanks, Charles, I'll make it short. *[Into O'NEIL's phone:]* Hello, yes, hello? Janet? This is Jerry Gerhardt–oh, you did, did you? I was wondering if you would mind doing me a big, big favor? 'You still up for that reunion? With me I mean? I could be there in five hours if I leave here right away, and we would get there in time for the dinner. What do you say, you want to save my life? *[He grimaces in great pain awaiting her reply then:]* You're a saint! I'll call you just before I get into town. Bye, now. *[He takes a deep breath]* 'Piece of cake. *[Tosses O'NEIL his phone back.]*

O'NEIL

You handled-

GERHARDT

Shh. Listen. Charles, listen. *[They listen]*

O'NEIL

I don't hear anything.

GERHARDT

No one's playing horseshoes?

O'NEIL

I thought you handled yourself very well in there today. What made you change your mind? Such a complete turn about?

GERHARDT

I've been a ghost for too long. Just a shadow of who I was, a dim reflection of who I still can become. Thank you, Charles. Thank you for standing behind me. Believing in me. Oh—and I discovered something else. In the cemetery.

O'NEIL

Cemetery?

GERHARDT

Where the collies were buried. But one of them wasn't a grave at all—the one unmarked? It should have been an easy clue, huh? I found the letters. From the German painter. I think someone had kept them from her; and before they died, they buried them so she would never find them in this old house. She knew every inch of it. They couldn't bring themselves to–

O'NEIL

Letters? What did you do with them?

GERHARDT

What would you think? *[He pauses]* Would you believe I burned them?

O'NEIL

You didn't? *[He looks at them and they laugh together]* You liar! What am I going to do with you?

GERHARDT

I don't know, because it looks as though you are stuck with me for a while.

O'NEIL

[The admiration cannot contain itself in his face]

Thank you. For everything. *[GERHARDT notices that O'NEIL has been crying, but does not mention it. O'NEIL, aware that GERHARDT has noticed the tears, cannot address it, but takes a deep breath and looks away, around the room. Noticing that the others have left:]*

GERHARDT

I bet you cry at movies! *[The two men laugh. At themselves.]* You go on ahead, Charles. I'm going to go change before I leave. Maybe–I don't know—into something *pink.*

O'NEIL

Mrs. Merrick will lock up. See you, tomorrow then? Have a safe trip. And Jerry . . . *[He holds up both thumbs, but the knot in his throat makes his voice break:]* Good show! *[His phone rings and he answers it as he exits. Into the phone:]* Yes, I'm so sorry, I meant to call you back–

GERHARDT

[All alone in the house. He walks around, waits. There is only a restful assurance of peace about the place. He recites from memory:]

These are the days when birds come back,
A very few, a bird or two,
To take a backward look . . .

Till ranks of seeds their witness bear,
And softly through the altered air
Hurries a timid leaf!

Oh, sacrament of summer days,
Oh, last communion in the haze,
Permit a child to join,
Thy sacred emblems to partake,
Thy consecrated bread to break,
Taste thine immortal wine!

[He waits, as though for someone to appear. Someone who does not appear. From his briefcase, he reveals a small stack of letters tied with a ribbon. He places them on the table as if to say, "These were yours." The room is silent. There is no ringing sound of horseshoes being played. The bright autumn leaves tap gently outside against the tall glass window above the stairs. Dr. Paul Gerhardt, the University Architect for the new Student Life Center and Parking Lot Complex nods with contentment. Smiles. And then from his briefcase takes out a yellow rose, places it tenderly on the table by the letters. Checking his watch, his pace is quick as he exits out the front doors of Elmwood.]

CURTAIN

POSTSCRIPT

Emma Parkes Watts

They came into the world together, Emma and Elmwood, in the same year, 1887. Across the street from what would become Eastern Kentucky University, the house stands as it did when Emma Parkes Watts lived: silent and full of intrigue to all that pass. Her father's initials carved into the stone over the entrance.

Figure 22

Figure 23

Emma Watts was born October 7, 1887, in Richmond, Kentucky. She was the only child of William Walker Watts, son of Charles Sinclair and Elizabeth Walker Watts, and Mary Parkes, daughter of John White and Elizabeth Buford Parkes. Their home was built by the French-Canadian architect Samuel E. des Jardins of the Cincinnati, Ohio firm DesJardins and Hayward.

Emma's house was named "Elmwood," because of the many elm trees that graced the estate. In

May 1886, Watts employed Sam Rice to make 600,000 bricks for the house. Built at the cost of $35,000.00, Elmwood is 9,000 square feet and 15 rooms. Interior paneling is golden oak with silk wallcoverings. Windows include Tiffany stained glass. Its grounds were a showcase with orchards, rose gardens, and a pond of exotic fish. A wind mill pumped water into the attic for plumbing purposes. Mary Watts wrote to her daughter, "The privacy of a home is one of its chief comforts for it means perfect freedom."

Figure 24 Elmwood

Elmwood was built upon the site of a double log house owned from 1819-1837 by Colonel William H. Caperton. In 1837, Union General John Miller, took down the log house and built a colonial brick house. Miller was killed in the Battle of Richmond, on August 30, 1862, a Confederate victory early in the Civil War. Miller was the son of Colonel John Miller and his wife Betsy Goodloe Miller, who founded the town of Richmond on their farm, and the county seat in their barn.[1] General Miller's widow sold the house to Major John D. Harris who lived there until William Walker Watts bought the house, raised it, and built Elmwood.

---

[1] French Tipton Papers, Townsend Room, (Richmond, Kentucky Eastern Kentucky University).

William Watts served in the Confederate Army. After the Civil War he made his fortune in Texas from cattle, cotton, and oil operations. Watts left Elmwood from Christmas to June and Emma wrote that while he was gone, she did not have to "Put on my company manners." His motto was *Forti non defict telum:* the strong man never lacks a sword.

Emma was a brilliant student and fine athlete. A tennis court was built in the Elmwood garden, and she played competitively. She attended the Madison Female Institute in Richmond, a school that had been temporarily a Civil War hospital during the Battle of Richmond. She played violin with the Stringed Instruments and was part of the Elocution team. There was a small summer house on the estate used as a playhouse for her beautiful collection of dolls that she kept into her adult years.

At age fourteen, she attended Hamilton College for women in Lexington, Kentucky. "When I first went to school, I believe I was the most homesick girl in Hamilton," she wrote. She found everything to be so different there; but as she made friends with the other girls, she grew to like the school and became very contented to remain there. She joined Chi Omega Fraternity and found that by being in contact with so many girls she had become "a little less selfish."[2] Her favorite classes were English, Latin, and French. She was part of the Athenea Society, played

Figure 25 The Elmwood fish pond

[2] Emma Watts, *My Commencement*, a gift book given to her by Tom Armstrong Knight, May 24, 1906.

Figure 26
Emma at Hamilton College 1906

the role of Delphline in the French play "Les Femmes Qui Pleurent," and played a violin solo "Overture from Mignon," by Thomas at the Senior Day exercises. President Jenkins bestowed upon Emma the Hamilton College one-year scholarship medal, May 1906.

During one summer while at Hamilton, it is believed that she took her first trip to Europe with her parents.
Philip Alexius de Laszlo was commissioned by the family to do their portraits, and Emma took private art lessons from him. But fearing the growing friendship of their young daughter and the art teacher, her mother booked them on an earlier voyage home.[3] They would later send Laszlo photographs of the family members for portraits.

Figure 27
Philip Alexius de Laszlo

Figure 28 "A Lady"
Unidentified Laszlo painting

[3] The Rev. Dr. John C. Cavendish, Private Conversations with Playwright, Minister of Miss. Watts, Christ Church Episcopal in Richmond, Kentucky.

Figure 29 Figure 30 Figure 31

In the fall of 1906, Emma enrolled at Vassar University in Poughkeepsie, New York. She and her mother wrote daily to one another. The letters of Emma that so often ended with "I love you better than anything in the world, my precious, precious Mother, darling, darling Mother," and "P.S. I send you lots of hugs and kisses" now at Vassar ended with simply "Affectionately yours."[4] At Vassar, she would eat her meals at The College Inn on Sundays, visit the theatre where she saw Madame Nazimna in Ibsen's *A Doll's House* and *Hedda Gabbler*, watch football: Harvard beat Yale 4-0, and the West Point games, and shop in New York City. Emma was elected to Phi Beta Kappa and the wording under her 1910 yearbook class photograph was quoted from John Milton, "Linked sweetness long drawn out."

Figure 32

[4] Emma Parkes Watts Papers, Letters to her mother, Townsend Room Archives, (Richmond, Kentucky: Eastern Kentucky University Library), from Cincinnati, Ohio March 3, 1898, and April 3, 1899.

Following her graduation, Emma attended regular reunions with her class of 1910. After roll call, the women all shared what they were doing: some were teachers, some social workers, some in business. Most of them like Emma responded, "Staying at home." When a friend, engaged to get married, inquired about her friends doing the same, Emma wrote, "We tell her that we could get off, but don't want to."[5] She was a Life Member of the Associate Alumnae of Vassar College. To celebrate her Senior year, her parents took her back to Europe in the summer of 1911, to tour Greece and Italy. Emma spent time on the trip with friends Thomas A. Knight, Ted Thome, and Juliette Worthly. The following year, Tom would write to Emma, "Last summer, you and I had opportunity to know each other better than ever before and simply because we cannot be together ought not to be any reason for our hearts and interests to drift apart."[6] At the death of William Watts, Tom wrote Emma's mother, "As long as I live, I shall always care for Emma as a sister, and in me I want you always to feel that she has a willing protector."[7]

William Watts' health declined on their return home and he died the following year, 1912. His wife, Mary, continued trips to Europe with Emma for many years, and on one trip, June 25, 1924, they attended the Thirteenth Alexandria Rose Day Empire Garden Party at Buckingham Palace, at the invitation of the Lord Chamberlain commanded by His Majesty King George V. On their trip to Scotland Emma took golf lessons from the famous Alexander "Sandy" Herd, who had won the 1902 Open Championship at Hoylake. Mary Watts died in 1934. Laszlo died three years later. Emma remained at Elmwood by herself. She never married. Tim Merritt and his wife Amelia worked at Elmwood for 48 years. Their son, John, and his wife Jeannette, worked in Frankfort for

---

[5] Emma Parkes Watts Papers, November 5, 1910.
[6] Thomas A. Knight , Letter from Palais d'Orsay, Paris, France, August 20, 1912, Emma Parkes Watts Papers, Letters to her mother, Townsend Room Archives, (Richmond, Kentucky: Eastern Kentucky University Library).
[7] Thomas A. Knight, Letter from Amsterdam, August 25, 1912.

the Kentucky Governor, but when Tim Merritt died, John and Jeannette left their work at the Governor's Mansion to care for Miss Emma at Elmwood.

Figure 33

Collies were the favorite pet of Miss Emma, and they lived long and happy lives with her, and after their deaths were buried in the garden. She is remembered fondly by friends, being chauffeured around in her Packard car at Christmas delivering presents. Through unkind anonymous typed letters, she became aware of a destitute but hardworking cousin Fanny Watts, and after consulting with her priest she bought the woman a house and gave her financial help; Fanny Watts (unaware of the threatening letters) responded with regular letters of gratitude and praise. Emma was also the benefactress of many young women attending college. Her wedding gift to Princess Elizabeth and the Duke of Edinburg in 1947, of C.A.R.E. food parcels to the poor was acknowledged with a hand signed thank you letter from the soon to be Queen of England. She helped lead the restoration of the Orlando Brown House in Frankfort. The African American community referred to her Elmwood as the "Colored Peoples' Heaven," for when people approached her for jobs on the estate, she gave them and kept the workers on; these expenditures were said to have added to the demise of her finances as she held onto a way of life that had passed with time.

James J. Neale, Jr. shared a seat with her on the Richmond Cemetery Board. On one occasion when the Board was challenged with an issue of conflict, Miss Watts called and shared her ideas with Neale. "I told my ideas to Bob, and Bob agrees with me!" she said. Neale responded, "That's good!" But Neale could not recall a Board member by the name of Bob. He thought, then asked, "But, Emma . . . who is Bob?" "My dog!" she replied. She had a delightful sense of humor.[8]

A newly published book appeared in the Eastern College library creating scandal for Emma Watts: it claimed that William Watts' Texas fortune and the fortune of his partner Igo was made by cattle rustling, i.e., stealing cattle that wandered onto their lands. In a panic, Emma called Igo's granddaughter, Betsy Ann Carr, and voiced her outrage and fear. "What will the world think of our families for making such a fortune!" she asked Betsy Ann. "What's the problem, Emma?" came the reply, "I'm enjoying mine, aren't you enjoying yours?" Emma promptly sent her servant to find the book in the College Library. The book disappeared from the library shelf, never to return.[9]

Robert Richard Martin was born on December 26, 1910, near McKinney in Lincoln County. He funded his own education through the Eastern Kentucky Normal Teacher's College by raising tobacco. He taught history at the Sardis High School in Mason County, and became principal of the Sardis Elementary School and then the Orangeburg High and Woodleigh Junior High of Mason County. He earned his M.A. degree at the University of Kentucky. During World War II, Martin served forty-one months as a weather observer-forecaster for the U.S. Army and then auditor of the State Department of Education. In 1948, he became head of the Bureau of Administration and Finance and earned his doctorate in education at the Columbia University's Teachers College in 1951.

Dr. Martin returned to Kentucky to help draft the Foundation Program for Education law enacted by the 1954 General Assembly. In 1955, he was elected State Superintendent of Public Instruction and then appointed as Commissioner of Finance in December, 1959, by Governor Bert T. Combs. Martin became President of the Eastern Kentucky Normal

---

[8] James J. Neale, Jr., Conversations with the playwright, 2015.

[9] Neale, Jr., "Conversations."

Figure 34 Dr. Robert R. Martin

Teacher's College on July 1, 1960, putting to use money for education that he had "squirreled away" under his appointment by Governor Combs.

Dr. Martin, made a persuasive proposal at a town meeting for Lancaster Road to be widened 60 feet, taking the footage from the Elmwood side that would take down the large trees and Miss Watts' rod iron fence that lined the street. But Miss Watts was not about to let loose of the land from her Elmwood lot. Attorney Jim Thompson spoke up: "Dr. Martin, what would you think of cutting 20 feet off Eastern's side and leave Miss Watts alone?"[10] This heralded a great response from the crowd at the meeting. It won Miss Watts's heart and Thompson became her attorney from that day forward. Her land was not touched. When Dr. Martin made a call at Elmwood asking her what she would "take for her little house," the reply, that has been told and cherished over the years, is that Miss Watts asked him simply, "What will you take for your little college?"

Miss Watts owned the Ramsey House built 1890, south of Elmwood that faced Lancaster Drive, and loaned it to the ROTC program of the College with the understanding that she would maintain the grounds and exterior and the College would maintain the interior. One day the ROTC students came to say goodbye to Miss Watts, explaining that President Martin had ordered the property vacated complaining that the house was "not fit to live in." She was hurt and felt betrayed by this and confronted the President over the telephone where she reportedly "called him everything but a white man." This ended her relationship with the college and from

[10] James E. Thompson, conversations with the playwright, February 16, 2016.

that time on she told her attorney, James Thompson, that when she died her house was never to go to the University "if you have to take it to the Supreme Court!"[11] What she may not have understood at the time was that President Martin had a secret plan to build a football stadium under the guise of a classroom building for the ROTC program.

Emma Watts was interested in politics and took James Neale, Jr. with her to Lexington to hear President John F. Kennedy speak; Mr. Neale sat in the front seat of her Packer with her chauffeur. Vice President Lyndon B. Johnson gave the address at the College commencement June 1, 1961. Because of her Texas connections, Johnson made a special call at Elmwood to visit Miss Watts. It is said that President Martin came with him and was left outside on the porch while Johnson was escorted into the Parlour, although Miss Watt's friends dispute this.

President Bob Martin introduced the country's Vice President at the commencement. Johnson spoke on the responsibility of the United States in Vietnam Nam to stop tyranny in the world. "If America proves unworthy of this task, there is no other nation in the world that can muster the power to stand in the breach. ... We must join with our friends all over Latin America in a creative campaign against poverty and illiteracy. . . . The United States will stand with all African nations that want to be master of their own destiny in freedom and in honor." Johnson was granted the first honorary degree given by the Eastern Kentucky College: Doctor of Laws. Afterwards, the Vice President helped break ground for the building of Alumni Coliseum.[12]

In 1963, Martin established the Colonel as the college mascot, designed by Louisville Courier-Journal cartoonist Hugh Haynie. In 1965, five separate colleges and a graduate school were created.

---

[11] Neale, Jr., "Conversations."

[12] Dr. Robert Grise, *The Richmond Register*, "Madison's Heritage: Lyndon Johnson Gave '61 Graduation Speech," (March 25, 1989).

July 1, 1966, Governor Edward Breathitt granted university status to Kentucky's regional colleges and Martin's school became Eastern Kentucky University. E.K.U. began offering master's degrees and a joint doctoral program in education with the University of Kentucky, and the law enforcement and nursing departments were created. President Martin was a brilliant crusader for the University and brought it to state and national acclaim with its career-oriented programs in vocational and technical education. The University's enrollment increased from 3,000 to 13,400 students. In 1971, he assumed the presidency of the American Association of State Colleges and Universities. He visited and studied the educational systems of Yugoslavia, the People's Republic of China and England and Northern Europe. Martin became president emeritus in September 1976, and went on to represent the Madison-Garrard-Mercer district in the state Senate.[13]

The Watts family had been faithful members of the Christian Church in Richmond. The Rev. E.B. Barnes had accepted their call as pastor and during his ministry had led the congregation in the construction of a beautiful new building. Unfortunately, his oratorical talents had not been so appealing. Due to the new grandiose size of the sanctuary, and before sound systems, many of the members including Mary Watts had found it too difficult to hear his sermons. William Watts had been of no help, Mary had written Emma while at college, because of his deafness; and as she had complained, he had sat in the pew just smiling for all to see. What had resulted was Barnes being asked to resign. It had created an unfortunate split in the church.[14] In later years, Emma became a faithful member of Christ Church Episcopal across the street. She is remembered by her pastor, the Rev. Dr. John Cavendish, for once arriving late for the Eucharist, but preceded up to the railing with her

---

[13] Charles Hay and Joyce Libbey, President's Office Records - Martin, 1914-1976, (Eastern Kentucky University, Special Collections and Archives, May 21, 2002).
[14] E.B. Barnes Letter, from the Seelbach Hotel, Louisville, KY, December 2, 1917; Emma Watts Papers, Letters from her mother, Mary Watts, Townsend Room Archives, (Richmond, Kentucky: Eastern Kentucky University Library).

apologies. After ROTC moved out of the Ramsey House on Lancaster Road, Miss Watts loaned it to Christ Church Episcopal for an educational center for college campus ministry, "Lancaster House, Episcopal Student Center." After her death, the University was able to acquire the house and tear it down for a much-needed parking lot.

Emma Watts died on Christmas Eve 1970, and her funeral was held inside Elmwood. When President Martin arrived inside the house, her attorney turned to James Neale, Jr. and whispered, "If Miss Emma knew he was here she would get right up out of that casket!"[15] Her remains were buried with her parents in the Richmond Cemetery. At her death, she left provisions in her will that her estate be maintained by the interest from her account, and that no state institution should purchase it. The Trust would terminate at the death of the last survivor of the Cope family, Emma's Texas cousins, Millard Lewis Cope Jr. and
Margaret Parkes Cope of Marshall, Texas.

The will of Emma Watts stated that her trustee "shall have no power or authority to sell or in any manner hypothecate any of my real estate located in Madison County, Kentucky, or any of the furniture, furnishings, linens, china, silver, glassware, books, ornaments or other tangible personal property located in Elmwood at the time of my death."

Dr. Martin died November 29, 1997, and is buried in a U.S. Veteran's grave at the Richmond Cemetery.

This play was written in 1999. In 2011, the trustee of Emma Watts' estate donated Elmwood and its grounds to the EKU Foundation to ensure it would be preserved.

[15] James J. Neale, Jr. "Conversations."

BIBLIOGRAPHY

Barnes, E.B., Letter dated December 2, 1917, given to playwright by James Neale, Jr.

Cavendish, The Rev. Dr. John C.: Minister of Miss. Watts, Christ Church Episcopal in Richmond, Kentucky. Private Conversations with Playwright.

Charles Hay and Joyce Libbey, President's Office Records - Martin, 1914-1976, Eastern Kentucky University - Special Collections and Archives, May 21, 2002.

Grise, Dr. Robert. Richmond, Kentucky: *The Richmond Register*. "Madison's Heritage: Lyndon Johnson Gave '61 Graduation Speech," March 25, 1989.

Merritt, Jeannette. Richmond, Kentucky: conversations with the playwright.

Neale, Jr., James J. Richmond, Kentucky: conversations with the playwright, 2015.

Thompson, James E. Richmond, Kentucky: conversations with the playwright, February 16, 2016.

Tipton, French. French Tipton Papers, Townsend Room, Eastern Kentucky University, Richmond, Kentucky.

Tom. Letter from Palais d'Orsay, Paris, France, August 20, 1912. Emma Parkes Watts Papers, Letters to her mother, Townsend Room Archives, Eastern Kentucky University Library, Richmond, Kentucky.

Watts, Emma Parkes. Emma Parkes Watts Papers, Letters to her mother, Townsend Room Archives, Eastern Kentucky University Library, Richmond, Kentucky.

The Dust of Summer

Introduction

As an historian, I was greatly pleased to have been asked to write an introduction to Richard Cavendish's play, "The Dust of Summer." You see, I feel like the play and I have a certain pleasant history. As a member of the Battle of Richmond Association, I was invited to read this play prior to its premier at Richmond's Battlefield Park by the Rose Barn Theatre group during the annual reenactment. My children were invited to play roles in the performance and what started with a mere acquaintance ended with the play feeling like a member of my own family. We spent a lot of time together after all from helping my children memorize their lines to practice and performances. And I designed and handmade the historical dress for the character of Elizabeth Armstrong.

The play explores on a dual level the intricacies of the Civil War on a national scope and how violence often visited farms and homes throughout the country. The family in this instance was Elizabeth Armstrong who lived at Pleasant View in Madison County in 1862 and her young children. Wars are supposed to be someplace far away, fought by men of valor and not visited upon a woman alone and her family. As someone who has spent the last twelve years teaching my community about our local history, this play is priceless in bringing that history alive. It is important to remember all our history; and most especially the most unpleasant pages.

One of the magical qualities of the premier performance was that it occurred exactly in the setting of the play itself. Just a few years before, there were bulldozers sitting around the old farmhouse ready to raze our history so that subdivisions could encroach. Local preservationists and the Battle of Richmond Association have been waging a war ever since to protect the land and our history so that we can continue teaching the history of both the Civil War and its effect on families such as the Armstrong's.

I would like to invite you to visit amazing, strong Elizabeth and her children on this land where the armies encroached. The park is open most days if you want to visit the house and walk the hills where the action takes place. There are wonderful and poetic lines throughout this work of art to match the beauty of the natural setting. I am most pleased to recommend "The Dust of Summer."

Emily Burns
President of Battle of Richmond Association 2015-16

On either side the river lie
Long fields of barley and of rye,
That clothe the wold and meet the sky;
And thro' the field the road runs by
To many-tower'd Camelot;
And up and down the people go,
Gazing where the lilies blow
Round an island there below,
The island of Shallot.

The Lady of Shallot, Alfred Lord Tennyson

The Dust of Summer

Characters

ELIZABETH, Mrs. Kavanaugh Armstrong
DEALEA, the house servant
SMITH, Maj. Gen. Edmund Kirby
BRAGG, Maj. Gen. Braxton
CLAY, Maj. Gen. Cassius Marcellus
NELSON, Maj. Gen. William "Bull"
MANSON, Brig. Gen. Mahlon Dickerson
SOLDIER
BETTE Armstrong, five-year-old
BISHOP Armstrong, four-year-old
LINCOLN, President Abraham
KAVANAUGH Armstrong

THE DUST OF SUMMER

By the light of a single kerosene lamp at stage Left, we see two Confederate officers in gray uniform, coats unbuttoned, ties discarded. Maj. Gen. Braxton BRAGG and Maj. Gen. Edmund Kirby SMITH. BRAGG is in his mid-forties, SMITH is in his late thirties. They sit at a table drinking brandy and smoking cigars; they have been discussing at length a map of the United States tacked to the wall of their hotel room in Chattanooga, Tennessee, July 31, 1862.

BRAGG

Major Smith, on the trains, I can get my whole army to Chattanooga ahead of Buell.

SMITH

And mine, too, Major Bragg. We're not going back to Knoxville and have all that mountain marching be for nothing. *[Slowly, the idea comes to him.]* Major Bragg . . wait a minute. *[He moves the lamp closer to the map, his hand tracing the plan.]* Wait a cotton pickin' minute, Major Bragg. *[For a moment, he does not move. Then, he quickly puts the lamp to the side of the table, and pulls down the map from the wall and lays it over the table.]* What if . . . ***just maybe*** . . . *[He puts his brandy sniffer on the map, and then takes BRAGG's brandy sniffer from his hand and places it at the side of the map.]* You have 30,000 men from Mississippi, Major Bragg, . . .*[As he places his brandy sniffer at the lower end of the map:]* and I have 20,000 men from Knoxville. *[Like playing chess, he moves BRAGG's glass below his own.]* Let's say that we move your men South and East of Buell to Chattanooga. And we move my men up to Cumberland Gap and *down* to join yours . . .*[He moves his glass.]*

BRAGG

[Envisioning it]

Secure Chattanooga, and take the Cumberland Gap–

SMITH

And liberate Nashville from the Yankees—

BRAGG

Offense. Jeff Davis will have to live with it.

SMITH

The nearest armies to come to Buell's aid would be, what? Grant? Sherman, and Rosecrane? All of them far to the West of the Mississippi.

BRAGG

By that time we could strike North into Kentucky! *[He moves the glasses up the map!]*

SMITH

Kentuckians have disowned the South to become neutral; the North has disowned them. It should make General Lee happy.

BRAGG

Morgan has said there was more favorable public opinion ahead—

SMITH

A victory for the Confederacy!

BRAGG

The whole war might be over in a few weeks. *[Proudly, he takes his glass.]* Looks like pure sunshine, Major Smith!

SMITH

[With sheer, calm confidence, his glass raised in a toast:]

There is yet still time for a brilliant summer campaign, Major Bragg!

[SMITH turns out the lamp, and we see ELIZABETH Armstrong at Center stage, lit only by the night and its crescent moon. A woman in her thirties, dressed in her nightgown, she wanders out into the garden of the Pleasant View farm, outside of Kingston, Kentucky. A few weeks later. The night of August 25, 1862.]

ELIZABETH

The night is warm. The road is full of shadows. *[We hear the sound of the servant DEALEA:]*

DEALEA

Miss. Lizzie? That baby kickin' again?

ELIZABETH

No, Dealea. *[She touches her belly.]* It was just the dream again.

DEALEA

You put that out of your head. You know what the Reverend Armstrong says about such things.

ELIZABETH

What harm is there in dreaming? It's just admiring, that's all.

DEALEA

Don't you be going down that road. He says 'you feel it in your heart, it's the same as doing it!

ELIZABETH

I have no plans of doing anything. *[To herself, with loathing:]* Or going anywhere. When do you think this fighting will be over? England says that our Union will lose the war.

DEALEA

There is such a price for freedom.

ELIZABETH

General Clay preaches emancipation. *[To DEALEA]* What do you think of emancipation, Dealea?

DEALEA

Everybody has the right to be free, he says.

ELIZABETH

Do we? *[She touches her belly.]* If Kavanaugh gave you your freedom, what would you do, Dealea? Would you go back to Africa? They tell me the freed slaves are captured and turned back to slavery there in Africa. General Clay is against colonization.

DEALEA

I wouldn't want to go to Africa. This is my home now.

ELIZABETH

That's right. This is our home. The war could never come here.

[By the light of a single kerosene lamp at stage Right we see two Union officers in blue uniform. Maj. Gen. Bill "Bull" NELSON, a heavy-set man in his late thirties, trying his best to ignore the pursuit of Maj. Gen. Cassius CLAY, a tall handsome man in his early fifties. In a tent along the Kentucky River, that same night of August 25, 1862.]

NELSON

General Clay, this is not a war against slavery.

CLAY

Major Nelson, we will never win this war with the sword in one hand and shackles in the other!

NELSON

General Wallace was in charge until I arrived. Well, I have arrived. Cash, I am in command now. No one wanted your views on emancipation in Russia and no one wants them here in Kentucky. We'd like to keep the Kentucky men in our forces, not run them off.

CLAY

Bill, our only hope is the River. The Palisades. Those passes are few and easy of defense. I have fished that river, from the three forks to the mouth.

NELSON

The Union government thanks you for your proffered services, General Clay.

CLAY

[Quickly:]

We can stop Kirby Smith and his Rebels.

NELSON

We are fighting for peace.

CLAY

You've been eighteen months carrying on this war with peace principles, and what have you gained? We are fighting as though we're afraid for either side to win.

NELSON

You can't just take charge of the Union troops as though they belonged to you!

CLAY

I was sent here by President Lincoln. General Lew Wallace gave me permission to lead the troops. But my charge came from a greater source than either Wallace or Lincoln.

NELSON

And who, may I ask, gave such a charge?

CLAY

John Adams. The Constitution of this country! Can we defeat the designs of God in regard to the great question of universal liberty? You must give to every man the same liberty you desire for yourself.

NELSON

[Holding his temple, carefully:]

As I have said, General Cassius Clay, you are relieved of your command. Thank you, and good night. *[CLAY starts to leave, MANSON enters, NELSON reaches to turn out the lamp.]*

CLAY

Draw your sword and restore the Union: allow four million good Union men in the South to cut our throats, all because you cannot lay aside a sickly prejudice. Never will I draw my sword to keep the chains upon another human being. *[In a fury, CLAY exits.]*

NELSON

[To MANSON]

You couldn't have a man like Cash Clay in charge here. He'd just as soon kill the Union soldiers as the enemy. And with his bowie knife.

[NELSON puts out the lamp as once again we see only ELIZABETH walking out into the night at her farm. She once again is wearing her night gown but carries a basket covered with a cloth. A few days later. The night of August 29, 1862.]

ELIZABETH

Come out from those bushes. I have a gun and believe me, I know how to use it. *[There is no movement of anything.]* I have food for you. *[She reaches into the basket and uncovers a plate. From the shadows appears a SOLDIER.]*

SOLDIER

I came looking for water, ma'am. *[As he draws closer to her, we see that he is a young man, his clothes dirty and tattered, no jacket or cap. He walks with a limp and carries a sack that he keeps close to him at all times.]*

ELIZABETH

General Manson has been told his soldiers can use our water. Sparingly. Many of the cisterns have gone dry this summer.

SOLDIER

Yes'am. Thank you.

ELIZABETH

I thought you might be hungry. *[She hands him the plate; and the SOLDIER quickly takes it, moves away from her, and sits on the ground eating the food with a starving hunger. She offers him a knife and fork, he looks at them but only proceeds to devour the food with his hands. She takes out a napkin but on second thought does not even bother and puts it back in the basket.]* Where're you from? *[The SOLDIER will not answer. She pours milk from a jar into a cup. We hear the voice of the enslaved, DEALEA:]*

DEALEA

Miss Lizzie? *[The SOLDIER jumps, ready to flee. ELIZABETH reassures him to stay seated.]*

ELIZABETH

[To DEALEA:]

I was dreaming again! The noise woke me up! I'm fine! Go back to bed! *[When it sounds as though DEALEA has retreated, ELIZABETH offers the cup of milk to the SOLDIER who grabs it and drinks.]* No one else knows you're here. I, ah, . . .don't really have a gun with me. But I have one *in the house*, and believe me, I know how to use it. *[As she watches him eat, now choosing to lie:]* My husband is asleep inside, but easily wakened. *[The SOLDIER makes no response. He has cleaned the plate and offers it back to her with the cup. She cannot help but notice his manners. He falls back in the relief of having eaten.]* General Manson's troops have been all over this farm for days. General Nelson commands them. "Bull" Nelson, they call him.

SOLDIER

[Looking around in all directions, he and ELIZABETH seem to be alone.]

Thank you for the food.

ELIZABETH

[His gratitude surprises her.]

You're welcome. And welcome to Pleasant View. That's the name of our farm. Pleasant View. In the daylight you can see all the way to Big Hill from here. We've only lived here a few years. We came from Casey County. My husband and children. Soon to be nine. *[She touches her belly. The name of the unborn:]* "Eli Crockett."

What is your name? *[The SOLDIER will not answer]* I am Mrs. Kavanaugh Armstrong.

[She offers her hand.] A gentleman should always receive a lady's hand when it is offered. *[He hesitates, and then succumbs to shake her hand. Their touch dissolves the barrier between them. She smiles at him. He eventually returns the smile.]* I've watched you for days. You can talk to me. I won't bite.

SOLDIER

I was watching *you.*

ELIZABETH

Oh?

SOLDIER

You were burying something in the garden. *[ELIZABETH is silent]* You won't tell anyone you saw me?

ELIZABETH

Not if you don't want me to. May I ask why? *[No response.]* Do you have a horse?

SOLDIER

I lost it days ago. What were you hiding here in the garden? *[She will not answer.]* So, you have your secrets, too. *[We hear sounds of war from the distance that make the SOLDIER jump in fear.]* 'You hear that? Rebels. Thousands of them. Don't you know where that road goes?

ELIZABETH

That road? *[With loathsomeness:]* It goes nowhere. It stays right here.

SOLDIER

At sunrise they will start marching this way. Up that road. In just hours from now.

ELIZABETH

How do you know?

SOLDIER

They captured me. Those Rebels. I heard them talking. Their Generals tell 'em that we Yankees have horns hidden under our hats. They tell 'em that we're *evil.* They tell 'em that God is on their side.

ELIZABETH

How foolish. And grown men. I can't believe they would say such nonsense. They should know better! . . . God is on *our* side. So, you escaped.

SOLDIER

No. They let me go "on a handshake:" that I'll go back to our troupes and have one of the prisoners released and sent back to them. An exchange, you see?

ELIZABETH

Why have you been hiding out here?

SOLDIER

I can't go down that road, and I can't go back. I'll be killed either way. And to stay . . . is to die over and over again. I'm cursed. You're not afraid of me?

ELIZABETH

Should I be? *[We hear the gunfire in the distance again.]*

SOLDIER

How can anyone sleep with that going on?

ELIZABETH

That's not what kept me awake. It was my dreams. I've been having the same dream now for some time.

SOLDIER

[He shakes his head and looks away.]

Me, too.

ELIZABETH

Have you?

Tell me about it. Please. I'll tell you mine if you tell me yours.

SOLDIER

I hope it's a pleasant one.

ELIZABETH

It is. Very pleasant. I dream of a young man with a beautiful plumed feather in his hat.

[She laughs at the embarrassment of it and looks for his acceptance. The SOLDIER listens.] A silver bugle at his side. Like General John Hunt Morgan when he rode through town. *[She remembers it with excitement]* It was so exhilarating: the people cheering, the flags . . .

SOLDIER

You're a *Confederate?*

ELIZABETH

[Whose enthusiasm has just wavered]

No. But it was exciting, just the same. *[He laughs at her. She laughs at herself.]*

SOLDIER

So, you dream of General Morgan?

ELIZABETH

No, not him. It is another man in my dreams, a younger man. *[She laughs at the silliness of it:]* I see him in my mirror–when I should look and see myself. And when I am awake, I cannot get him out of my mind. I try, but he invades my thoughts. He has captured my heart, this young soldier in the mirror. What is your dream?

SOLDIER

Nothing like that.

ELIZABETH

Tell me.

SOLDIER

It's a woman. She is digging, digging up what she buried in the garden. And finding it still there. But when she finds it, she's not happy. She should be, but for some reason she's not. It makes her sad. *[She waits for more.]* That's all there is. It's where she put it. But she's sad when she finds it.

ELIZABETH

Humm.

SOLDIER

She's . . a lot like you.

ELIZABETH

[Jokingly]

She must be very beautiful.

SOLDIER

She is. *[ELIZABETH looks away with embarrassment.]* I don't think your husband is asleep inside.

ELIZABETH

He is—

SOLDIER

I think he's gone and left you here by yourself. *[She turns away. He moves closer to her.]* You must be very lonely. I know how you feel. *[He moves in closer. She lets him.]* A beautiful woman like you . . . you shouldn't be left alone.

ELIZABETH

[She suddenly escapes the lure of him.]

I lied when I said my husband was inside. I haven't seen him for days. And there has been no word from him. You see . . . you see . . .I am so ashamed! *[She controls her tears with bitterness. As though it explains everything:]* He served with "Colonel" Metcalfe. *[In case he does not know, has not heard:]* Colonel Metcalfe's troops ran like cowards. They turned back and left the Colonel to charge the enemy alone. *[She starts to sob, but hides her face in her handkerchief.]* What kind of soldier runs from battle!

SOLDIER

Boys and farmers. Shootin' a deer is not the same as shootin' a man. Can you blame them for running? To face the gunfire, the canon, . . . the blood. . . Which is cowardice do you think? To face death or to face life?

ELIZABETH

Bull Nelson has ordered them captured and taken to prison. He makes them run around tree stumps for twenty-four hours . . . I think they will be hanged. And my Kavanaugh with them!

SOLDIER

What makes you think they are not hanged already?

ELIZABETH

You think you know someone . . . You give him children, make a home for him all these years and yet . . . We never really know them at all. I was hiding my silver. I buried it in the garden. That's what you saw. It's the silver that has been handed down through my family.

SOLDIER

You were hiding it from the Confederates.

ELIZABETH

Yes. And no. I was hiding it from him when he comes back.

SOLDIER

But why—

ELIZABETH

I don't trust him. Not now. Not after this. Who knows what he will do? 'Could do? I can't leave this house. I am a prisoner here.

SOLDIER

You are free to go anywhere you please.

ELIZABETH

No. *[She laughs]* I can go to my loom, to my needle and thread. I am free to pray for the soldier that will wear each button I sew onto a uniform. To tend to my children. My house. To weave my dreams into my tapestries. Men march and fight. We women, we sit and watch. Like I said, that road stays right here. *[She realizes the similarity between them.]* I am cursed, also.

SOLDIER

I was with your husband.

ELIZABETH

Kavanaugh Armstrong?

SOLDIER

Yes, Lieutenant Kavanaugh Armstrong. I know him well. The firing was hot on both sides for about an hour. But the position of Metcalf in a stand-up fight was just too strong . . . just too strong: they were all scared and turned back and fled. Hundreds. But

Lieutenant Kavanaugh was not one of them.

ELIZABETH

Are you telling me the truth!?

SOLDIER

The rest . . . ran. Skedaddled in the most cowardly manner. Colonel Metcalfe escaped. But not Lieutenant Kavanaugh.

ELIZABETH

[To the Heavens.]

Oh, thank you, God. Thank you! *[She crouches to think she might have been heard inside the house, then grabs the arm of the SOLIDER to anchor her emotion.]* Thank you.

SOLDIER

What? You're glad the Confederates took him prisoner? *[He shrugs what he hears to be idiocy. She grabs his face and kisses his cheek.]*

ELIZABETH

He was not a coward! *[Laughing through her sobs:]* Thank you for telling me. You are a saint—

SOLDIER

No. . .

ELIZABETH

An angel sent by God,—

SOLDIER

[Moving away from her.]

No, no—

ELIZABETH

You are. You are! *[To herself, convincing herself of the truth.]* You were with Colonel Metcalfe. You fought alongside of him. With my Kavanaugh. *[Now to the SOLDIER, with gratitude and remedy:]* You can come and live here with us! Work the farm with us—

SOLDIER

NO! *[They both shutter to find if DEALEA has heard them. But cannons in the distance drown out the thought.]* I was captured with them because I was shot. That's why they released me. "On a handshake." 'That I would go back and send them one of their prisoners. On my "honor." But I didn't, you see? I gave my word, and I didn't. I wasn't shot from my horse for charging with them. *[He stops]*

ELIZABETH

You don't mean—

SOLDIER

Yes. Yes, I was one of those cowards from the Seventh Calvary. Fleeing for my life.

ELIZABETH

You were one of *those* men? *[She moves quickly away from him now.]* One of the ones who turned and ran—and left Colonel Metcalf to die? . . . and Kavanaugh?

SOLDIER

You don't know Colonel Metcalfe. He was the devil. There at Big Hill, a little slave girl climbed up to watch us march. Someone shot her dead, like you'd shoot a bird. She just fell off that fence, like a feather. And the troops, just marched on. Marched right on . . .

ELIZABETH

Why did you run?

SOLDIER

Why did you think your husband a coward! Why didn't you trust him to be brave! No, you didn't, did you? *[He realizes that this was cruel.]* I'm sorry. *[The silence after battle.]*

ELIZABETH

So, that's why you are hiding in our woods.

SOLDIER

That's why I'm hiding in your woods. Like a coward. Running from Bull Nelson's army. *[The silence after the confessions]*

ELIZABETH

What's in that sack?

SOLDIER

[He pulls out his blue wool Union jacket.]

I'm not fit to wear it. *[Shamefully]* I even lost most of its buttons.

ELIZABETH

[Reaching into her pocket, she produces two brass buttons and a needle and thread.]

Hand it to me.

SOLDIER

How can you see–

ELIZABETH

I can sew with my eyes shut. *[She starts to sew the buttons.]* I knew you had not come from Manson's men.

SOLDIER

You did? How?

ELIZABETH

You betrayed yourself with the food. His men would not be so hungry.

SOLDIER

You thought me a Rebel.

ELIZABETH

No. You betrayed yourself there, too: you thanked me for the food. A Rebel would expect it. You Union soldiers keep yourselves clean and washed. The Southern *chivalry* expect their servants to do it for them, or else they'll go filthy—and even then they'll demand to be invited into your home and seated in your parlour and served from your best silver.

SOLDIER

I am not so clean these days. Why don't you take the silver with you?

ELIZABETH

I'm not going anywhere.

SOLDIER

You can't stay here. In a few hours, this whole area will be nothing but fighting and killing.

ELIZABETH

I'll not have the Confederates in my house!

SOLDIER

You must leave. I tell you, you must.

ELIZABETH

I can't.

SOLDIER

You are afraid of dying, too.

ELIZABETH

What do you mean?

SOLDIER

It's always safer to stay. Once you go down that road, you see that there's a lot more answers to our pea-size questions.

ELIZABETH

I can always come home.

SOLDIER

But it won't be the same. The woman you were will have floated down the stream, only to be discovered by a world that crosses itself in fear and prays God's mercy . . . And notices how lovely was once your face . . .

ELIZABETH

What are *you* going to do? You can't stay here.

SOLDIER

[Revealing his despair:]

I don't know. *[He looks down the road.]* I can't go back. *[He turns and looks the direction of the house behind him]* I'm afraid of Bull Nelson . . . *[Revealing his self-loathing]* I don't know.

ELIZABETH

I have a friend in Lexington, a lady, who spit on Bull Nelson when he paraded through town. He demanded that she curtsy and apologize or he would turn her house into a hospital. *[Sadly]* She curtsied and apologized. *[There is a silence between them.]* May I tell you something? *[She looks at the small crescent moon.]* The soldier in my dreams . . . it was you. *[She looks to see if he finds this scandalous, but he does not. She is pleased. Her mirror has cracked a deep divide between two images. She looks him straight in the eye:] That soldier* is a man of courage. *[We hear the sounds of war in the distance.]*

SOLDIER

In a few hours, your farm will be littered with the bodies of Union soldiers. You think I should be one of them?

ELIZABETH

At least you would have a chance. Did Colonel Metcalf know you had deserted? Did Kavanaugh?

SOLDIER

No.

ELIZABETH

Then why tell anyone? Let the coward die. Be that reflection in my mirror. *[We hear a rooster crow.]*

SOLDIER

[Looking to the sunrise]

The sun is rising. Shadows of the world appear.

ELIZABETH

As many as the dust of summer. I am tired of shadows. *[She hands him back his jacket complete with buttons. He admires her work, stands and puts on the jacket. He looks to her for strength, takes his cap from the sack and puts it on his head, turns]*

SOLDIER

When this is over, and I live, . . . *if* I live . . . I'll come back and steal that silver. *[Before ELIZABETH can leap to swell with pride for his choice, she is stunned by the differences between them, and the thought of his dream. He looks ahead and passes into the early morning. She watches him disappear in the night up the road, and then she passes into the house.*

[It is daylight. At Stage Right we see CLAY enter to MANSON who sits at his desk and puts out the night's lamp.]

CLAY

It's daylight and General Nelson is not here?

MANSON

I am waiting for his orders.

CLAY

You've sent our men across the River and the Confederate's are charging up from Big Hill? Where is General Nelson?

MANSON

I don't know.

CLAY

What?!

MANSON

He didn't tell anyone where he was going. He just told us not to move until he gave the orders.

CLAY

But the Confederates are charging–

MANSON

I cannot give them orders until he tells me–

CLAY

Where is he? *[Losing his temper]* **WHERE IS HE!**

MANSON

[He matches his rage]

I DON'T KNOW! . . . No one does.

CLAY

For God's sake, man! *[Backing away, finding his own words unbelievable:]* You don't even know where he is. *[It is out of his control. It is too late. He goes to the map]*

There is a farm there. Right in the middle. *Pleasant View.* How ironic.

[The morning light fades away CLAY and MANSON while we see ELIZABETH once again, but this time in her morning dress. We hear the voice of her servant, DEALEA:]

DEALEA

Miss Lizzie? Breakfast 'be ready in a few minutes. *[We see now the CHILDREN, five year old BETTIE and four year old BISHOP. They circle, sing, and fall to the ground and laugh.]*

CHILDREN

Ring around the rosy, A pocket full of posy, Ashes, ashes, we all fall down!

BETTIE

[Looking down the road]

Where 'they coming from, Mama?

ELIZABETH

Who, honey?

BETTIE

Those people coming up the road?

ELIZABETH

Some are farmers like your daddy, taking their crops to town to be sold down the river. There's a preacher going to the church. Those girls in their sun bonnets are heading to market to buy new dresses. People have gone up and down this road for a long time.

BISHOP

Even before I was born?

ELIZABETH

Even before you were born, Bishop.

BETTIE

Even before I was born?

ELIZABETH

Oh, yes, Bettie, dear. Even before you were born. Before I was born. Why, years ago the early pioneers traveled down that road.

BETTIE

And before that?

ELIZABETH

Before that? Why the Indians, of course.

BISHOP

And before that?

ELIZABETH

Before the Indians? Why, the buffalo, I guess, and the deer . . .

BETTIE and BISHOP

And before that?

ELIZABETH

Before that? Oh, that is a long time ago. Before that, I guess it was just God walking down that road.

BISHOP

And they never came back?

BETTIE

'Course they came back, stupid. What goes up must go down.

BISHOP

I'm not stupid!

ELIZABETH

Bettie, don't call your brother, stupid. That's not nice.

BISHOP

But nobody goes down the road. They're all comin,' but there's nobody going.

ELIZABETH

[He's right. The people are refugees coming their direction. Quickly:]

I want you to listen to your mother. We could join the parade. Would you like that? I want you all to get into the wagon. We are going right away. *[The children squeal and run off]* Dealea! Henry! We are leaving this house. Bring the wagon around. Now.

DEALEA

Miss Lizzie, breakfast–

ELIZABETH

Do as I say. And hurry! *[The lights slowly fade out on the Pleasant View farm.]*

[Once again, we see Cassius Marcellus CLAY, now dressed in civilian clothing, standing before President Abraham LINCOLN seated at his desk at the White House, Washington D.C. It is a few days later.]

CLAY

Mr. President, a thousand or so of our Union soldiers were killed or wounded there in my hometown. The troops were untrained, unprepared, unable to even work their equipment. I thought you should know. *[LINCOLN does not respond; his eyes are cast down upon the papers in front of him on the desk.]* There is a proclamation on your desk. Yes, it will only stop slavery in the South. But that's a start. It will weaken their forces. I see this proclamation is missing a signature. *[He motions to the ink well]* Is the well empty? Is it not filled with the blood of my young countrymen? The old Union cannot be restored. A new one has to be embraced. Now is the time, to change tactics. Emancipation. Now or never. *[No, he rethinks it:]* Now and *forever. [CLAY exits as the lights slowly fade on LINCOLN.]*

CURTAIN

POSTSCRIPT

Figure 35 Pleasant View

Kentucky was the birthplace of both Presidents of the Civil War: Abraham Lincoln of the Union and Jefferson Davis of the Confederacy. Lincoln lost the Kentucky vote each time he was elected to the United States Presidency. His wife, Mary Todd Lincoln, was from Lexington, Kentucky, where Jefferson Davis had attended Transylvania University. Kentucky was the home of abolitionist Cassius M. Clay, whose Battalion protected the White House in the early days of the Civil War. Clay served under Lincoln as minister to Russia and negotiator for the purchase of Alaska, and might have stopped the Civil War at the Kentucky River. In Paint Lick, Kentucky, just a few miles from Richmond, Harriet Beecher Stowe gathered information from the Kennedy plantation for her novel *Uncle Tom's Cabin*, that inflamed the North and outraged the South.

Kentucky lay between the Confederate states and the Union states. Richmond, the county seat of Madison County, is almost equidistant from Cincinnati and the Ohio River on the North, and the Tennessee border to the South. The House of Representatives in Kentucky adopted a resolution on May 16, 1861, "That this state and the citizens thereof should take no part in the civil war now being waged except as mediators and friends of the belligerent parties; and that Kentucky should, during the contest, occupy the position of strict neutrality." But this neutrality was violated by each side[1]

During the early part of the Civil War, Lincoln saw the Appalachian Mountains and the Cumberland Gap as supreme importance for the defense of central Kentucky. He wrote to a friend, "I think to lose Kentucky is nearly the same as to lose the whole game."[2] His plan was to strongly fortify the Gap with a railway and army; but this plan was never carried out, and adequate defense was never provided for central Kentucky.[3]

In late July of 1862, General Braxton Bragg and Major General Edmund Kirby Smith met and devised a plan to advance the Confederacy into Kentucky. Bragg had troops of 30,000 from Mississippi and Smith had 20,000 from Knoxville. If Bragg moved his men South and East into Chattanooga, and Smith moved his men up to the Cumberland Gap and down to join them, they could secure Chattanooga and take the Cumberland Gap and liberate Nashville from the Union forces. Both Bragg and Smith realized that their plan would be met by the forces of Grant, Sherman and Rosecrans, all of whom were far West of the Mississippi River. It was a plan that would allow the troops of Bragg and Smith to meet and strike North into Kentucky.

When Cassius Clay returned to Washington from Russia in August of 1862, and saw how the war was progressing, he began to think that if the slaves were freed, the Union would win the war. He pressed upon Lincoln the important of emancipation of all slaves in the southern states,

---

[1]James S. Chenault, "Introduction" to Dean Warren Lambert's *When the Ripe Pears Fell: The Battle of Richmond, Kentucky* (Richmond, Kentucky: The Madison County Historical Society, 1995), pp. xv—xxii.

[2] Dean Warren Lambert, *When the Ripe Pears Fell: The Battle of Richmond, Kentucky* (Richmond, Kentucky: The Madison County Historical Society, 1995), pp. 3-6.

[3] Nathaniel Southgate Shaler, *Kentucky: A Pioneer Commonwealth,* (Boston and New York: Houghton, Mifflin and Company; The Riverside Press, Cambridge, Massachusetts, 1884), p. 286.

and Lincoln sent Clay to Kentucky to see how the Legislature stood in support of the Union. When Clay reached Lexington, Kirby Smith was marching on Richmond, Clay's hometown. Clay suggested to Union General Lewis Wallace that the defense should be on the bluffs of the Kentucky River, "the passes were few, and easy of defense." Wallace put him in charge of the infantry and artillery. Borrowing pistols and a sword, Clay posted his troops on the

Figure 36 Cassius Clay

Figure 37 "Bull" Nelson

north bank of the River, but Field Commander General William "Bull" Nelson showed up at the River and relieved Clay of his position. Nelson may have done this because he knew Clay would kill Confederate soldiers on the spot and not take them prisoners. When Cassius Clay returned that night to his home, Whitehall, in Richmond, the protection of the River and Lexington went with him.[4]

Joseph Barnett had built the Pleasant View house in 1825, on his farm of 578 acres of land. Kavanaugh Armstrong bought the house and 198 ½ acres in 1856, from William D. and Theodotia McCord at a

[4] Lambert, "*Pears,*" pp.20-21.

price of $11,910.00. Armstrong had been born in 1821, and had lived in Casey County with his wife Elizabeth Dinwiddie and their two children and her brother John. Kavanaugh was a farmer and Elizabeth a seamstress.[5] During the Battle, Kavanaugh and Elizabeth lived at the Pleasant View Farm with their eight children, expecting their ninth.[6]

In 1860, the Pleasant View Farm would have included the following: 200 acres of improved land worth $12,000.00, ten horses, three mules, eight milk cows, four oxen, seventeen cattle, sixteen sheep, fifty-four swine, one hundred fifty bushels of wheat and fifty bushes of rye, ten pounds of tobacco, fifty pounds of wool, ten pounds of beans, twenty pounds of Irish potatoes, fifteen pounds of sweet potatoes, three hundred pounds of butter, six tons of hay, thirty-one gallons of molasses, and $180.00 worth of slaughtered animals.[7]

At sunrise on Saturday, August 30, 1862, the Confederate troops began their march to the Kentucky River and Lexington by way of the Pleasant View farm. Being unable to locate Nelson, Manson in desperation called for the Union troops to cross the River and head South. Kavanaugh Armstrong, is thought to have joined the Union troops. Elizabeth loaded up two enslaved persons and her eight children and sent them to the Thomas Palmer house nearby. She buried her family silver in the yard for fear of it being confiscated by the Confederates.[8] The Confederate forces took control of the Pleasant View house as a "lookout" and hospital. Legend has it that an upstairs bedroom contains bloodstains

---

[5] 1850 U.S. Federal Census, District 2, Casey County, Kentucky, July 28, 1850, page 575.

[6] Robert C. Moody, Chapters XVIII "Battle Action at Kavanaugh Armstrong's," Chapter XXV "Kavanaugh Armstrong, Master of Pleasant View," (Richmond, Kentucky: unpublished book but copyrighted, 2014).

[7] 1860 Madison County Agriculture Census, Eastern Kentucky University Archives, Richmond, Kentucky.

[8] Robert C. Moody, Chapter XXV "Kavanaugh Armstrong, Master of Pleasant View" (Richmond, Kentucky: unpublished book but copyrighted, 2014).

from a dying Confederate officer and that a butter churn was used as a chamber pot.

What has been called "The Battle of Richmond" was a huge victory for the Confederacy. The Union soldiers were too inexperienced in spite of the equipment they were given. The Confederacy took Richmond, Kentucky using the courtyard fence as a prison for Union captives and controlled the city for three months. It is estimated that some 4,300 Union soldiers were taken prisoner and more than 1,000 were either killed or wounded. The Confederates lost 128. The "Pleasant View" on the farm the last weekend of 1862 was the view of a dark and bloody ground.

Kirby Smith moved his 11,000 men to Lexington and occupied the city for weeks. The large Medical Hall of Transylvania University on the corner of Broadway and Second was burned to the ground that following May, the hospital full of wounded Union soldiers at the time.

Upon having his command taken from him, Cassius Clay rode to Frankfort on August 27, and addressed the Kentucky Legislature urging an Emancipation Proclamation that he had pressed upon Lincoln. Upon hearing of the tragedy to his friends in Richmond, Clay visited President Abraham Lincoln in Washington D.C. and gave to Lincoln a verbal report of the bloody battle.

> "Lincoln said but little; but, on the 22nd day of September, 1862, issued his immortal Proclamation of Freedom for the slaves in all the rebel states. Thus my good star stood high in the heavens; and whilst my enemies sought by unworthy means my ruin, I seemed by Providence to have been called for he culminating act of my life's aspirations."[9]

---

[9] Cassius M. Clay, *The Life of Cassius Marcellus Clay. Memoirs, Writings, and Speeches, Showing His Conduct in the Overthrow of American Slavery, the Salvation*

During that summer, Professor A. W. Blinn wrote his "Political Recollections" of Cassius M. Clay, stating: "I believe that Mr. Clay was among the foremost to urge upon Mr. Lincoln the measure of Emancipation."[10]

In October of 1865, the Armstrongs celebrated the marriage of their oldest daughter, Rosa Belle to Evan G. Moore. The family silver must have been used to entertain the guests. Kavanaugh's brother and father were both Methodist ministers and may have performed the ceremony. Evan and Rosa made their home in Casey County until their house burned and they returned to the Pleasant View farm.[11]

The Armstrong family sold Pleasant View Farm to William Gibson on October 24, 1873, and at that time the farm consisted of 203 acres, an increase attributed to the changing of the old road when the Turnpike was added. The Armstrongs moved to Texas.[12]

The Battle of Richmond was the second largest Civil War battle in Kentucky and it was one of the most decisive and complete Confederate victories of the Civil War. "In no other case during the war was an army so completely annihilated in a single day's battle," wrote historian Nathaniel Southgate Shaler in 1884.[13]

There is no evidence that Kavanaugh Armstrong was a Lieutenant who fought with Colonel Leonidas K. Metcalfe. Lambert records that Lt. Col. W. M. Odin was abandoned by the frightened Calvary of 400 alongside Col. Leonidas Metcalfe at Big Hill, Rockcastle County,

---

of the Union, and the Restoration of the Autonomy of the States, Volume 1 (Cincinnati, Ohio: J. Fletcher Brennan & Co., 1886), pp. 304-312.

[10] Clay, *"Memoirs,"* p.312

[11] Robert C. Moody, Chapter XXV "Kavanaugh Armstrong, Master of Pleasant View," unpublished book but copyrighted, 2014.

[12] Moody, "Kavanaugh Armstrong.".

[13] Nathaniel Southgate Shaler, Kentucky*: A Pioneer Commonwealth (*Boston and New York: Houghton, Mifflin and Company; Cambridge, Massachusetts: The Riverside Press, 1884), p. 293.

August 23; Odin and Metcalfe escaped thanks to the covering fire of the Third Tennessee Infantry Regiment.[14] Metcalfe estimated that ten men were killed and forty wounded and taken prisoners.[15] There is no evidence at present found as to how Armstrong served in the War. The SOLDIER in this play is completely fictional, but represents many of the soldiers who were killed in the Battle of Richmond. These ideas were created solely for the purposes of framing the story in this play.

When Bragg and Kirby Smith met in their hotel room in Chattanooga, Tennessee, July 31, 1862, reportedly the map was attached to the wall and not laid on a table. The incident of the little enslaved girl who was shot off a gate post at Big Hill is recorded by Howell Carter in his *A Cavalryman's Reminiscences of the Civil War*, although it is not clear from which unit Union or Confederate came this meanness.[16]

In 2001, the Madison County Historical Society purchased the Pleasant View farm of 62 acres at public auction for $564,764.00. It was then sold to the Madison County Fiscal Court and has been developed as Battlefield Park. In 2007, 300 acres were purchased and added, and with the Battlefield Golf Course included, a total of almost 600 acres has been preserved for the Richmond, Kentucky Civil War Battlefield Park.

---

[14] Lambert, "*Pears,*" p. 17.

[15] Richard H. and Lewis Collins, *History of Kentucky*, Vol. 1. (Covington, Ky.: Collins & Co., 1874), pp. 109-110.

[16] Howell Carter, *A Cavalryman's Reminiscences of the Civil War,* (New Orleans: American Printing Co., Ltd., 1900, pp. 25, 161.

BIBLIOGRAPHY

Carter, Howell. *A Cavalryman's Reminiscences of the Civil War.* New Orleans: American Printing Co., Ltd., 1900.

Chenault, James S., "Introduction" to Dean Warren Lambert's *When the Ripe Pears Fell: The Battle of Richmond, Kentucky.* The Madison County Historical Society, Richmond, Kentucky, 1995.

Clay, Cassius M. *The Life of Cassius Marcellus Clay. Memoirs, Writings, and Speeches, Showing His Conduct in the Overthrow of American Slavery, the Salvation of the Union, and the Restoration of the Autonomy of the States.* Volume 1. Cincinnati, Ohio: J. Fletcher Brennan & Co., 1886.

Clay, Jr., Henry Clay. *Josephine Clay: Pioneer Horsewoman of the Bluegrass.* Louisville: Harmony House Publishers, 2005.

Collins, Lewis. *History of Kentucky.* Revised by his son Richard H. Collins, Covington, Ky.: Collins & Co., 1874.

Ellis, William E.; Everman, H. E.; Spears, Richard D. *Madison County: 200 Years in Retrospect.* Richmond, Kentucky: The Madison County Historical Society, 1985.

Lambert, Dean Warren. *When the Ripe Pears Fell: The Battle of Richmond, Kentucky.* Richmond, Kentucky: The Madison County Historical Society, 1995.

Madison County Agriculture Census, Richmond: Eastern Kentucky University Archives, 1860.

Moody, Robert C. Chapter XXV "Kavanaugh Armstrong, Master of Pleasant View." Richmond, Kentucky: Unpublished book but copyrighted, 2014.

Moody, Robert C. Chapters XVIII "Battle Action at Kavanaugh Armstrong's." Chapter XXV "Kavanaugh Armstrong, Master of Pleasant View." Richmond, Kentucky: Unpublished book but copyrighted, 2014

Shaler, Nathaniel Southgate. *Kentucky: A Pioneer Commonwealth.* Boston and New York: Houghton, Mifflin and Company; Cambridge, Massachusetts: The Riverside Press, 1884.

Tennyson, Alfred Lord. *The Lady of Shalott*, 1833-42.

U.S. Federal Census. Kentucky: District 2

The Two Villages

Introduction

The paintings, portraits, and water colors of Paul Sawyier are found in many homes throughout Frankfort, Kentucky, the town where the artist grew to manhood. Since his death in 1917, there have been several written accounts of Sawyier and his art. Building on the research of authors Willard Rouse Jillson, Arthur R. Jones and especially the recent Sawyier biography by William Donald Coffey, playwright Cavendish (pen name of Russell R. Rechenbach) has melded Sawyier's romantic tragedy into a beautiful and poignant one-act play. Sawyier based a set of paintings on the Rose Terry Cook prose poem, *The Two Villages.* The "villages" represent Frankfort and the Frankfort Cemetery on the hill above town. By the close of the play, the reader has learned much of Sawyier's life and the dilemmas he faced in his attempt to be independent of his family, his lover, and most of all, with his art. His art was everything to him. His passion for painting was greater than his loyalty to family, friends, and his years-long relationship with his love, Mayme Bull.

Cavendish lets his characters define themselves in their own words. The wise old stone mason, Gus, is recognized as the town philosopher. Mayme, or Mary, as Paul affectionately calls her, is confronted with frustrations of her aging beyond child-bearing years and an extended courtship with no future. And Paul, fearful of accepting the responsibilities of marriage that in his mind would shift him away from his true love, art.

Sawyier saw his artistry as representing his heart and soul "...a piece of my life." Through his work he captured forever the places he roamed: Elkhorn Creek, the Kentucky River, the Tyrone area, High Bridge and several quaint communities in central Kentucky. He stamped all of his work with *his* visuals and *his* colors. Though some have tried, no one seems to have surpassed the uniqueness of Paul Sawyier's work.

This is a play of tenderness, tragedy, pride, passion, and loneliness. Mayme says "she can't help the way I am." Paul says "We can all help the way we are. There are no excuses...If we are victims then we have made ourselves victims." And yet with all the drama, Cavendish has sprinkled in moments of humor. This play not only defines the plight of the protagonists, but evokes readers to look back through their own past experience, pondering choices, failures and victories.

This edition of the play contains extra short scenarios of the lives of Paul, Mayme and Gus with an important source bibliography. Cavendish's play was performed for the 2015 Kentucky Playwrights Workshop at the The Bard's Town Theatre.

Russ Hatter
Frankfort City Historian at the Capital City Museum

Russ Hatter had a 40-year career as a radio announcer, (37 years as "the morning man" in Frankfort) before joining the Frankfort Parks and Recreation Department's Division of Historic Sites in 2001. Starting in 1958, he has directed and performed in many plays, recorded television commercials, appeared in KET educational productions, and appeared in several locally produced films.

The Two Villages

Characters

Paul SAWYIER, the artist
Uncle GUS, the town philosopher
MAYME Bull, the fiancée

We see the inside of a houseboat, about twenty feet long. At stage Right is a small front porch where the boat is tied to the dock. Immediately inside is a small kitchen, neatly arranged. There are easels and canvases and paints set up at one end used as a studio. It is particularly neat. Immaculately painted and arranged; a canvas of art all its own. To the extreme Stage Left is a small back porch that looks out over the Kentucky River. The sun is setting but a full moon has appeared. The two men sitting on the sofa playing cards are drinking bourbon. One man is the artist who lives on the boat, Paul SAWYIER, in his mid-forties, nicely dressed in pressed white shirt and tie; the other is an African-American, Uncle GUS, now an old man, wearing a coyote fur hat, cotton shirt and overalls. It is late afternoon, although this time of day by these people is commonly referred to as "evening." June 23, 1910.

SAWYIER

So, what *is* love, Gus?

GUS

You think you be in love with this girl, Mister Sawyier?

SAWYIER

I don't know. *[SAWYIER is distracted from the game.]*

GUS

How'd you come to meet this girl "Rose?"

SAWYIER

I was out paintin'. She and her friends came by in a wagon, and they stopped to watch. It annoyed me at first, but then Rose and I started talkin' . . .

GUS

[Noticing SAWYIER looking towards the door.]

You be expectin' someone this evening, Mr. Sawyier?

SAWYIER

No. What makes you say that?

GUS

Oh, . . . I donno. What about Miss Mayme?

SAWYIER

What about her?

GUS

You and Miss Mayme 'known each other a long time. She's libel to expect things . . .

SAWYIER

She expects to be the most important thing in my life.

GUS

Every woman wants to be the most important thing in her man's life. Miss Mayme's a woman. How many years you and Miss Mayme 'been together now?

SAWYIER

Twenty-three years.

GUS

Long time to be courtin' one girl.

SAWYIER

Yeah.

GUS

You and Miss Mayme's engaged. And when'd you say the wedding's gonna be?

SAWYIER

We haven't set a date.

GUS

Guess it is kinda early: you only been engaged for a *couple* ***years?***

SAWYIER

Eighteen months.

GUS

'Long time to be engaged. Don't you think, Mister Sawyier?

SAWYIER

I guess . . .

GUS

'Girl wants to get married. Have a family. Have a home.

SAWYIER

Yeah.

GUS

Her Daddy's dead. Your Daddy's not long for this world. Those obligations 'be gone soon.

SAWYIER

Yeah. But she's still got to look after her mother.

GUS

She got brothers and sisters, ain't she?

SAWYIER

Yeah, but she's the oldest. You know Mary.

GUS

[He laughs. This roar of a laughter has a symphony all its own. Hearty, rich, and singing from the reserves of times and places stored deep within a soul.]

Yeah. I know Miss Mayme Bull. Now–everybody else calls her Mayme, but you call her "Mary." 'Always been meanin' to ask you: why you suppose that is?

SAWYIER

I don't know.

GUS

She writes you pretty much every day, don't she?

SAWYIER

Yeah.

GUS

'Lots of letters. You write her back?

SAWYIER

Sometimes.

GUS

You painted her that big bunch of paintings . . .

SAWYIER

The Two Villages.

GUS

That's right. Mr. Sawyier?

SAWYIER

Yeah?

GUS

Don't think Miss Mayme knows about Miss Rose, does ya?

SAWYIER

I don't know.

GUS

My, oh, my! What you think she gonna think of Miss Rose? "Mister Sawyier and Miss Rose?"

SAWYIER

[Laying down the cards, he takes a drink.]

'What you think, Gus?

GUS

I think maybe a fella might not be fixin' to buy the milk if he can get it for free from the cow.

SAWYIER

[He takes a smoke from his cigar.]

I wouldn't hurt Mary for nothin'.

GUS

Miss Rose, she's a lot younger than Miss Mayme.

SAWYIER

Yeah, but that has nothing to do with it.

GUS

No?

SAWYIER

No.

GUS

You in love with Miss Mayme? Or you in love with Miss Rose? *[He laughs]* My grandpa used to say, "Can't never ride two donkeys with one ass." *[SAWYIER laughs]* What you gonna say to Miss Mayme when she comes 'round?

SAWYIER

Why do I have to say anything?

GUS

Sometimes silence is an answer. Sometimes the truth. Sometimes a lie.

SAWYIER

If she wants an answer, I don't know what the question'd be. *[There is a knock at the door]* Who's that this time of evenin'?

GUS

Maybe that be the question, Mister Sawyier. *[GUS laughs and gathers up the cards. MAYME Bull enters. She is an attractive woman, also in her forties, a few months younger than SAWYIER; she wears a white puffed blouse with long skirt of the period, a gold watch on a chain around her neck, her hair up, all very fashionable. But her countenance does not match her dress: she is upset. Upset to have come to the riverboat, upset because of what she has heard, upset for not knowing what to say or do on this late afternoon.]*

SAWYIER

Mary. What a surprise . . .*[GUS looks away so as not to have his smile betrayed.]* Come in. Come in.

MAYME

'Evenin,' Gus.

GUS

[GUS has removed his hat and stands]

'Evenin,' Miss Bull. *[MAYME smiles and nods.]*

SAWYIER

Won't you have a seat? We were just playing some cards. You could join us. *[He motions to the sofa. She slowly sits on the edge of the sofa.]* Would you like something to drink? Or I could fix some tea . . .*[He pours a glass of bourbon and hands it to her. She takes it with no intention of drinking, as though thinking by going through these motions she will find her voice.]*

GUS

Nice to see you, Miss Bull. *[To SAWYIER]* I think I best 'be going.

SAWYIER

No, Gus. You don't need to go—

GUS

I need to check the lines down the ways. 'Let you two visit . . .

SAWYIER

Come right back, Gus.

GUS

'Evening, Miss Bull. *[GUS bows and exits. SAWYIER and MAYME are alone. The silence is awkward.]*

SAWYIER

What do you think of the houseboat? I read that Claude Monet has a houseboat on the river.

MAYME

It looks different.

SAWYIER

I've painted since you saw it last. 'Rearranged things. This is of course, The Parlour. And the Kitchen. And the Dining Room. *[She is quiet. He moves to the other side of the boat and gestures of the tour:]* The Drawing Room—my studio. The only one where we may withdraw and draw at the same time.

MAYME

It looks like a work of art in itself.

SAWYIER

Oh, it'll do.

MAYME

'Smells like biscuits 'been cookin'.

SAWYIER

[Darting for the stove]

You want some? I got country ham and—

MAYME

–Red-eyed gravy. No. I'm not hungry. You still drinkin' Boone Knoll?

SAWYIER

Yeah.

MAYME

What've you been paintin'?

SAWYIER

A portrait of the President of Transylvania . . . The Bishop. *[He guides her around the paintings in the room, and holds up the portrait of the Bishop.]* What do you think?

MAYME

'Very lifelike.

SAWYIER

'So lifelike I have to shave him every morning!

MAYME

You never did finish Mother's painting.

SAWYIER

I know. I need to do that. *[He moves around looking for that portrait.]* It's all finished but for the hands . . . and the book . . . and the chair . . .

MAYME

You brought your mother's sofa from the house. 'Looks nice here.

SAWYIER

One of the few things . . .

MAYME

It's almost like your mother's right here with us. 'Waiting for one of Doc Sawyier's patients to come knock at the door.

SAWYIER

All hours of the day and night. *[SAWYIER moves to the kitchen area to fix a plate of biscuits for MAYME anyway.]*

MAYME

How is he?

SAWYIER

Father? Half the time he doesn't know who I am. The other half he doesn't know who he is.

MAYME

'He still in the hospital? In Louisville?

SAWYIER

Yeah. I go up every week.

MAYME

He was always such a fine man. I know it's a worry for you.

SAWYIER

Yes. And your mother? How's she?

MAYME

We have a mutual relationship in everything. I do everything. She complains about everything. *[SAWYIER nods. He hands her a small plate of ham and biscuits which she places in her lap but never touches.]* You made a promise to your mother that you wouldn't leave town until after she was gone. Now you are free to follow your dream. The river. Privacy. Miles from town. You can paint to your heart's content out here. *[Curtly:]* You're never less alone than when you're by yourself.

SAWYIER

In the morning, the sun comes up over the ridge and shines on the water . . . Come out on the Veranda. *[He moves to the Left and out on the back little porch of the boat. MAYME puts away the plate but follows him with her drink. The two look out over the river in awe without saying anything for a moment. On both sides of the river are the breathtakingly tall limestone cliffs.]*

MAYME

The Palisades. *[She turns, sees the High Bridge in the distance, and shrieks! SAWYIER laughs at her surprise. The size of the bridge is enormousness. She laughs at herself.]* So, that's The High Bridge.

SAWYIER

Pretty amazing, isn't it?

MAYME

Trains will run across that?

SAWYIER

Yeah, and you'll be able to walk across it.

MAYME

All the marvels of God and man. I can see why you'd want to be down here. What's that over there? *[She gestures across the river.]*

SAWYIER

That's the landing for the Shakers. They send all their goods out, 'bring in new supplies.

MAYME

There aren't many of them left anymore. Not like they once were. They don't believe in having children. *[She had no intention of mentioning this.]*

SAWYIER

[Changing the subject, he looks up at the Palisades.]

I can't imagine the Grand Canyon being better than this.

MAYME

'No way to capture this in a painting.

SAWYIER

I can try. Look: there's a full moon. *[He looks around, his back to the railing.]* The sun goes down earlier here on the river. The river runs backward. Up to the North. And empties into the great Ohio. And starts from a tiny stream. *[With his hands holding his drink, he leans against his forearms on the railing.]* You should see it in the winter. The cliffs all white with snow. The leaves all gone, you can see right through the branches. 'See what's been hidden all summer. The sky so beautifully gray . . .

MAYME

I prefer color.

SAWYIER

All the life of color is there. In the shades of grays and browns. The green cedars here and there . . . the sky so cold, the air so dry . . .

MAYME

'Sounds depressing.

SAWYIER

No. It has a beauty all its own.

MAYME

My girlfriends and I, we went swimming on one of those gray days. We couldn't wait; we jumped in without our stockings. And you came along. You sat on the bank and just talked and talked to us. We kept hidden under the water, with only our heads stickin' out. You were all a gab—I thought you'd never shut up. By the time you finally left we were almost frozen blue!

SAWYIER

Why didn't you all get out?

MAYME

Without our stockings on? We would rather have frozen to death. *[Looking out over the river.]* I was baptized in this river.

SAWYIER

So was I.

MAYME

And yet . . . it has a terrible undertow. Lots of folks 'been drowned . . .

SAWYIER

Including the Bishop. *[MAYME looks in surprise]* The wind blew His Reverence off my easel the other day. I bet his Reverence is drifting toward that sweet old town of Frankfort.

MAYME

[She looks down at the river, and quotes from a favorite poem:]

"For underneath its restless flow,
Too black for light's full noon to show,
Lie broken rocks no mortals know.
So quiet is the river."

Do you bring Rose here?

SAWYIER

Mary . . .

MAYME

Do you? Have you? Tell me about Rose Stoddard.

SAWYIER

So, that's why you came. *[He walks around the porch. MAYME puts her drink down.]* What have you heard?

MAYME

What are you going to tell me? *[SAWYIER avoids her eyes.]* You've been seen with her. They say you see a lot of her.

SAWYIER

We are friends—

MAYME

'Seen with her practically every day. And she lives nearby.

SAWYIER

She lives in Cincinnati with friends: the Doughertys. He's here building the bridge. He's the one I told you about that's been helping me sell my paintings–

MAYME

You know what I mean.

SAWYIER

He takes my paintings up to Cincinnati and they exhibit them—he's sold several for me. Rose is a companion to his wife. They're nice people. They'll be gone before long.

MAYME

You spent New Year's with her.

SAWYIER

I spent New Year's with *them.* I invited you.

MAYME

I couldn't leave Mother. Paul, we are engaged.

SAWYIER

I know.

MAYME

We still haven't set a date.

SAWYIER

I've been painting.

MAYME

You are always painting. Do you love her?

SAWYIER

Don't be cross with me, Mary—

MAYME

[Sternly]

Do you love her? *[SAWYIER does not answer.]*

MAYME

You are old enough to be her father! Is that the attraction? She makes you feel young? Well, I was young once, too, you know. Don't you remember?

SAWYIER

Of course—

MAYME

And I waited for you. All these years. Hoping for tomorrow to come . . . For us to marry. *[SAWYIER, having heard this a hundred times before, walks away into the houseboat and fills his glass. MAYME stands in the doorway to the porch and faces him.]* For us to make the Old Red Brick our own home. To have our own children. What was I waiting for, Paul? Waiting and growing older. Now, I'm too old to have children.

SAWYIER

I can't get married until I have a steady income–

MAYME

We've been engaged for a year and a half and we haven't set a date. When are we going to get married, Paul?

SAWYIER

I need to sell some more paintings. . .

MAYME

Are we going to get married, Paul?

SAWYIER

I've told you: I'm not going to raise a family in poverty.

MAYME

I got a letter from your sister the other day. *[Oh, how he dreads to hear this!]* She says she knows President Taft. Weren't your families good friends at one time?

SAWYIER

Yes. A while back. Billy and I used to play together.

MAYME

"Billy?" *[Surprised that he is so familiar with the President.]* He's done well for himself—

SAWYIER

Yes, he has.

MAYME

Your sister says she can convince The President to exhibit your paintings in Washington–

SAWYIER

Oh, please, don't do me any favors!

MAYME

In Washington, Paul. The Capital.

SAWYIER

I'd rather starve, thank you.

MAYME

Why?

SAWYIER

I don't need charity.

MAYME

From the Tafts? Or from your sister?

SAWYIER

From either of them. All of them. Especially her. I can make it on my own.

MAYME

Why won't you let them help you? You could be a success!

SAWYIER

I'm not a failure, Mary.

MAYME

I didn't say you were. *[They are silent.]* I just thought—

SAWYIER

No.

MAYME

You need the money–

SAWYIER

No. I'm not complaining. My life is good. A great sport. I have my work. This boat. The river. Lots of people don't have that. I bet Billy wishes he had.

MAYME

I don't see the harm in letting the Tafts exhibit your work–

SAWYIER

My sister would do better coming back here and helping her father. 'Too late for her mother.

MAYME

Your mother was a fine lady.

SAWYIER

My father made her life hell. Borrowing all that money, losing his practice,—

MAYME

Only in these last years—

SAWYIER

[Losing his temper:]

Do you want to end up like my mother? So poor you can't even afford to live in your own house because you have to rent it out? Living in the preacher's parsonage that flooded every time the river rose! She had to bake cakes just to pay the water bill.

MAYME

I like baking cakes.

SAWYIER

Yeah, but not for a living. And you wouldn't like running your Father's Shoe Shop the rest of your life, either.

MAYME

I don't mind it.

SAWYIER

I didn't mind working in the Mill. But not for a living.

MAYME

If you got a real job you'd have a real income–

SAWYIER

This is a real job.

MAYME

Paul . . . *[Carefully:]* You paint pictures of the river. Of horses and wagons the way they used to be. Of bridges that are gone.

SAWYIER

So?

MAYME

You get pennies for your work. You did better working in your Father's Mill.

SAWYIER

Selling twine? I'm not doing that again. My life is more than hemp. People don't understand about a painting. It's not a photograph. It's a piece of the artist's heart and soul . . . 'A piece of my life.

MAYME

I think your problem is pride.

SAWYIER

What?

MAYME

You never grew up in poverty. Your father was a doctor. Your grandparents 'bankers and lawyers.

SAWYIER

Father was gone all the time–

MAYME

Yes, **working,** so that you could live in a fine house in town and know the finest people. 'Go to the finest parties.

SAWYIER

And look where it got him: he lost his mind. Look what the Shoe Shop did to your father—he worked himself to death.

MAYME

Your brother went all the way to Mississippi to find a job. He married: they were poor but happy—my brothers told me so.

SAWYIER

Yes, and he stopped painting. And he died at twenty-seven.

MAYME

You never talk about your brother. *[And he still will not.]* The bank makes allowances for you because of your family's reputation. The Church let you live for free in their parsonage because of it.

SAWYIER

That's why I moved out of the parsonage and bought this boat.

MAYME

I heard it was the drinking.

SAWYIER

The agreement was made with my mother. My mother is gone, and so is the agreement.

MAYME

The Baptist church didn't approve of your drinking. You played the organ on Sunday mornings; they could smell it on your breath. That's what I heard.

SAWYIER

Well, you heard wrong.

MAYME

Your father never drank.

SAWYIER

No, but maybe he should have. He might have been happier. My father was miserable. His only dream growing up was to be an artist; Grandfather forced him to be a doctor. That's why Father wanted us to paint.

MAYME

A luxury *you* could not afford on your own. Look at you. The only artist who dresses in shirt and tie to paint.

SAWYIER

I dress to go to work.

MAYME

It's just you and your paints. Who cares if you dress up every day?

SAWYIER

I care. I do it for myself. And my art.

MAYME

Your art! *[It always comes down to this. MAYME comes back into the room. SAWYIER offers to refill her drink but she refuses. Going toward the sofa:]* So, you are still receiving rent from the house?

SAWYIER

Yes.

MAYME

The Old Red Brick. I would like to have seen it before the train came through and they built the depot across the street. I had hoped that one day. . . *[She stops.]* And all the lovely furniture? Did your sisters take it?

SAWYIER

A few of the old things. The rest were cried off.[2] Except Mother's sofa.

---

[2] Auctioned off to the highest bidder. Willard Rouse Jillson, *Paul Sawyier and His Paintings*, prelude address for the Centennial Exhibition of the paintings, etchings, and miniatures of Paul Sawyer at the Speed Memorial Museum, delivered March 1, 1965, p. 14.

MAYME

It looks good here. We had our first kiss in the parlour on this sofa; you spilt your tea . . . *[She searches closely for the spot. Yes, it is there.]* You can still see the stain. It never really left. Nor has the memory of that kiss. It was my first kiss.

SAWYIER

Mine, too.

MAYME

What did it make you think of?

SAWYIER

Grandmother. *[MAYME is quickly offended!]* The sofa belonged to my grandmother. I think of her. I think of lying in her lap. Painting on paper with her. A purple vase.

MAYME

On this sofa is where your art began?

SAWYIER

In a way, yes. With my grandmother.

MAYME

So, this is the culprit that ruined our lives. *[SAWYIER laughs. MAYME tries not to, but she gives in and laughs at herself]* And then your father sent for that artist. What was her name?

SAWYIER

Miss Hutchins–

MAYME

Yes! Miss Hutchins of Cincinnati. She came to tutor all of you. You were her best student—far better than your sisters.

SAWYIER

It was expected.

MAYME

I can see her now sitting on this sofa. Wouldn't it be amazing if *all the people* who ever sat on could come back . . . for just one evening? What stories they would tell! *[She strokes the arm of the sofa, as if it were a cherished friend.]*

SAWYIER

From both villages.

MAYME

[She goes back to the door of the porch, unwilling to let go of the last glimpse of the river. Retrieving her plate, she takes the top off the biscuit and eats.]

The lightning bugs make the prettiest reflections on the water. Oh, how we used to love to catch them! To keep the light . . . Until they. . . *[SAWYIER joins her once more on the porch looking out over the river at dusk and the Palisades.]* We were the perfect couple. That was the day. Our unguarded moment.

SAWYIER

You liked the paintings didn't you? "The Two Villages?" You said you did.

MAYME

Some girls get roses. Some girls get diamonds. I get paintings of the cemetery up on the cliff with the town down below. Of course, I like them. Why did you paint them?

SAWYIER

I knew how much you loved the poem.

MAYME

I do love the poem. But I think you painted them to *keep* them. The way we tried to keep the lightening bugs. The way you kept the old covered bridge: they tore it down and built a big new steel one, but it stays the same in your paintings. The river flows, always changing and moving away, but in your paintings it stays the same. The way you captured me in the canoe. Just sitting there. Waiting.

SAWYIER

You make it sound like a bird . . . in a cage.

MAYME

Birds don't fly away if they are kept in a cage. They can't come near. *[She recites the poem:]*

When the night is starry and still,
Many a weary soul in prayer
Looks to the other village there,
And weeping and sighing, longs to go
Up to that home from this below;
Longs to sleep in the forest wild,
Whither have vanished wife and child,
And heareth, praying, this answer fall:

[They say the last line of the poem together:]

"Patience! that village shall hold ye all!

MAYME

You painted the cemetery on the hill, the town below in the valley. And the river divided them. And we rode the river. Here we are still riding the river. You painted that man in there.

SAWYIER

Uncle Gus.

MAYME

He's not your Uncle.

SAWYIER

The children call him that.

MAYME

It's a portrait of a colored man, a common rock breaker.

SAWYIER

'Not to the kids in town. He holds them all in the palm of his hand when he weaves his stories. The rich and the poor alike. White and Black. I bet he's better known—and respected—in town than the Governor. He's more approachable.

MAYME

He wears that same coyote hat summer and winter. People in town talk about the kind of people you have out here.

SAWYIER

Then their lives must be awful boring.

MAYME

Is that why you moved your boat down here to the High Bridge?

SAWYIER

I'm a painter. I'm not ashamed of it. Some people like my art. And I like the people who like my art.

MAYME

We're all just a big painting that you're keeping. And there are too many people in it. *[SAWYIER is reminded of this side of her that he does not like.]* There's no room on your canvas for me. I get painted in as an afterthought. Down at the bottom where you sign your name.

SAWYIER

That's not true. Why do you say such things? We've been taking care of our parents. That's been our lives.

MAYME

You've been trying to pay off your Father's debts for so long that you haven't had a life of your own. It isn't fair to you. It wasn't fair to your mother. All she knew was taking care of him.

SAWYIER

She's dead now. It's over. Let's put it behind us.

MAYME

It's not over. You're still paying his debts. You are, aren't you? He's probably running away right now like he did last time, and to the Banks who will issue him more and more money, so you can be more and more in their debt! They've got you by the throat.

SAWYIER

He wanted Natalie and me to study in Europe. We signed the note with him.

MAYME

[This is a strange piece to the puzzle.]

You never told me that.

SAWYIER

No, . . . I . . . Well, we did. But Father was sure he could pay it back. He always had before.

MAYME

Natalie went to Europe and studied. But you didn't.

SAWYIER

No, by that time Father was sick.

MAYME

And your sister Natalie gone. And you left holding the note.

SAWYIER

Yes, something like that. Yes.

MAYME

But then he took out another loan, didn't he? It was all a lot of money. Where is all that money?

SAWYIER

Wherever his mind is, I guess.

MAYME

Oh, Paul . . .

SAWYIER

We sold our shares in the Mill. When he passes, I'll have the house. I'll mortgage it and finish paying the debts.

MAYME

You never told me about the note. You never told me about Rose Stoddard. We used to tell each other everything.

SAWYIER

You would like Rose if you met her. You would. In some ways you are both a lot alike.

MAYME

Ha! I doubt it.

SAWYIER

The way you used to be. Before you changed.

MAYME

If I've changed it's because you made me like this!

SAWYIER

No. You made yourself like this.

MAYME

You brought this boat up here to get away from me! You went to Cincinnati to get away from me!

SAWYIER

I went to Cincinnati to study Art! Why are you like this?

MAYME

Like what?

SAWYIER

[Losing his patience]

Like this! You're so full of anger all the time. It's like poison to be around.

MAYME

Poison? What about you!

SAWYIER

Whenever we go anywhere, I can't have a conversation with anyone but you finish my sentences for me from across the room. It's like if I'm out of your sight for a minute you lose control of me. I come down here and you follow me to see what I'm up to, as if you're going to miss something. People aren't supposed to smother other people. 'Control them. It's just no good that way. *[He walks away, turns and takes a deep look at her.]* Sometimes. . . Sometimes it's just a relief to be away from you. To be here alone on the river.

MAYME

I can't help the way I am!

SAWYIER

We can all help the way we are. There are no excuses, Mary. If we are victims then we have made ourselves victims. That's what Gus says. *[MAYME moves away from SAWYIER and goes back into the boat. She stands near the sofa where Gus had sat. She looks at the cards. SAWYIER lights a lamp.]*

MAYME

Oh really? What else does Gus say?

SAWYIER

That you need to marry a rich man, who can give you all the things you dreamed of, and let you write your poetry. I can never do that.

MAYME

I can't leave my Mother, Paul . . .

SAWYIER

I would never ask you to. I wouldn't want you to. I wouldn't love you the way I do if you did.

MAYME

Do you love me, Paul?

SAWYIER

We've grown up together.

MAYME

[Walks around the room. Looks at the canvases.]

Since we were kids in school. We shared everything. Our friends. Our first dance. Our first kiss. But I'm not your art. And your art is your first love. I'm tired of waiting, Paul. Do you realize that this is the only evening we've ever spent together unchaperoned. There's always a flock of people around—

SAWYIER

Gus is here—

MAYME

Who cares! I'm forty-five years old. Over twenty years we have been together and played the rules of society to please them all. For what? For what, damn it! What has it got us? Where has it got us! Another night watching the river pass us by. The moon on the river. So quiet is the river.

SAWYIER

It was your decision to wait.

MAYME

Well, maybe I just got tired of waiting. Is there anything wrong with that? Did you sleep with her? *[But there is no answer.]* That's it, isn't it? *[He turns from her and is silent. Her rage rises, and steaming tears with them. She goes at him with her fists; he stops them.]*

SAWYIER

Stop it! *[Too emotional, MAYME can't get her breath, bends over gasping for it.]* Now, breathe. Just breathe. *[He waits while her breathing returns. She sits on the sofa. He pours her a glass of water and takes it to her.]*

SAWYIER

You always get so worked up over things. You are my best friend. I wanted to tell you about Rose. I tried to.

MAYME

[She drinks from the water and is calmer. It helps float her back to her poetry, to the sweet old town, to the way things once were long before. Things she had forgotten.]

When I was very little, we used to go sit and listen to him weave his stories. "Uncle Gus," we used to call him. We thought he was a hundred years old then. He would tell us of faraway places and animals. It was all so . . . quaint . . . and exciting . . . and *innocent.* We were intoxicated with it. And I thought life would come to me like that. Eventually. *[She takes a deep sigh, gets up from the sofa. Wanders around the neat, artistic studio. Her housekeeping would probably never live up to his standards.]* Later I learned that he had fought in the War. 'How they had separated the colored soldiers from the whites. 'How they treated them. It was anything but innocent–*[She rummages through the canvases looking again for her mother's portrait. One particular painting steals her attention. Then another. Another–]* My paintings . . .

SAWYIER

[They are copies of The Two Villages.]

Yes. I've been commissioned to do two more sets of them. I guess they saw yours and must of really liked them. *[The undertow of the river.]*

MAYME

I'm glad I've served a purpose in your commercial enterprise. *[This current has helped her catch her footing. And in it she finds her breath.]* I didn't come here today to protest Rose Stoddard. I came to protect her.

SAWYIER

Protect her?

MAYME

You can't love the way a man should love a woman—the way I want you to love me. And you will never love her that way either. I know that. You know that. Paul, . . . you must be honest with her. You owe it to her. Don't find yourself with her twenty years from now, the way you find yourself with me now.

SAWYIER

I should have told you.

MAYME

I think I've known all along. But she needs to know the truth. We can at least spare her our pain. *[She places the glass by the sink and goes to the table of cards below the sofa. She takes off her ring.]* You were always a brother, a friend. I never meant to tell you that I loved you. *[She places the ring on the table.]* Time loves a new day. *[She takes a deep breath of its memory. Warm and comforting. But the sun has set on that day. She looks at her watch that reminds her of what has gone and can never come again.]*

SAWYIER

Let's set a date for the wedding.

MAYME

[But she can't hear this. And it has come too late. Like a piece of driftwood that has floated too quickly out of reach.]

The driver is waiting, and the Terhune's are expecting me for supper. I'll take the train home in the morning . . . Mother needs me. *[She would like to laugh at the irony of her last words but cannot. Instead, she opens the screen door, looks out from the porch to the moon as it starts to reflect on the river. She knows that when she takes these feeble steps from the door they will never return to Paul again.]*

SAWYIER

I'll get a lantern.

MAYME

No.

SAWYIER

I'll go with you—

MAYME

No. I can make it up the bank by myself. *[So much she would like to say, but cannot. All the things that have been too many times said before. He has been a permanent staple for as long as she can remember, but somehow, she knows now that she will never see SAWYIER again in her lifetime.]* The day after is never tomorrow, is it? *[MAYME exits, passing GUS at the door. All is silent. GUS walks into the boat. SAWYIER fills his glass with bourbon and takes a heavy drink.]*

GUS

Ain't no fish on the lines. Unless they got away. *[SAWYIER leans his head over the sink.]* 'You all right, Mister Sawyier? You look as if your best dog done died. *[SAWYIER gets his guitar and takes it to the back porch. He strums the guitar. The strings of his heart, like the strings of the guitar, are in tune but have not the same old tone. His grief follows these cords, follows the flow of the river. GUS sits on the sofa, sees the ring on the table.]* You got it wrong, Mister Sawyier. All wrong. *[SAWYIER stops strumming the guitar.]* That aint' the dog that died. You be the dog that died.

SAWYIER

How's that?

GUS

You can't remember the War, can you?

SAWYIER

[Watching the river.]

No, I was born the year it ended.

GUS

Well, many a soldier in that war give his life so as his friend could return to that village of the living . . . in the valley. They went to that village on the hill.

SAWYIER

Your point being . . .?

GUS

That's what love is. *[SAWYIER plays a bit more. Stops.]*

SAWYIER

It's much greater than that when it's been your whole life.

GUS

Then it's greater love. *[SAWYIER puts the guitar down. The fingers of one hand now playing his gold ring on the little finger of the other.]*

SAWYIER

It shouldn't have to hurt so much.

GUS

Naw, you're right, it shouldn't, Mister Sawyier. I had a little squirrel once. I nursed it on the thumb of a glove—used to climb on my shoulder. 'Used to keep him in my pocket. 'Til one day I figured, that squirrel could never live the life a squirrel is meant to live unless I set it loose. So, I set it free. Oh, it like to killed me. But when I think of it out there running around with all its little friends, . . . it does my heart good. You see, I loved that squirrel. *[SAWYIER walks over to the sofa, takes her ring into his fist. GUS laughs:]* Sometime, . . . that little varmint 'come by my window 'a evening just to check on me . . . And then he be gone. *[SAWYIER puts her ring in his pocket.]* Funny she a showin' up here tonight like that. Miss Mayme aint one to come uninvited. You don't fool me none, Mister Sawyier.

SAWYIER

No. I guess not. How'd you get to be so wise? *[GUS laughs and deals the cards. SAWYIER lights a cigar and pours a drink. The river flows. The moon reflects on the river.]*

CURTAIN

The Two Villages

By Rose (Terry) Cooke 1827-1892

Kentucky Theater Association's Roots of the Bluegrass Play Writing Competition

Over the river, on the hill,
Lieth a village white and still;
All around it the forest-trees
Shiver and whisper in the breeze;
Over it sailing shadows go
Of soaring hawk and screaming crow,
And mountain grasses, low and sweet,
Grow in the middle of every street.

Over the river, under the hill,
Another village lieth still;
There I see in the cloudy night
Twinkling stars of household light,
Fires that gleam from the smithy's door,
Mists that curl on the river-shore;
And in the roads no grasses grow,
For the wheels that hasten to and fro.

In that village on the hill
Never is sound of smithy or mill;
The houses are thatched with grass and flowers;
Never a clock to toll the hours;
The marble doors are always shut,
You cannot enter in hall or hut;
All the villagers lie asleep;
Never a grain to sow or reap;
Never in dreams to moan or sigh;
Silent and idle and low they lie.

In that village under the hill,
When the night is starry and still,

Many a weary soul in prayer
Looks to the other village there,
And weeping and sighing, longs to go
Up to that home from this below;
Longs to sleep in the forest wild,
Whither have vanished wife and child,
And heareth, praying, this answer fall:
'Patience! That village shall hold ye all!'

POSTSCRIPT

PAUL SAWYIER
1865-1917

Figure 38

At the age of five, Paul Sawyier came with his family to "that sweet old town" of Frankfort, Kentucky. He had been born on Table Rock Farm near London, Ohio, March 23, 1865, just a couple weeks before the signing of surrender at the Appomattox Courthouse that ended the Civil War. Frankfort had been the home of his grandfather, Nathaniel Sawyier, Sr., who had been admitted to the practice of law in Franklin County by 1819.

When Kentucky became its own state in 1792, Reuben Anderson was awarded several large land grants on the Elkhorn Creek and in Frankfort, its capital city. He built a handsome Federal brick house for his family at what would become 112 East Broadway, in the heart of the select part of Frankfort reserved for upper class society. A large addition was later built to accommodate the growing family. The quaintness of the neighborhood changed when the railroad tunnel was cut into the hillside nearby bringing the train into town for the first time and through their front yard in 1850, with the depot built across the street. Sneed's drawing of the Penitentiary in 1860, shows the Anderson House as the only house then on the street.[1] The Anderson House was given to Reuben's daughter, Penelope as a wedding present when she married banker Henry Wingate, and Penelope's daughter Ellen was Paul's mother. Reuben's other daughter, Pemelia, would marry Nathanial J. Sawyier, Sr., and her

---

[1] Sneed, *The Kentucky Penitentiary*; Carl E. Kramer, *Capital on the Kentucky*, "Bird's Eye View of the Penitentiary from the Blanton's Hill (1860)," (Frankfort, Kentucky: Historic Frankfort, Inc., 1986), p. 163.

son was Paul's father. Paul Sawyier's parents were first cousins.[2] Thus, the Anderson House was the ancestral home to both Paul's father and mother. And so it was that when Penelope was left widowed and alone in the old Anderson House, her nephew Dr. Nathanial J. Sawyier, Jr., his wife Ellen Wingate [her daughter], and their three children made it their permanent residence with her on June 20, 1870.

Paul grew up in the Anderson House learning piano, guitar, and painting. He began elementary school in September of 1871, under Principal Samuel P. Browder. At twelve years of age, Miss Elizabeth S. Hutchins of Cincinnati was employed as private art instructor to the Sawyier children during the summer months. Paul made more rapid progress than the other children, as Ellen remarked, "It was expected."[3] In the fall of 1881, Paul was enrolled into the Dudley Institute in South Frankfort where he graduated high school in 1883. Professor Thomas M. Turner noted that Paul was "not of a very bookish inclination," and taking notice of Paul's fine artwork, scribbled amidst his Latin and Math notebooks, saw that it "indicated a very decided preference of the young man for art."[4]

In the fall of 1884, Paul was registered as student at the Cincinnati Art Academy under Thomas Satterwhite Nobel studying figure and portrait painting. Then he and Avery Sharp worked at a commercial portrait studio in Cincinnati. But in 1886, Paul was called to the Kentucky River Mill to assist his father as salesman for hemp production. In the fall of 1889, he was enrolled in the New York Arts Student's League and studied under William Merritt Chase. Chase is thought to have had a strong influence on Paul's later impressionistic style, believed Paul was talented, and given him the advice: "Be yourself, Paul—be

[2] Willard Rouse Jillson, *Paul Sawyier and His Paintings*, prelude address for the Centennial Exhibition of the paintings, etchings, and miniatures of Paul Sawyer at the Speed Memorial Museum, delivered March 1, 1965, pp. 8-9.
[3] Ibid., p. 10.
[4] Ibid., p. 9.

your individual self; be Paul Sawyier."[5]

In April 1890, Paul returned to Cincinnati, Ohio to study under portrait painter Frank Duveneck. During this time, his older brother, Henry Wingate Sawyier, also a painter, moved to Greenville, Mississippi with Mayme Bull's brothers and died there September 17, 1890. Henry was 27 years old.[6]

Figure 39

In the summer of 1891, Paul returned to the Anderson House and four years later opened a studio upstairs of H.G. Mattern's photography shop where he exhibited his works for sale. Other locations for his exhibits included Todd's Store on St. Clair Street, Capital Trust Company building corner of West Main and St. Clair, with raffles at Frank Stagg's Hardware Store on Ann Street.[7] He also played the organ for the First Baptist Church.

Paul's father began to experience dementia, lost his medical practice, and borrowed large sums of money from the bank. The First Baptist Church offered their vacant parsonage to Ellen Sawyier so that she could care for her husband there away from the dangerous train tracks; this allowed her

---

[5]Mary Sawyier Neiss-Waner. Arthur R. Jones, The *Art of Paul Sawyier* (Lexington, Kentucky: The University Press of Kentucky), 1976, p. 10.
[6] Jillson, "*Paul Sawyier and His Paintings,*" p 13; William Donald Coffey, *Paul Sawyier--Kentucky Artist* (Frankfort, Kentucky: Frankfort Heritage Press, 2010), pp. 42, 175.
[7] Jillson, "*Paul Sawyier and His Paintings,*" p.12.

Figure 40

to rent out the Anderson House and bake cakes to help pay expenses. The parsonage was located at 205 St. Clair Street directly behind the Church. Ellen fell and broke her leg and became unable to care for her husband, and as Dr. Sawyier's dementia worsened, Paul was forced to admit him into the Lakelane Insane Asylum in Louisville. Ellen grieved over the situation and died April 13, 1908.[8]

The Sawyiers had many friends, both white and black, who came to assist and show respects to the family at Ellen's death. Paul's sisters, Lillian, Natalie, and Mary, all returned for the funeral and took pieces of furniture, and what was left was "cried out," or auctioned to the highest bidder. Paul lived for a while with his cousin Russel McRery at the corner of Steel and Third Streets in South Frankfort, as the arrangement with the parsonage had been made for Ellen while she was alive.[9]

Paul contracted with C. F. Bower and Company, a household furnishings store in Lexington, giving them exclusive rights to sell his paintings. He bought a houseboat and moved it up to High Bridge Landing in August 1908. In the spring of 1909, he met Rose Stoddard of Cincinnati, Ohio and they became friends. Rose was twenty years younger than Paul, and was a paid companion to the wife of Curtis Dougherty, architect for the bridge expansion. On June 23, 1910, Paul's lifelong sweetheart and fiancée Mayme Bull came unexpectedly to the houseboat to confront him about Rose. They parted that night never to see each other again. That

[8] Ibid., pp. 13-14.
[9] Ibid.

following November 17, Dr. Sawyier died in the Louisville hospital with Paul at his side.[10]

Paul enjoyed the company of other men and was known as the "Prince of Good Fellows." His houseboat entertained many visitors, "men-only."[11] John Wilson Townsend, Kentucky historian, twenty years younger, met Paul in 1909, and became a strong supporter of Paul's talent and introduced him to collectors; Townsend would often stay at the boat. As did John J. King, also in his twenties, who was the wealthy owner of the Frankfort Hotel and commissioned Paul for many paintings.[12] Two large Sawyier oil paintings were built into the walls of the hotel lobby of the Frankfort Hotel.[13] When Paul moved to New York and boarded at the home of his sister Lillian and her husband, he shared third floor rooms with a fellow student from the Art Students League.[14] When he moved into the old chapel/studio on the Highmount estate of
Mrs. Marshall L. Emory in New York, he shared it with Belgian artist, Edward Buyck.[15]

Boone's Knoll was the favorite bourbon drink of Paul Sawyier, "to ward off the river's Ward off the river's chill."[16] Edward J. Curley founded the distillery in 1860s. Born from Irish immigrants, Curley was a recruit to the Union Army stationed in Lexington, Kentucky. Outside of Lexington was an installation Camp Nelson, Jessamine County, that recruited emancipated Blacks for soldiers. One of Curley's partners in the distillery was Dwight A. Aiken, captain in the Commissary

---

[10] Coffey, "*Paul Sawyier--Kentucky Artist,*" pp. 95-97, 106-107;
Jillson, "*Paul Sawyier and His Paintings*," p.16-17.
[11] Mary Darby Fitzhugh, letter to Willard Rouse Jillson, dated 1939;
Coffey, *"Paul Sawyier--Kentucky Artist*, p. 102.
[12] Coffey, "*Paul Sawyier--Kentucky Artist,*" pp. 98, 102-103, 109-110.
[13] Interview with Jouett Sheetinger, who rescued the paintings from the Frankfort Hotel as it was being demolished and later sold them to Mrs. Louis B. Nunn for the Kentucky Governor's Mansion.
[14] Lillian Sawyier Hill, "My Memories," December 1939;
[15] Jones, "*The Art of Paul Sawyier*," p.29.
[16] John Wilson Townsend, Coffey, "*Paul Sawyier—Kentucky Artist,*" p. 118.

Department of the Union Army. Curley's distillery was built near Camp Nelson on "Boone's Knoll," a favorite ford across the Kentucky River to legendary pioneer Daniel Boone; the drink was bottled "Blue Grass Whiskey" and exported overseas. His second distillery was built just across the river and known as the "Boone's Knoll Distillery." Curley sold his industry in 1889, and its new manager, August C. Gutzeit, bottled "Boone's Knoll Bourbon." Prohibition put many distilleries out of business, but parts of Boone's Knoll survived for medicinal purposes. In the 1960's it was sold to produce Canada Dry soft drinks.[17]
Julian Van Winkle, III, continued its name and production in Lawrenceburg 1990, exporting it to Japan. Another recipe of his grandfather "Pappy" Van Winkle was resurrected after prohibition and is now being produced by Buffalo Trace Distilleries in Frankfort, an elite bourbon aged fifteen, twenty, and twenty-three years.[18]

On August 22, 1913, Paul sold the Anderson House and stayed with his sister Lillian, Mrs. Hawthorn Hill, at 329 Lincoln Road in Brooklyn, New York, painting realistic landscapes in oil. In 1914, Paul retreated to the Catskill Mountains at the invitation of an elderly Belgian lady, Mrs. Marie Shields Myer and stayed in the summer home of her sister, Mrs. Marshall L. Emory. In October, while visiting art dealer Edward Jackson in his store, Paul received a wire of Mayme Bull's death; he went into a rear room requesting to be left alone, then he took the train to Frankfort for the funeral. He asked only for Mayme's eyeglasses and later wore them with his own lenses. At the cemetery, he began a painting of Mayme's gravesite painted to the lyrics of a popular song "Absent" by Catherine Young Glen and John W. Metcalf.[19] Mrs. Emory loaned Paul the use of her chapel to use as a painting gallery for the winter, and there Paul stayed with fellow artist, Edward Buyck.

---

[17]Jack Sullivan, E. *J. Curley Turned Boone's Knoll into a Distilling Marvel*, Thursday, January 22, 2015.
[18] Interview with Buffalo Trace Distilleries, Frankfort, Kentucky, June 2015.
[19]Coffey, "*Paul Sawyier--Kentucky Artist*," pp. 124-5.

In the spring of 1916, Paul took rooms with Mr. Philip F. Schaeffer a store merchant of the nearby town of Fleischmanns, New York, near the Delaware River. There he was given their attic for a studio. Mrs. Myer wrote a check to the Schaeffers to cover his indebtedness, and often sent him pocket money, clothing, and art supplies.[20]

Suffering from heart problems, Paul fell ill and was nursed by the Schaeffer family and many friends until his death in November of 1917. Paul's sisters removed his belongings from the Schaeffer home and found personal letters belonging to Paul that he had carefully preserved and stored in a trunk; they quickly burned the bundles of letters to keep his private life from being "exposed."[21]

On June 9, 1923, the body of Paul Sawyier was brought to Frankfort and laid in the Frankfort Cemetery, of which Paul had painted in his collection, *The Two Villages*.

---

[20] Jones, "*The Art of Paul Sawyier,*" p. 31.
[21]Natalie Sawyier Bentz to a friend, 1933; Coffey, "*Paul Sawyier--Kentucky Artist,*" p. 149.

MAYME BULL

1865--1914

Figure 41

Mary Thomas Bull was the fourth of nine children, born to Samuel C. Bull and Jacqueline Page in Frankfort, Kentucky, on July 25, 1865. Family and friends called her "Mayme," but Paul Sawyier always called her "Mary." Samuel Bull was a book dealer who bought William M. Todd's bookstore, and was choir director of First Presbyterian Church and Superintendent of the Sunday School. He was proprietor of the City Mills, milling business, from 1873-1877, then sold the business and bought his own shoe store. In 1891 he was bookkeeper at R.K. McClure, life insurance agent, and served on the Board of Commissioners of Kentucky Institute for Education and Training of Feeble-Minded Children.[22]

In 1881, Mayme's two older sisters Jennie Page and Annie Tilford died of fever, fourteen days apart. After her father died January 19, 1905, with her older brother Samuel Jr. married and living in Greenville, Mississippi, Mayme was left in Frankfort as the eldest of the Bull children and cared for her mother, siblings and their children.

---

[22] Coffey, "*Paul Sawyier--Kentucky Artist,*" p.175.

Mary attended the Second Street Elementary school where she would have known Paul Sawyier. Emma Morris is said to have reintroduced Mayme to Paul in 1887, at the home of Dr. William Morris near Knight's Bridge, which led to the start of their romance.[23] For years they went to dances and parties as a couple and were engaged to be married Christmas of 1908. On the afternoon of June 23, 1910, after twenty-three years of dating and eighteen months engaged, Mayme appeared at Paul's houseboat docked at High Bridge and called off the engagement. They never saw each other again.[24] Mayme died four years later October 6, 1914, from "nervous prostration." Paul returned to Frankfort for the funeral; he would join her in death three years later. Both would be buried in one of The Two Villages that Paul had painted for her: the Frankfort Cemetery.

Mary was a poet. Paul painted for her a nineteen-page portfolio of watercolor paintings illustrating one of her favorite poems, *The Two Villages*, by Rose (Terry) Cooke. Three sets of these paintings exist today, one set having been donated to the Historical Society by Miss Ann Thomas. Ann's brother, Western, great nephew to Emily Tubman, was close friends with Paul and Mayme.

---

[3] Ibid., p. 32.
[4] Ibid., pp. 103-104.

UNCLE GUS

"After a long day at school, what a relief it was to stroll idly homeward along the dusty pike, lingering for a talk with old Uncle Gus, the colored philosopher, as he sat on the rock pile breaking rock by hand," wrote Ermina Jett Darnell of her childhood memories in Frankfort in her book, Filling the Chinks. "A unique public character, he has long since been immortalized by Paul Sawyier's remarkable portrait, "The Rock Breaker.""[25]

Figure 42

Paul painted this town celebrity in pastels and dated the work at the top, May 26, 1903. The man is said also to have been known as Henry Waters, who—thinking himself so unattractive in the portrait—remarked that Mr. Sawyier need not fear it being stolen. Other sources call the man "Uncle Jo."[26]

THE TWO VILLAGES was commissioned by Kentucky Playwrights Workshop and premiered at the Bards Town Theatre, Louisville in August 2015. It was performed by Theater on the River summer 2017 at the Ward Oates Amphitheater in Frankfort beside the river that Paul loved.

---

[25] Ermina Jett Darnell, *Filling the Chinks* (Frankfort, Kentucky: Roberts Printing Co., 1966), p.127.

[26] Coffey, "*Paul Sawyier--Kentucky Artist*," p. 78.

BIBLIOGRAPHY

Coffey, William Donald. Paul Sawyier–Kentucky Artist. Frankfort Heritage Press, 2010.

Darnell, Ermina Jett. *Filling the Chinks*, Roberts Printing Co., Frankfort, 1966.

Glenn, Nettie. *Love to All, Your Paul*, Science Press, Ephrata, PA; copyright Mrs. John Glenn, Frankfort, 1974.

Jillson, Willard Rouse. *A Bibliography of Paul Sawyier, American Artist, 1865-1917*, 1939.

Jillson, Willard Rouse. *Paul Sawyier and His Paintings*, prelude address for the Centennial Exhibition of the paintings, etchings, and miniatures of Paul Sawyer at the Speed Memorial Museum, delivered March 1, 1965.

Jones, Arthur R. *The Art of Paul Sawyier*, The University Press of Kentucky, Lexington, Kentucky, 1976.

Kramer, Carl E. *Capital on the Kentucky*, "Bird's Eye View of the Penitentiary from the Blanton's Hill (1860)." Historic Frankfort, Inc., Frankfort, Kentucky, 1986.

Index

PREFACE

THE BOTANIC GARDEN

EMMA OF ELMWOOD

THE DUST OF SUMMER

THE TWO VILLAGES

About the Author

Richard Cavendish, is the registered pen name with Dramatists Guild of America for the Rev. Dr. Russell Richard Rechenbach, II, a native of Frankfort, Kentucky. He graduated from Transylvania University with a Bachelor of Arts degree majoring in Drama and Religion and completed the Master of Divinity and the Doctor of Ministry degrees from Lexington Theological Seminary. He attended Mansfield College of Oxford, England. He retired from ministry in 2011, to write historical dramas. Dr. Rechenbach has restored The Old Parsonage of Andrew Tribble built in 1794, located in Richmond to be used for community events. His play *Botherum* was chosen Best Ten-Minute Play 2017 with Kentucky Theater Association's Roots of the Bluegrass Play Writing Competition, and his plays *Night Music of the River* 2016, *The Botanic Garden* 2018, and *Beatin' the Dark Home* 2019 were chosen first place finalists.

Printed in the United States
by Baker & Taylor Publisher Services